D0394913

Opera on Screen

Opera on Screen

Marcia J. Citron

Yale University Press   New Haven and London

Frontispiece: Robert Helpmann and Ludmilla Tcherina in *Tales of Hoffmann* (1951). Directed by Michael Powell, in collaboration with Emeric Pressburger. (Courtesy British Film Institute)

Printed in the United States of America.

Library of Congress Cataloging-in-Publication Data
Citron, Marcia J.
Opera on screen / Marcia J. Citron.
p. cm.
Includes bibliographical references and index.
ISBN 0-300-08158-8 (alk. paper)
1. Operas—Film and video adaptations—History and criticism.
2. Musical films—History and criticism.   I. Title.
ML1700.C57   2000
791.43'6—dc21   99-048686

A catalogue record for this book is available from the British Library.

The paper in this book meets the guidelines
for permanence and durability of the Committee
on Production Guidelines for Book Longevity of
the Council on Library Resources.

10 9 8 7 6 5 4 3 2 1

In memory of my mother,
who took me to see *Don Giovanni* at the Old Met.

Contents

Acknowledgments

I am grateful to the staff of the stills archives at the British Film Institute and the Museum of Modern Art. Bridget Kinally was most helpful in providing assistance at the London facility. In New York, Mary Corliss offered sound advice as well as guidance in the selection of shots. Charles Silver, of the film research library at MOMA, was also generous with his time and steered me toward important resources, especially microfilms of scripts and correspondence for *Tales of Hoffmann*. The British Film Institute similarly granted access to important archival materials, and its Joseph Losey collection filled in the background for *Don Giovanni*.

On the home front I was fortunate to have the assistance of capable graduate students from the Shepherd School of Music at Rice University, where I teach. To David Michael Bynog, Rachel Rhinehart Champagne, and Wendy Lin, I express warm thanks for your dedication and hard work on behalf of the project. I also owe a great deal to the Shepherd School students who have populated my seminars on opera over the years. We have learned many things together, and opera videos have allowed us to find common ground for interpretation.

A special word of appreciation goes to Ellen Burns, president of the Lyrica Society for Word-Music Relations. Her invitation to participate on a paper session devoted to screen treatments of opera, back in 1992, supplied the jump-start that has culminated in this book. Indeed, her enthusiasm for screen opera in general has nourished scholarship in the area, and her organization of two major scholarly events in 1998 attests to her continued presence. She is a patron who makes things happen—Ellen, we owe you a lot!

On a more specific level, I extend thanks to Oxford University Press for permission to reuse my article, "A Night at the Cinema: Zeffirelli's *Otello* and the Genre of Film-Opera," which in reworked form is the basis of chapter 3 in *Opera on Screen*. The essay first appeared in *The Musical Quarterly* 78/4 (Winter 1994): 700-41. I am also grateful to Dr. Eberhard Scheele of Forum Media, Munich, for several stills of Peter Sellars's productions. Winnie Klotz, photographer for the Metropolitan Opera, kindly supplied a photograph of Zeffirelli's telecast production of *Turandot*. And Catherine Ashmore, of Zoë Dominic Photography in London, provided stills of the Royal Opera House's production of *Otello*.

Harry Haskell of Yale University Press shepherded the project over bumps and hurdles with grace. Mary Hunter provided the kind of expert readership that every author would hope to have. I am grateful for her wisdom, thoroughness, and thoughtfulness, and above all her ability to understand what I was trying to do in this book even as she called for major changes.

Last but not least, I want to express heartfelt appreciation to Mark Kulstad, who always kept the big picture in mind and reminded me of it. Your support has been indispensable.

I

Introduction

I fell in love with opera on screen in the early 1980s at a double bill of Bergman's *Magic Flute* and Losey's *Don Giovanni*. Viewing two Mozart works on the big screen, with fellow spellbound moviegoers, was exhilarating. I was fascinated by those larger-than-life figures, the variety of the two films, and hearing these beloved works in a movie theater. There was something special about seeing them in a casual setting. Soon there appeared Zeffirelli's *La Traviata,* a film critics loved and audiences flocked to see. I went with high hopes but came back with mixed emotions. Once again I felt that something special had happened. Yet I was angry at being reduced to tears when Violetta died at the end. This, I thought, was excessive. The director was exploiting film's expressive potential by overpowering me with huge close-ups of her sickly face as Verdi's sentimental music played on. I had lost control as a rational viewer. I was being manipulated by some larger force and cinema had won. It was clear that the medium wielded enormous power to shape interpretation and my response to it.

Screen opera also had an impact in the classroom. When I started to teach seminars on opera in the mid 1980s, students used audio recordings to become familiar with works. This was fine as far as it went. Discussions of operas centered on musical or factual details or on critical interpretations of them. A few students commented on a production they had seen, but for others an actual performance was only to be imagined. Houston Grand Opera, the local company, might stage a work we were studying, but that would be a rare coincidence. Something was missing. Gradually that missing element materialized, in the form of opera videos. They soon replaced audio versions as the representatives of the work. We now had a shared visual experience of the opera. We also had a sense of the work as a drama enacted in a specific place, performed by seen bodies who move, emote, and interact with each other. As a class we could consider critical elements of staging, direction, and interpretation and their impact on the work. Today it is hard to imagine how we managed without them.

Opera videos soon became much more than representatives of the work. Their interpretations took on a life of their own and generated thoughtful questions. What happened to the opera when it was adapted for the screen, and were these legitimate or successful changes? Why were the changes made? Why were some operas more conducive to screen versions than others? How was the notion of the original opera affected by this treatment? How are we affected by the camera? And so on. For me these questions led to others, but they stayed at the level of aesthetic rumination for several years. In 1992, however, my thoughts were channeled in a scholarly venue by an invitation from Ellen Burns, of the Lyrica Society for Word-Music Relations, to contribute a paper to a session on opera-film that she was organizing for the annual meeting of the Modern Language Association. Thus began a formal dialogue with the genre and a complicated relationship with a perplexing film, Zeffirelli's movie *Otello* (1986). The presentation was expanded into an article, "A Night at the Cinema: Zeffirelli's *Otello* and the Genre of Film-Opera."[1] The piece explored general issues associated with adaptation and theorized about the fit between a given opera and screen treatment. It also discussed spectatorship, gender, and the relationship between film music and operatic music adapted for film.

It soon became clear that the article raised as many questions as it answered, and a larger study was needed. The idea for *Opera on Screen* was born. Without attempting to be comprehensive, for that is impossible at such an early stage in the field, the book aims to explore many of the major concerns behind screen opera in cinema, television, and video: how it works, how it relates to film and television and to staged opera, how we attend to it, how it fits into culture at large, and how it modernizes old works in a media-intensive age. I like to think of it as a prelude to a general theory of screen opera. If any theme is paramount it is the role of medium—cinema, television, video—in constructing a new operatic text. This drives the organization of the chapters and the emphasis on certain issues for certain works.

As these concerns suggest, the range of *Opera on Screen* is broad and draws on a variety of theories and approaches from several fields. I consider this an advantage because screen opera is a new area of scholarly inquiry and crosses many disciplinary borders. One of the major goals in the study is to sketch fruitful ways of applying critical methods to screen opera. Narrative theory, media theory, sound theory, feminist theory, and psychoanalytic theory all have something important to contribute to the critique as now one and then another provides useful modeling for the works under discussion. I have no stake in any one theory or theoretical perspective, for the featured works form a repertoire with a rich field of signifiers. Despite the eclecticism, the volume is informed throughout by a musicological perspective. My disciplinary home is music. For *Opera on Screen* this means a standpoint that practices criticism with ear and mind that are alert to music and to the historical position of opera. Screen treatments of opera can be (and have been) explored from a variety of perspectives.[2] But we need to remember that opera *is* musical drama, and to ignore music in a major study of media treatments is to distort the meanings of these fascinating cultural products.

The exploration of the genre takes place in interpretive essays on selected works. Over its long history screen opera has produced a rich history (see chapter 2) and there are many works one can study. In general I have gravitated toward works that play out telling characteristics of a medium. Thus for cinema I discuss films that make use of the outdoors (Rosi's *Bizet's Carmen* and Losey's *Don Giovanni*) and exploit motion pictures' affinity for fantasy (Powell and Pressburger's *Tales of Hoffmann* and Syberberg's *Parsifal*). I also prefer works that have become influential—high points as it were of a screen-opera canon—and that disclose pitfalls as well as advantages of crafting works for the screen. But as much as anything I have chosen works that excite me. Some may infuriate me at times, but all the featured works are provocative and exploit their medium to expand the borders of opera and cinema/television. They engage intriguing issues, whether aesthetic, generic, technological, or social. These productions may not offer clear answers to the questions they raise but this quality makes them attractive for analysis. I was also interested in studying operas from different countries. The works embrace several traditions: Italian, French, German, "American" by way of Peter Sellars, and a very loose version of "British" by way of the anglicized *Tales of Hoffmann.* Regardless of my personal tastes, the featured works embody the best of what the combination of opera and visual media has to offer musically, visually, and dramatically.

Ten productions receive detailed study. Eight operas make up the group, with two of them—*Otello* and *Don Giovanni*—in two different versions (the former in a direct comparison, the latter in separate contexts). Except for *Tales of Hoffmann,* which appeared in 1951, all the screen treatments are recent, produced since the late 1970s. I did not begin with the express goal of stressing recent works, but various factors led to that result. For cinema I was interested mainly in full-length treatments. Although many were made before 1970, recent examples form a critical mass that suggests important connections between cinema and opera. And, not unimportantly, they are available on video. This means that readers can find them easily.

A similar argument applies to television. The relay telecast became viable technologically only since the mid 1970s; earlier efforts lacked the resources to transmit a performance successfully from the opera house. Of course, an early studio production such as *Amahl and the Night Visitors* (see chapter 2) would have contributed important insights for the study. But as of this writing it is not available on video. Many of these productions were broadcast live, and if they were recorded, as were the later telecasts of *Amahl,* the film or videotape may be in poor condition. Thus while scholarly interest argues for inclusion of early examples, practicality suggests otherwise. Readers would lose a great deal if they were unable to see the productions.[3]

The source operas are interesting chronologically. While the dates of composition range from 1724 to 1887 they fall into two groups: eighteenth-century works (one Handel and three Mozart) and late-nineteenth-century works (four operas). The latter category, it turns out, covers a period of only twelve years, from 1875 (*Carmen*) to 1887 (*Otello*). This was not intentional, and I was surprised when I realized the narrowness of the spread. If a study of opera is to be representative, then surely there should be examples from a wide range of periods. But this is misleading because certain periods and styles have been captured by the camera more than others. The late nineteenth century has drawn the most interest. *Carmen,* for example, has received more treatment on screen than any other opera. This is no accident. Works from this period have achieved great popularity with the public. Operagoers flock to *Carmen, Tales of Hoffmann,* and *La Bohème,* and late-nineteenth-century music has also found a secure place in mainstream culture. The public has also become familiar with the style through its use as film music. Its opulence, tunefulness, and use of recurring motives have worked well, particularly in classical Hollywood film.

There appears to be another reason why operas from the late nineteenth century have been used so often. Their affinity for continuous music is suited to visual representation. For cinema especially, continuous music connects the images and injects a feeling of naturalism into the artifice of opera. Frequent instrumental passages enhance the utility of the style and move it closer to ordinary film music. Puccini typifies this model (see chapter 2). But as Zeffirelli's *Otello* suggests, problems can arise when certain continuous operas are subjected to certain manipulations for the camera. Furthermore, many operas from this period do not have continuous music. Nonetheless, the prominence of continuous music in late-nineteenth-century opera has been a major reason for its popularity in opera on screen.

COUNTERPOINTS

I am obviously a big fan of screen opera and believe in its integrity as an independent genre that combines opera and technology. This does not mean that it is unproblematic, however. Like many hybrids it bears the tensions of its components, some of which may not reconcile themselves easily with the others. Opera, for example, tends to unfold more slowly than cinema or television. As librettists know, music requires time to function successfully as a dramatic discourse—to express emotion, to limn character, and to shape drama.[4] Literary genres build their dramatic impact through the cumulative impact of words. Adaptation from a wordy source such as a play or novel means a great deal of cutting. Moreover, opera consists of reflective numbers that are relatively static. Cinema and television depend much more on movement and action, and thrive on a faster pace. When these media combine with opera, the reconciliation of differences creates a formidable challenge. No single formula ensures success, and the characteristics of the opera and the aims of the project will guide the treatment. Nonetheless, some works will be more successful than others in negotiating difficulties.

Screen opera brings the viewer into an intimate relationship with characters and singers. In the movie house figures are larger than life, but we seem close to them. On television figures are smaller than we are, and relatively close. We are probably watching them in a domestic setting. Both venues encourage an easy bond with the narrative onscreen. For some critics, however, this may not be a salutary effect. Sam Abel, for example, finds the connection too comfortable. It effaces the epic quality of opera and masks the idea that opera involves live bodies that exude a sexual presence.[5] Technology imposes a false familiarity on a communal ritual that depends on sexual resonance between performers and audience who occupy the same space at the same time. For Abel, therefore, instead of narrowing the gap between viewer and performer, screen opera actually increases distance. He worries that media treatments of opera become another way in which technology wipes out live human interactions, all the while promoting itself as modern and the wave of the future.

Abel's critique of reproduced art extends the arguments put forth in Walter Benjamin's famous essay of the 1930s, "The Work of Art in the Age of Mechanical Reproduction."[6] For Benjamin reproduced art compromises the "aura" or aesthetic vitality of live or real art works and creates in its stead a copy that is unchanging. Yet he sees the camera in film as a means of compensating for the loss of live human beings as it allows the work to "meet the beholder halfway" (p. 220). This interplay of artifice and reality threads its way through *Opera on Screen,* especially in relation to the compensatory function of film music and psychological consequences of the sound-image relationship.

The connection plays out in other ways in screen opera. Opera establishes a theatrical world of pretense that is framed by the proscenium arch and articulated by an unnatural means of communication. Cinema, in contrast, promotes a greater sense of realism and fosters the illusion of a space without limits. As in the real world, speaking is the principal medium of discourse. Although television is more bounded spatially, it also thrives on realism—in fact, the use of videotape often creates a feeling of "hyper-realism." Yet the realism-artifice relationship is inverted when it comes to sound. Opera delivers real and embodied sound: it is emitted at the same time it is heard, and the physical source is generally knowable. For cinema and most of television, sound is emitted at the time the work is recorded, not when it is screened. In the case of film versions of opera, the situation extends even further. Here the music is usually prerecorded and later lip-synchronized to playback when the film is recorded by the camera. Singers become vessels from whom sound appears to originate, even though they only mouth the words. This artificial means of dealing with the music of the opera brings to mind the artifices of opera, but of course it is cinema's demands for realistic movement and consistent sound quality (as well as error-free performance) that cause this idiosyncrasy.

What Abel and others worry about is that reproduced opera will replace live opera. This is a misguided fear. Live and screen opera do not compete with each other but enhance each other. Screen opera expands the interpretive potential of opera in all its forms as it makes the genre available to millions who might not otherwise see it. Abel worries about the palliative effect of technology and fears that this will tempt audiences away from the opera house for good. While I recognize the hypnotic quality of screened phenomena, I do not believe it will snuff out the desire for live art. Each format appeals to different aspects of aesthetic experience. Moreover, their differences create tensions that inject new life into the other and invigorate opera in the larger sense. *Opera on Screen* is not a call for the triumph of reproduced opera at the expense of live art. It is a study of the newer format in the hopes of showing how opera is an inclusive concept that embraces diverse kinds of aesthetic experience. In our media-saturated culture, the proscenium arch cannot contain this extravagant art form.

While stage and screen opera both belong to the larger category opera, screen opera is an independent genre with its own properties. It involves cinema, television, and video, and creates its own ways of dealing with narrative, discourse, and representation. Leftist critics would argue that the new works are so independent that they have nothing to do with the source opera or staged opera in general. We should study them as entities unto themselves, or as pure films or telecasts, without reference to opera. If opera is accorded priority it means that media treatments are derivative works and the aesthetics of the stage limit what can be done interpretively. Music will colonize a screen treatment and assert a primacy that characterizes stage opera. Innovation will suffer, and hence the shackles of the source must be removed. Jeremy Tambling's study, *Opera, Ideology and Film*, tacitly endorses this position.[7]

I view the situation differently. Screen treatments are essentially independent texts that have to be approached with their own theory, which is drawn from a variety of disciplines. But one of the disciplines is opera. Hence I take a more centrist position. *Opera on Screen* develops ways of interpreting screen opera that place works in their own aesthetic categories, but it also recognizes the role of the source opera and opera in general in forming the categories and affecting the success of the outcome. Opera is not accorded primacy in my approach to screen opera, but it is recognized as something that cannot be ignored. The extent of involvement depends on individual circumstances.

THEMES

Earlier I sketched major concerns of the study, but how are they fleshed out in the readings? At the heart of the focus on medium lie differences between cinema and television and their impact on what is made, how it is made, and its relationship with the viewer. For example, the venues of the two media create different viewing conditions and encourage different expectations and responses from a viewer. These can reinforce or contradict a dramatic interpretation. For example, as explored in chapter 3, regressive aspects of Verdi's *Otello*—especially the idealization of the past—are reinforced by certain tendencies in the viewing experience of cinema. Zeffirelli's film exploits this potential and thus depends on a trait of the medium to shape his interpretation. In contrast, the Moshinsky-Large telecast exudes a cool and rational countenance that reflects one of television's main characteristics, its sense of presence. The study of Peter Sellars's settings of Mozart and Handel continues the discussion of television's capabilities as a medium. One characteristic that is reinforced in his productions is television's affinity for direct address. Sellars uses the device to break the fiction of the narrative and add a new layer of meaning to his conception. Video enters the discussion in both chapters: in *Otello* for its effects as a leveling device between cinema and television, and in the Sellars essay for its centrality in media culture and as a guide to the behavior of the camera. Despite the impact of a given medium, however, the book also shows that there is substantial cross-influence between cinema and television.

Screen opera affords great latitude in setting; locations can be indoors, outdoors, or contrived as in animation. I am concerned with the meaning of theatrical and non-theatrical locations and their effect on the way the work is fashioned by the camera. Productions from the opera house obviously use interior settings and the camera is restricted in angle and movement by the proscenium. Interior locations in cinema stress theatricality and forgo the sense of documentary realism that comes with nature or architecture. These differences apply to the four movies that are explored in chapters 4 and 5. Both films of chapter 4 use the confines of theatrical locations to highlight how fantasy can be marshalled for interpretation. In *Parsifal* the aim is mainly ideological. *Tales of Hoffmann* is more complicated in its goals and the film emerges as a mixture of parody and entertainment. It even re-enacts performance as a theatrical event and deploys ballet as a major discourse alongside opera. Both films are clearly cinematic, however, and would not be mistaken for stage productions. They demonstrate that cinema owes a debt to theater—a fitting relationship given the origin of opera in the theater.

Cinematic opera can also rely on exterior locations and on the naturalistic movement between indoors and outdoors. Rosi's *Carmen* takes place in Andalusia and uses nature and architecture for a frank and uncynical interpretation. The understated treatment of the setting guides the film as a whole, especially its music and image, and proves the adage that less is more—in this case an extremely successful version of Bizet's opera. The other film of chapter 5, Losey's *Don Giovanni*, uses Palladian buildings and surrounding countryside in the Veneto to erect a

Marxist critique of class relations. In comparison to Zeffirelli's flamboyant use of scenery in *Otello,* these films tone down the sense of spectacle.

The function of the camera in shaping narrative and meaning assumes thematic status in the readings. A powerful tool, the camera guides what we see and how long we see it. In this way it controls not only the content of the image but its rhythm. This suggests a close connection with the rhythm of the music, and the manipulation of this relationship can lead to interesting results. Rosi's restraint in visual cutting, for example, blunts the dramatic fluctuations in the music. Losey sometimes imposes visual cuts that contradict the dramaturgy of Mozart's score, perhaps for ideological reasons. Peter Sellars applies a schizo-phrenic pace in the camera—sometimes it cuts very quickly, sometimes it lingers much too long—and this is meant to re-flect the manic nature of contemporary culture. Syberberg pro-vides a visual analogue to Wagner's slow-paced music in his tendency to prolong camera shots. Jean-Pierre Ponnelle, him-self a director of many treatments of screen opera, sums up the situation when he likens the rhythmic aspect of the camera to a contrapuntal relationship with the score.[8]

The camera can also point out detail to establish dramatic relationships. Sellars takes this potential to extremes as he ex-ploits facial close-ups to probe moment-by-moment reactions. He also has tight shots of symbols of violence to show the deca-dent world he is subjecting to critique. Syberberg and Rosi, on the other hand, consciously avoid detail in order to keep the narrative detached from the audience. This means that the camera is creating an objectified subject position for the viewer, one of an infinite variety of positions of identification that the camera can create. Indeed, many of the directors discussed here keep the viewer at a distance from the world of the story (the diegesis): a Brechtian technique that is used in the service of interpretation. This does not work as well for relay productions from the opera house, especially if the camera shows house, audience, and conductor. Such shots pull us inward, not outward, as they urge us to identify with the audience and its participation in the event. For all the treatments the camera creates a sense of scale that is different from live opera. The size and focus of images depends on the particular medium and its relationship with the viewer.

The rhythmic interaction between image and music is only one aspect of a larger concern regarding the relation of image to sound. Sound in general clarifies space through distinctions in volume. But in many treatments of screen opera sound confounds or does little to confirm a sense of space. The playback method precludes such distinctions. Most film treatments are structured this way, and lip-synching conveys the illusion of emitted sound. The technique demonstrates the manufactured nature of the relationship between sound and image and the technological basis of opera on screen. Even the transmission from the opera house entails technological manipulation. Singers appear to be singing the music, but the sound is modified electronically and is probably recorded rather than live (at least in recent versions).

Some film treatments foreground the constructed nature of the relationship by emphasizing the separation of image and music. Of course, lip-synching by its very nature means a separation, but some films stress the quality more than others. *Parsifal* not only has poor synchronization between moving lips and music in much of the film, but offers the sensational feature of a man's voice seemingly emitted by a female character. *Tales of Hoffmann* contains numbers in which music is heard but no moving lips are seen. These devices serve varied ends and sometimes lead to multiple identities in the narrative. Perhaps it is no coincidence that most of the roles in *Parsifal* and

Hoffmann are portrayed on-screen by actors. This offers a clue to the separability of heard music from its actual sources, who do not appear in the film. I like to think of the use of actors as an honest way of signifying the manufactured relationship of sound and image. It openly acknowledges the disembodied status of the voice in cinematic treatments of opera.

For many critics of cinematic opera, the use of actors indicates that image has triumphed over music in a hybrid genre with irreconcilable elements. To such opponents image and music are engaged in a struggle for primacy in screened opera, and image usually prevails.[9] While I do not subscribe to this oppositional premise, a few treatments seem to suffer because one element is so overwhelming that it compromises productive interaction between them. A possible example is Zeffirelli's *Otello*. While most examples of screen opera make changes to accommodate the camera and the aims of the project—all of the films emphasized in this study do so—*Otello* reflects a mismatch between source and transformation. Perhaps only unsatisfying versions of screen opera make one aware of an imbalance; otherwise the inevitable accommodations between image and music pass unnoticed because of an imaginative vision for the whole.

The relationship between sound and image also involves the use of noise. Noise has an effect on the interaction of narrative and illusion in screen opera. It injects realism into the diegesis and suppresses idealistic elements of narrative and operatic discourse. Rosi's *Carmen* typifies this effect as the film offers frequent noises of everyday life—dogs barking, birds singing, people gossiping—and de-idealizes operatic music. At the other extreme is Syberberg's symbolic *Parsifal*, where we are enveloped in the soundtrack of Wagner's music and have few aural markers of an outside world. Zeffirelli's *Otello* stands somewhere in between as it gives us occasional references to real life but often keeps us saturated in Verdi's music. We would expect television productions from the opera house to include noise. Yet as the Royal Opera House version of *Otello* demonstrates, many do not, and in this way they take on an aspect of cinema that denies television's affinity for presence—in this case the presence of aural markers of real events.

Opera on Screen is also concerned with the place of the viewer in relation to the spectacle. As noted earlier, screen opera can create a variety of subject positions for the viewer and affect how he or she identifies with the drama played out on screen. Zeffirelli's *Otello,* for example, reinforces cinema's tendency to promote psychological regression in the viewing of film. Through flashback and other symbols of anteriority, the viewer is persuaded to identify with the narrative's glorification of the past. Whereas Zeffirelli's film draws the viewer in, however, many treatments push the viewer away. These may be allied with a strong ideological component. Losey's depiction of a cruel upper class in *Don Giovanni* is meant to alienate the viewer from capitalism and the liberal tradition that supports it. Syberberg takes aim at Wagner and German guilt in *Parsifal,* although the excessive array of symbols and references may itself alienate the viewer. Although Rosi treads more lightly with respect to ideology in *Carmen,* his cinematic techniques keep the viewer at a distance from the narrative.

Television encourages other kinds of relationships. With a small screen and domestic venue, television promotes familiarity and intimacy. While cinema dominates and overwhelms the viewer, television creates an environment in which the viewer can identify with the narrative on a more equal footing. This quality suggests one reason why the relay from the opera house has been a popular format. Sellars's obsessive use of close-up trades on the medium's affinity for intimacy and shows the influence of a particular television genre, soap opera.

Although it may be maligned by critics as frivolous, soap opera heightens bonds of intimacy with the viewer and serves Sellars's purposes of emotional exaggeration and the viewer's response to it. Nonetheless, other elements in his productions counteract this tendency toward pulling the viewer in. In the end, Sellars's productions forge complex relationships with the viewer, as do many of the treatments under discussion. Some subject positions in screen opera result from tendencies of the viewing medium, some from the particular interpretation, and many from the interaction between the two. Furthermore, as the discussion of *Tales of Hoffmann* points out, subject positions are flexible and can change in a short period of time.

Spectatorship is closely connected with another theme of the study, namely, gender. In *Hoffmann,* gender assumes dynamic form as it contributes to the way we perceive personas inside and outside the narrative and how we relate to them. The female voice receives special attention as an independent entity and also as an integral element in the unified representation of a woman. The latter has major implications for the meaning of cinema as a medium. Zeffirelli's representation of gender also entails the medium of cinema, but he builds on its ability to evoke regressive desires in the viewer. The idealization of the main female figure, Desdemona, can set in motion desires for a pleasure that is associated with the imaginary stage of psychological development—that idyllic period when the maternal voice promises utopian pleasure. Although female viewers may respond differently from men, the visual and auditory pleasures of the maternal principle—or what is called the lost maternal object—are powerful and are affirmed by other elements in the film.

The readings of individual films also explore gender in the object itself, that is, in the narrative, the discourse, and the representational apparatus of the treatment. In *Hoffmann* the fact that ballet permeates the film and is generally associated with the feminine adds a gendered tone to the film. More concretely, dance becomes the vehicle through which the quest for the eternal feminine principle unfolds. The other fantastic film of chapter 4, Syberberg's *Parsifal*, also places gender in a central position that affects meaning. The character of Parsifal is constituted by two figures of different genders, although each lip-synchs to the same male voice. While notions of androgyny, heterosexuality, and multiple identities are invoked by the structure, one important result is that Kundry moves closer to the center of the narrative and becomes transfigured healer rather than punished penitent. The prominence of gender and the feminine in an opera that has strong homosocial and misogynist overtones leads to a radical treatment of Wagner's final work.

As in staged opera, music functions as a major discourse in screen opera. Yet the presence of the camera and the prominence of image inevitably affect the role of music and how it shapes narrative and meaning. This occupies our attention in many of the readings. Several questions arise. What kinds of musical construction work well in cinema and television, respectively? How does music operate amid other discourses that create meaning, especially image and noise? And what adjustments are made to accommodate medium and the interpretive goals of the director? In chapter 3, for example, we see how Zeffirelli's *Otello* makes significant changes to Verdi's continuous opera to accommodate certain aims of the director. Whereas Zeffirelli's alterations are questionable, the cuts and rearrangements in Powell and Pressburger's *Tales of Hoffmann* do not pose a problem because the music of Offenbach's opera can be modified more easily. This difference emphasizes the influence of the source on the way the work is adapted for another medium; some operas lend themselves more readily to certain kinds of transformation than to others.

Opera itself becomes a topic for interpretation in screen opera. Whereas *Hoffmann* uses parody to pay homage to the stage origins of opera, other treatments offer different kinds of allusions. Losey, for example, isolates a major number and sets it on an actual stage in order to stress the artifice of opera. Although Sellars has been vilified for ruining classic works, his transformations perform a ritual of homage as they attempt to restore a meaning for contemporary audiences that is comparable to the "shock value" the operas had for eighteenth-century audiences. Furthermore, his updated versions take place on the stage and in this way signal a commitment to opera as a medium.

In this study Sellars's treatments serve as the most obvious examples of media culture: a vague but meaningful term that applies to various combinations of technology and popular culture. Broadly speaking, screen opera is a product of media culture. It modernizes old works as it passes them through technology and distributes them by means of popular channels of communication. The genre unfolds on a screen and partakes of contemporary ways of knowing the world, which include the Internet. It resonates with other aspects of a digital age: an emphasis on playback, fragmentation (especially with video), and personal manipulation of material and its venue for transmission. This epistemology is obviously most meaningful to younger generations, who feel comfortable with computers and the acquisition of knowledge and culture through electronic means. For these reasons screen opera provides a special opportunity to "make opera visible" (to paraphrase Wagner and Syberberg) and allow it to resonate with larger audiences. It has the potential to keep opera alive in a technological age.

Screen opera offers a modern form of the *Gesamtkunstwerk* and challenges the boundaries between high art and mass media. It has already carved out a major niche for itself and shows signs of continued vitality in the future. I hope that *Opera on Screen* contributes to this process as it helps us to understand how the genre works and how successful versions come to be made.

2

A Stroll Through History

Opera has been captured on camera since the beginning of the twentieth century. This has produced a rich history, but like most histories the course of screen opera has been uneven. It could be argued that the most creative projects occurred near the inception of cinema and television, respectively, and what came later represented a decline.

On the whole the genre of screen opera has been propelled by diverse aims. Many treatments of operas on screen are arranged to showcase the talent of particular singers. Some serve as promotional devices for audio recordings. Some are thought to add prestige to an essentially commercial venture. But motivation has also been high-minded. In the early years of American television, for example, emigrés promoted opera as a means of educating the public and improving its taste. Sensing a rare opportunity in the populist medium, the pioneers of screen opera attempted to instill the European affinity for opera in an America in search of its own operatic expression. Such utopian ideals were not confined to the United States, however. Many countries hoped to rejuvenate opera through new works for the new medium. Opera's potential for social critique has also attracted many film directors who are searching for imaginative venues to advance their social agendas. Opera films since the 1970s, in particular, betray a strong directorial presence, reflecting the auteur tradition of European cinema. Perhaps filmmakers are attracted to the challenge of combining two media that have significant aesthetic differences. Some directors—Franco Zeffirelli, for one—believe that the possibility of attracting a large audience is a major reason for making a film of an opera. Many recorded versions, of course, are made mainly to entertain.

Although screen opera has an international presence, its visibility and impact have not been uniform. The history of the genre differs in Europe and the United States, largely because of the cultural positions of opera and cinema in each place. In the United States opera has attracted audiences at least partly because it exudes a cosmopolitan flavor—a sign of upper-class trappings in a purportedly classless society. In Europe, however, opera has served as a more natural product of the culture and forged bonds more easily with the public. Cinema also functions differently in America and in Europe. Dominated by the commercialism of Hollywood, American film has stressed entertainment and promoted ideals that are fundamental to American society: individualism, progress, and happiness. European cinema on the whole is more serious and gravitates toward themes that are political or introspective. European film endings may be ambiguous rather than definitive, and the director is more likely to inscribe a personal vision into a film. In Europe one speaks of a filmmaker or cinéaste much as one would an artist.

Economic support has shaped the two traditions. In the United States commercial interests have sustained visual media and the arts. In Europe governmental support has played a major role in supporting these ventures. One cannot overestimate the significance of this difference for projects that involve opera. Financial success, as gauged by mass appeal, guides the former. The latter allows for a variety of goals, which may stress experimentation, cultural literacy, or national identity rather than filling the pocketbook. Obviously the broad differences sketched here oversimplify the situation. For example, European countries do not share a uniform history or sources of financial support. Nonetheless, their similarities form a contrast with the United States.

The combination of opera and film has not been restricted to screen opera. As a melodramatic genre, opera has also influenced general films. Some films incorporate operatic music in the story (diegetic music) or use it as accompaniment in the background (non-diegetic). Others assume an exaggerated plot reminiscent of opera, as in *Moonstruck* and *8 1/2*. Occasionally a film features an opera scene, as in the culminating sequence of the Marx Brothers' *A Night at the Opera*. A few films revolve around an opera singer and the world of opera, for example, the cult film *Diva* and the various versions of *The Phantom of the Opera*. The world of opera may also reside in a secondary character, as in the singer Susan Alexander, protégé of the title character in *Citizen Kane*. And less frequently a film appears that adopts the continuous-music premise of opera. *The Umbrellas of Cherbourg* is the most famous example, but such musicals as *Tommy* and *Evita* also have continuous music. For some filmmakers of the early sound era, the 1930s, the future of opera and film was embodied in motion pictures with a newly composed score of continuous music with words. Their goals were partly realized in the lush underscoring of Erich Korngold and others in the golden age of Hollywood film. Many scores amount to full-length instrumental pieces, like Korngold's award-winning music for *The Adventures of Robin Hood* (1938).[1] These scores consisted of mostly continuous music, but it was *The Robber Symphony* (1936), a film of a new opera composed expressly for cinema, that fulfilled the goal completely. The filmic *Gesamtkunstwerk*, however, would not take hold on any major scale.

Screen opera has also influenced staged opera. The most obvious effect is the use of film or slides in a production. Although new operas are more likely to include recorded images, traditional operas may also incorporate the technique—for example, David Alden's production of Verdi's *Macbeth* for the Houston Grand Opera (1997). A precursor can be found in the original stage production of Wagner's *Parsifal* (1882), where a painted backdrop moved continuously in one direction during the transformation music of Acts I and III. Alban Berg's *Wozzeck* (1925) suggests cinematic montage in its juxtaposition of snapshot-like scenes, and his later opera *Lulu* (1937) includes an actual filmed sequence. But media culture has probably infiltrated the opera house in other ways. Movement and gesture, for example, might be paced more quickly to reflect the speed of MTV, commercials, and television. Stage productions prepared for the camera might be especially prone to this influence, but there is probably a similar effect in stagings not geared to recording. As time passes and more directors and singers come to opera as consumers of television and video culture, the impact of visual media should become more apparent on the stage. Moreover, the disruptive juxtapositions that can result from creative film editing may also affect the narrative organization in staged opera.[2]

The connection between opera and media (cinema, television, and video) over their century-long history can be characterized as fluctuating relationships of continuation, dependence, enrichment, and competition. The complex interactions are inflected by the counterpoint between live and reproduced art, populist and elitist art forms, Eurocentric and New World sensibilities, and commercial and idealist aims. These themes underlie the historical overview of screen opera presented in this chapter. Proceeding roughly chronologically, I trace the major phases of the genre: the silent and sound eras in cinema, the early and later years of television, the modern film-opera, and recent developments. My aims are to discuss the main achievements and influential works, to show how each medium imprinted its stamp on screened works, and to explore the impact of culture on what was made and how it was made.

ORIGINS AND THE SILENT ERA

The main technological components that make up screen opera developed at about the same time. The phonograph, patented by Thomas Edison in 1878, reproduced music, while moving pictures on film reproduced image. The visual process was developed in several countries, especially in France by the Lumière Brothers and in America by Edison. Both technologies transformed art from a live experience to an electronic reproduction—from an original to a copy—and ushered in profound change. As Walter Benjamin observed, the *Ersatz* situation seriously compromises the "aura" of art—its uniqueness and directness—and hence its cultural authority.[3] He felt that bourgeois complacency can set in and art consequently becomes a palliative kitsch devoid of real meaning.[4]

Although the reproduced nature of cinema makes it quite different from live opera, cinema could be viewed historically as the successor to late nineteenth-century opera. Both stress spectacle and melodrama, and both have mass appeal. Both offer a vast canvas of emotions, and both air political and social concerns.[5] Silent film takes on the excess and exaggeration of this kind of opera. It too has stylized gestures, heightened lighting and makeup, and overheated musical accompaniment.[6] Given the similarities it seems natural that early motion pictures would combine the elements of opera and film. Peter Franklin suggests that early opera on film reflects the merging of high and low art that took place in Italian opera at about the same time. Such verismo works as *Tosca* (1900) and *Cavalleria rusticana* (1890) appealed so strongly to mass taste that they broke down what Franklin called the "great divide" between opera and popular idioms.[7] A similar kind of merging occurred in early cinema with its incorporation of opera and operatic elements. This helped not only to popularize opera but also to legitimize the new medium. When cinema was more firmly entrenched, verismo was categorized along with film music as entertainment pandering to mass taste and therefore of poor quality. Both were considered effeminate,[8] a marginalizing term to indicate abnormality.

Thus early cinema kept alive the spirit of verismo opera and depended on it for survival.[9] But for some the relationship was less benign. Some German modernists—Arnold Schoenberg among them—saw cinema as a dangerous force that threatened to replace opera.[10] They felt it would lure away audiences and composers of opera and cheapen the quality of art music. The fear of replacing an established medium with a new one becomes thematic in our history. Cinema is feared and denigrated by supporters of the "legitimate theater" and opera; television by proponents of cinema and theater; video by advocates of cinema and television; and screen opera by fans of live opera. In any case, the advent of cinema served as a populist force that would lead to major realignments of art forms. Cinema did not cause the death of opera; it heralded new meanings for the medium.[11]

"Soundless opera," as E. H. Bierstadt called opera on the screen in 1915, enjoyed a lively career in silent film. As early as the 1890s Edison had envisioned a place for opera in his new medium, as he wrote in *The New York Times* in 1893: "My intention is to have such a happy combination of photography and electricity that a man can sit in his own parlor, see depicted upon a curtain the forms of the players in opera upon a distant stage and hear the voices of the singers."[12] It's interesting that he spoke of a private kind of viewing—a foreshadowing of television.

Edison's company produced a version of *Parsifal* in 1904 that was quite ambitious for its day. Directed by Edwin S. Porter, it contained eight scenes and was meant to be accompanied by phonograph records distributed with the film. Its run was curtailed because of a lawsuit to protect the rights of an author against unauthorized use of the script.[13] In France, meanwhile, cinéaste Georges Méliès, building on the innovative filming techniques of the Lumière Brothers, produced fantastic films steeped in opera. An operaphile who lived near the Opéra and the Opéra-Comique, Méliès created several works that are seen as milestones in the early days of filmed opera. In 1903, he produced *Faust aux enfers* based on Hector Berlioz's *Damnation of Faust,* and the next year a thirteen-minute *Damnation du Docteur Faust* on Charles Gounod's *Faust.* They were distributed with scores that include film cues for the pianist. Like the director's work in general, both films feature fantasy and stage machinery and include a devil, played by Méliès himself (fig. 2.1).[14]

Opera was often combined with film in these early years to promote phonograph recordings, another new medium. A scene or aria would be filmed to showcase a famous opera star, like Enrico Caruso, and the phonograph recording would accompany the film—or rather the film would accompany the music. In 1908 a large number were released by Pathé and include scenes from *Pagliacci, Manon Lescaut,* and *Lohengrin,* among others.[15] The star vehicle motivated many other projects. Perhaps the most famous is the 1915 version of *Carmen,* starring Geraldine Farrar and directed by Cecil B. DeMille. Some sixty minutes in length, the film received a great deal of publicity because of the enormous fee paid to Farrar for her trek to Hollywood. In his review Bierstadt considers the film a calculated effort "to interest that part of the public . . . which still regards moving pictures as essentially a cheap and vulgar form

Fig. 2.1 Georges Méliès in *Faust et Marguérite* (190?). Directed by
Georges Méliès. (Courtesy Museum of Modern Art)

of amusement. That they have succeeded in so doing will un-
doubtedly be proved by a long line of automobiles drawn up
before the house where the 'Carmen' pictures are playing."[16]
Because of tight control of the opera by Bizet's heirs, DeMille
relied on the literary source, Prosper Mérimée's *Carmen,* more
than on the Bizet. Even within the thirty or more film versions
of the opera—probably the largest number of any opera[17]—
DeMille's film represents an early classic of opera on film.

Farrar went on to star in fifteen films between 1915 and 1921.
Although no one matched her success, other opera singers—including Lucien Muratore, Lina Cavalieri, and Richard Tauber
—appeared on the screen. Silent film opera also became a vehicle for movie actors. Theda Bara, known as "The Vamp," created a memorable performance of Carmen in a 1915 film. In the
sound era many other opera singers appeared in films—among
them were Grace Moore, Lawrence Tibbett, John McCor-
mack, Gladys Swarthout, Lily Pons, and Beniamino Gigli.[18]

In 1926 a film version of Richard Strauss's *Der Rosenkavalier* appeared, first in Dresden, in the very theater where the opera had premiered in 1911, and a few months later in London. Hugo von Hofmannsthal and Strauss both had a hand in the arrangement. A few details of the story were changed (the Feldmarschall, for example, makes an appearance), and the composer arranged and conducted the music. Strauss claimed that he was writing a film for his music rather than musical accompaniment to a film.[19] At approximately one hour and fifteen minutes in length the film was rather substantial. The director, Robert Wiene, was a celebrated filmmaker, having made the *Cabinet of Dr. Caligari* of 1919, a milestone in German expressionism. Although composer and librettist were willing participants, the publisher of the opera opposed the film. He saw it as direct competition to the stage version and therefore to the commercial viability of the original score.[20] The film has enjoyed a revival; in early 1994, a screening in New York was accompanied by Strauss's arrangement, conducted by Leon Botstein, and a few years before Armin Brunner used his own music to accompany the film.

As in the DeMille *Carmen,* many silent films returned to the literary source and used music from the opera as accompaniment. For example, an American-made *Manon Lescaut* (1914), with Cavalieri and Muratore, was based on Prévost's novel. Some four years later another striking version of *Carmen,* directed by Ernst Lubitsch, returned to the Mérimée and featured Pola Negri, a famous film star.[21]

Opera would also figure in films with independent plots. Gillian Anderson, for example, has identified several quotations from *Carmen* and *Pagliacci* in the score of Chaplin's movie *The Circus* (1928). The practice provided a link with tunes in the audience's memory and emphasized the centrality of music in the creation of a coherent narrative.[22] It also indicates that opera and film were not far apart culturally and that some operatic numbers had a firm hold in popular consciousness.

The combination of silent film and opera raises important aesthetic issues. It highlights the relation of sound to image, particularly their separation. It could be argued that silent film serves as the source of this technique that will be prominent in later opera films. Films of the sound era have a soundtrack that is integral to the film and is seemingly wedded to the image. Lips move and sound is emitted. In most films of opera, characters do not actually sing but lip-synch to prerecorded music. These shadowy likenesses of real people are only miming and resemble ghostly vessels that transmit sound, or rather appear to transmit sound.[23] In silent film the music is emitted live or on phonograph; in later practice it is integrated into the soundtrack. Both involve a time-shift and silent lips.

Opera in silent film also reminds us of the fluid practices toward music generally in silent film.[24] Music can change from one showing to the next, as in the restored *Rosenkavalier*. This makes music a performative element that challenges ideals of unity and fidelity that were valued in the late nineteenth and early twentieth centuries. These include the legacy of the *Gesamtkunstwerk*, with its unifying hand. Of course, such ideals pertain to art music more than to popular idioms such as cinema and vaudeville, the latter a likely model for the live musical accompaniment. In any case, silent film practices recall the borrowing and substitution that characterize eighteenth-century opera. In other words, the opera-film relationship in the silent era rests on a premodernist aesthetic of flexibility. Unlike the uniform product of the sound era, when one showing resembles another, the silent era fostered spontaneity and uniqueness. It created a variety of opera texts and discourses around opera and demonstrated that opera could be a major player in the electronic revolution. It also suggests that opera played a key role in the acceptance of film.

THE SOUND ERA

By the beginning of the sound era, at least in the United States, ornate movie palaces served as substitutes for the grand opera houses of Europe. Many movie theaters had boasted large orchestras in the silent era, and many had the lavish decoration found in old world temples of music. For some opera lovers these houses held out the promise of a rejuvenation of opera. Writing in *The Etude* in 1936, Harrison Lawler dreamed of a special kind of "screen grand opera" to dazzle audiences: with singers who look good on the screen and who know how to act for it. He predicted that this would have a salutary effect on staged opera. He thought it would improve performers' acting (an opinion seconded by Lawrence Tibbett), and that the Metropolitan Opera would turn to Hollywood for its talent. In the end Lawler looked to film as the salvation of art music, which was "becoming lost in a jazz age"[25]—a suggestion of cinema as a lesser threat than the feared jazz.

The advent of sound in film precipitated obvious changes for the combining of opera and film. Prerecorded and presynchronized sound replaced live performance and live playback. In fact the new relationship created a model for how music might function in motion pictures. Early on, even in the silent era, it was believed that music was needed to overcome the sense of film as a technical apparatus and to breathe life into the ghostly figures on the screen—in other words to humanize the mechanical images and to create the fiction of reality. Music would also provide a connective between cuts and hold the structure together. The question was exactly how music would be used in a sound movie.

Opera, and by extension opera in film, provided a useful model. Therefore it is not surprising that opera became a popular choice for filmic adaptation. Opera also furnished an opulent musical style for use in film. Wagnerian Leitmotif technique provided a powerful Romantic tool and became a staple of underscoring. Such Hollywood composers as Max Steiner, Miklos Rosza, and Bernard Herrmann depended on this aesthetic, which would dominate Hollywood film for decades. Although the style imparted an air of old world prestige, its use in a popular medium also democratized (some would say diluted) the idiom and converted it into kitsch: the very realization of Schoenberg's fears. The musical style would not be heard the same way again.

The incorporation of sound into film also brought about a reconsideration of opera in film. Idealists like composer George Antheil proposed a new kind of "opera for the movies." With newly composed music and other adjustments tailored to the medium, "motion-picture-operas" would be more suitable than a condensation of a stage work.[26] In 1936, the same year as Antheil's article, such an opera movie, *The Robber Symphony,* was produced in Britain. The film included newly composed music by Friedrich Feher, who also directed the film. With a fairy-tale plot, *Symphony* emphasized fantasy and included a famous dream sequence. The film had a disappointing premiere but has recently achieved a kind of cult status.[27] *Symphony* was not the first screen opera to contain newly composed music; the silent film *Jenseits des Stromes* (1922) preceded it. The German movie called for live soloists and orchestra to be synchronized during screening, whereas *Symphony* had a prerecorded track.

Antheil also mentioned plans made by studio owners for producing many opera films, but in fact few were made during this period. From this point Europe far outpaced Hollywood in the number of operas put on film.[28] Hollywood favored opera in small doses, as in a scene or aria inserted into a film. More typically the combination of song and image blossomed into that most American of forms, the musical. Jeanette MacDonald and Nelson Eddy helped to popularize the operetta, which also flourished on the Continent.[29] So-called "biopics" of an opera composer or singer also appealed to audiences, and they offered attractive vehicles for stars. Opera singers and opera proved useful to the industry at this time. They buttressed the reputation of cinema when many thought the addition of sound spelled the demise of the medium.

Some notable opera films were created in the 1930s. Fortune Gallo's version of *I Pagliacci* (1930) represents one of the earliest complete operas on film, particularly from the United States. From Germany came Max Ophuls's *Die Verkaufte Braut* (1932), which capitalizes on the outdoors and the possibility of a true cinematic conception. Some seventy-six minutes long, *Braut* typifies the early opera film in that it does not present the complete opera but has extensive cutting and rearrangement.[30] Another landmark of the decade is *Die Dreigroschenoper* (1931), directed by Georg Wilhelm Pabst and starring Lotte Lenya as Jenny. Pabst's movie was controversial because composer Kurt Weill and playwright Bertholt Brecht believed that the film betrayed their principles of epic theater.[31] In separate legal actions Brecht lost but Weill won. In 1935 Hollywood produced the (in)famous *A Night at the Opera,* with the Marx Brothers. Although a standard movie rather than a film of an opera, the film reveals a great deal about the social role of opera. The latter part of the story, revolving around a performance of *Il Trovatore* in an opera house in New York, mocks the genre "as a site of anarchy," as Gerhard Koch aptly describes it.[32] In the film,

Fig. 2.2 Harpo Marx (center), Chico Marx (right), and Margaret Dumont (rear) in *A Night at the Opera* (1935). Directed by Sam Wood. (Courtesy Museum of Modern Art)

operatic ritual is portrayed as a vehicle through which America aspires to the aristocratic polish of Europe (fig. 2.2).

Many films amounted to operas "in prose," that is, spoken treatments built on the literary source, with operatic music as support. A fine example is *La Vie de Bohème* (1942). Directed by Marcel L'Herbier and starring Louis Jourdan, the movie returns to Henri Murger's story on which the Puccini version is based. The opera supplies background music, all instrumental. Unfortunately, by the time it was released, after World War II, its light mood was out of favor and the film was severely criticized.[33] Another major French film, Abel Gance's *Louise* (1938), suffered at the hands of critics. Directed by the creator of the epic *Napoleon* (1927), *Louise* featured Grace Moore in Charpentier's opera. In the movie Gance attempted to meld film and opera into a "film lyrique." The composer was also involved in the project, and most of the recitatives were converted into dialogue.[34]

It is not surprising that Italy, birthplace of opera, developed a strong tradition of opera on film. By the 1940s the country boasted several important directors. Carmine Gallone, a formative figure in Italian neo-realism, made several films around opera. *Rigoletto* (1946), for example, stresses the stage origins of opera. He also produced biopics, such as *Verdi* in 1938 and *Puccini* in 1953. Gallone directed several films that Ermanno Comuzio called "parallel works." In these films, the life of a fictional singer merges with that of the role she or he is playing, and the updated story usually entails newly composed music. Two examples by Gallone are *Il Sogno di Butterfly* (1939), based on the Puccini opera, and *Amami, Alfredo* (1940), a variation on *La Traviata*.[35] An Italian opera film that has achieved a measure of cult status is Clemente Fracassi's *Aida* (1953), with Renata Tebaldi's voice lip-synched by Sophia Loren. It features grand spectacle and, at only ninety-five minutes, cuts a great deal of Verdi's score.

The connection between Italian culture and opera emerges in general films as well. In *Senso* (1954), a landmark in cinema, director Luchino Visconti uses opera in interesting ways. The story is set in the last years of the Risorgimento and the characters find themselves pitting their personal passions against nationalist loyalty—a recurrent theme in Verdian melodrama. The influence of Verdi is apparent from the beginning of the film as the title credits roll over a stage performance of *Il Trovatore;* we see Manrico assemble the insurgents and sing the stirring "Di quella pira." This incites a riot in the theater, as leaflets from Italian patriots rain down from the balcony. The Austrian military in attendance are placed on the defensive. Visconti's use of this Verdian conceit sets the stakes for the entire film. In contrast to the satiric use of *Il Trovatore* in *A Night at the Opera*, in *Senso* Verdi's opera has a serious function. It becomes a site of political action — a place where social upheaval can be launched. The exaggerated quality of Bruckner's Symphony No. 7, which serves as underscoring at key emotional places, also lends an operatic intensity to the film.[36]

In the United States the film musical continued in popularity. Some films, such as *The Student Prince* (1954), resembled the operetta, and others portrayed opera singers, as in *The Great Caruso* (1951) with Mario Lanza (Lanza's voice was dubbed into *Student Prince*). But the opera film as such became an endangered species. Nonetheless, two landmark films of opera were produced in America in the early 1950s: *The Medium* (1951) and *Carmen Jones* (1954). Produced and directed by Otto Preminger, *Carmen Jones* is an updated, Americanized version of Bizet's opera, and is based on Oscar Hammerstein's Broadway musical of 1943. The cast and characters are black and the plot parallels the Bizet. The story is set in South Carolina (Bizet's setting is Andalusia) and begins at a factory on an army base. The killing of Carmen takes place outside a boxing ring in Chicago instead of a Spanish bullring. Produced by a major studio, *Carmen Jones* was produced as mass entertainment. It has a wide-screen format, a feature of many Hollywood epics in this period. The film is clearly a musical and not an opera, and it fits in Rick Altman's category of a folk musical.[37] *Carmen Jones* contains a great deal of reworked material, including colloquial lyrics. Musical numbers may be transposed, eliminated, truncated, or used in other ways — for example, as a diegetic number (the Seguidilla as a cocktail-piano piece in a hotel suite), as non-diegetic underscoring, or as a hummed or whistled tune for recall or foreshadowing (fig. 2.3).

Although highly imaginative, *Carmen Jones* can be a troubling work, especially for late-twentieth-century audiences. In

Fig. 2.3 Dorothy Dandridge and Harry Belafonte in *Carmen Jones* (1954). Directed by Otto Preminger. (Courtesy British Film Institute)

its time it was considered a novelty, not for its operatic elements but for its focus on black life in the United States. Preminger and Hammerstein stated that they had idealistic motives behind the project (including the Broadway version).[38] The result, however, can be seen as an objectification of black culture. Part of the problem, as James Baldwin noted in his review when the film appeared, is that the world we see in the film is populated only by blacks, while Bizet's *Carmen* contains gypsies in conflict with Europeans in authority. Baldwin contends that the black-only characters in *Carmen Jones* were not imbued with characteristics that reflected real black culture, or its problems. The film promotes a they're-just-like-us feeling for white audiences, while simultaneously distancing the characters through demeaning "dats" and "deres" in the lyrics of the songs. Bald-

Fig. 2.4 Leo Coleman and Anna-Maria Alberghetti in *The Medium*
(1951). Directed by Gian-Carlo Menotti. (Courtesy British Film
Institute)

win worries about the "color vacuum" that "each spectator will
fill with his own fantasies," and the appropriation by Great
Art "of the exceptional Negro and using him for questionable
purposes."[39] Despite the difficulties, however, *Carmen Jones* is
appealing in many respects. Dorothy Dandridge is persuasive
as Carmen, and Pearl Bailey injects life into the film as Frankie.
Carmen Jones may be problematic but it is seductive.[40]

The Medium is a rare example of a full-length film-opera
produced in the United States (fig. 2.4). Composed by Italian-
American Gian-Carlo Menotti, the opera premiered on Broadway and enjoyed an extended run.[41] The film may have the distinction of being the only film-opera directed by the composer-
librettist of the original opera. Its birth outside the opera house
hints at the light, melodic style of much of the English-language work, but it also suggests a bias against American opera.

In any event, the populist nature of the story, the language, and much of the music may help explain why it was made into a film. Unlike *Carmen Jones,* however, *The Medium* is not a musical. It involves continuous music, conventional operatic voices (except for the role of Monica), and at times a modernist score that is angular and dissonant.

Menotti created a cinematic interpretation that is remarkably effective. He shot the movie in black and white, with chiaroscuro and extremes in lighting—a visual style reminiscent of Orson Welles and Jean Cocteau.[42] These mannered devices heighten the hysteria of the story. As the composer noted, this is a drama about the difficulty of sorting out one's belief in relation to the real and the unreal,[43] and hallucination and insanity are only a breath away. Menotti favors the close-up, as in the lingering tight shot of Mrs. Gobineau's eyes as she sings of her dead boy. The continuous music changes kaleidoscopically as it shifts from underscoring to vocal accompaniment to diegetic number and gradations in between. One reason this organization works so well is that the score has recurring motives, akin to Leitmotifs. For the film Menotti added a substantial amount of music, mostly as accompaniment for visual and transitional effects, and the success of the film is due in no small measure to this fit. It can be argued that *The Medium* offers the second major embodiment of the ideal envisioned in the 1930s for opera on the screen: a truly new opera for the screen, tailored specifically for the medium. I say this while recognizing the existence of the stage opera *The Medium.* Nonetheless the film version, with composer-librettist at the helm, amounts to a new work for cinema.

The 1950s witnessed other interesting projects. In Britain an imaginative version of *The Tales of Hoffmann* was produced by the team of Michael Powell and Emeric Pressburger in 1951 (see chapter 4 for a detailed study). Although Britain had produced relatively few films of opera, *Tales* builds on a British tradition of ballet-film, and most of the leading roles are filled by dancers. Dance and mime are prominent and overshadow the music in many places. A substantial portion of the cast and production team came from *The Red Shoes,* Powell and Pressburger's *hommage* to the lure of dance. This 1948 movie enjoyed great success in the United States, especially among aspiring ballerinas, and eventually led to an operatic sequel, the scintillating *Tales.*

The Soviet Union boasted significant filmmaking in this period and stressed works that glorify the country. Among the major opera films were Vera Stroyeva's versions of Mussorgsky's *Boris Godunov* (1955) and *Khovanshchina* (1959). Roman Tikhomirov, another major filmmaker, produced Tchaikovsky's *Eugene Onegin* (1958) and *The Queen of Spades* (1960). Earlier, director-writer Sergei Eisenstein and composer Sergei Prokofief collaborated on two memorable operatic films: *Alexander Nevsky* (1938) and *Ivan the Terrible,* Parts 1 and 2 (1943 and 1946, respectively). Pauline Kael described *Ivan* as an opera without song; with its operatic extremes of plot, the film resembles a sequence of stills on the verge of erupting into an aria.[44]

Paul Czinner's version of *Der Rosenkavalier* (1960) might be considered a capstone to the first half-century of opera on film. It combines the talents of major figures—Herbert Von Karajan, Elisabeth Schwarzkopf, and Sena Jurinac—in a recreation of a major Salzburg production. Czinner, a Hungarian emigré to Britain, had didactic and preservationist concerns in mind with this film. Plot summaries, for example, appear before each act to facilitate understanding (no subtitles appeared in the original video version). Some of the introductory matter serves questionable ends, however. Adoring shots of Von Karajan's entrances into the pit inject a self-serving element and set the reverent tone of *Der Rosenkavalier* as Masterpiece German

Culture: an unfortunate element in an otherwise moving artistic experience. As for the rest Czinner fulfills his mission of preserving a fine performance, and Schwarzkopf shines in one of her signature roles as the Marschallin. The interaction of camera, staging, and music emphasizes the setting in the theater. Although several cameras are placed around the hall (or rather the studio re-creation), the camera remains static and keeps a respectful distance from the singers. Medium shots predominate and close-ups are few. The movie glorifies opera in the theater, a hint at what television will take up vigorously in the coming years.

TELEVISION

The arrival of television created great excitement for the production of opera and eventually shifted the center of gravity from the large screen to the small. Television offers an intimacy and informality that contrast with the more ritualistic venues of cinema and opera house. Because it is usually watched in a domestic setting, television is a powerful force for social cohesion. Its affinity for directness and reportage imbues it with a sense of reality that cinema is hard-pressed to match. Opera on television builds on these characteristics to create a variety of representations for the small-scale medium—whether live, videotaped, or on film, whether originating in the studio, opera house, or outdoors.

Televised opera has certain technical needs. All aspects of theatrical craft must be tailored to the medium. It deploys multiple cameras and requires intensified lighting, especially for the relay from the opera house. As in cinema, the sound-image relationship must be carefully structured. Scale, composition, and perspective have to be planned for the small screen. Canadian television director Peter Symcox, for instance, considers the longitudinal orientation of television fundamental in planning productions.[45] Further adjustments are needed if an audience is present when the work is being taped.

Socially television reaches vast numbers of people and has the potential to be populist and democratic. It can minimize difference and encourage unity. Indeed, idealism has fueled many televised productions. Artistically, this includes a wish to educate and improve the taste of audiences. Practically, televised opera has helped sustain opera in an era of growing financial strain for the genre and relied on a variety of sources for funding. Many projects have found support in partnerships with recording companies and video distributors. In the United States, producing opera for television is difficult because of the commercial nature of the medium and the relative lack of interest in opera. Many European countries, however, have state-supported television. This system can accommodate projects for a variety of reasons, be it artistic experimentation, national pride, or cultural literacy. Many ventures on both sides of the Atlantic depend on a combination of public and private support. Nonetheless, the financial traditions characteristic of each region affect the kinds of projects that are made and broadcast.

There are three main types of telecast opera: the studio production, the film, and the relay (live or delayed) from the opera house. The boundaries can be ambiguous, however. Many of Jean-Pierre Ponnelle's films, for example, were shot in a studio and belong to two categories. Furthermore, the boundary between television and cinema can be blurred, as in Ingmar Bergman's *The Magic Flute*, originally produced for television (1975) and subsequently shown in movie theaters. It has assumed such an independence from television that it is often considered the first modern film-opera, a status encouraged by Bergman's position as cinéaste.

Opera on television did little to help establish television as a medium in its early days—a situation quite different from opera's influence on early cinema. As we have seen, opera played a major role in the establishment of cinema. Filmmakers adapted opera's narrative structures to early films; opera provided models for melodrama and the combining of music and image on film. The difference between opera's influence on cinema and on television seems to be a function of medium and chronology. Many of the social and aesthetic characteristics of early cinema had a lot in common with opera. Television, however, arose in the mid twentieth century and depended on values of speed, convenience, and distraction, which have little in common with opera.

Early History

Advocates of opera on television had high hopes in the early years. Perhaps some saw television as a way of redressing the failure of cinema to establish a tradition of opera on film.[46] Visionaries in the United States, especially emigrés Peter Herman Adler and Herbert Graf, considered television a means of making opera available to all. They felt it could elevate public taste and encourage a specifically American kind of opera, one more populist and accessible than that of the European tradition. Such operas were to be written and tailored for television. They might also rejuvenate an interest in opera in the United States—just as screen opera in the 1930s was meant to rekindle interest in live opera. In addition to a genuine desire to include opera in the new fare, some executives saw opera as a way of gaining goodwill for the new commercial medium.[47]

Beginning in 1936, scattered experiments in televising opera or excerpts from opera occurred on the BBC and NBC and also at a new station in Schenectady, New York. Although such activities were suspended at the BBC during the war, NBC hired stage director Herbert Graf in 1944 to create viable productions for the new medium. He discovered that certain effects work well for television, especially English translations, sensitive camerawork, and naturalistic acting. His condensed version of *Pagliacci* set a precedent. In response to a ban on live instrumental music on television, which was a provision of a labor agreement, singers lip-synched to a prerecorded version.[48] After the war, the BBC resumed broadcasts of opera, and by 1947 these included relays from the opera house.[49] In November 1948, ABC telecast the opening-night performance of *Otello* from the stage of the Metropolitan Opera. Approximately 500,000 homes tuned in to the event, an astonishing figure given that so few owned a television set. Although hailed as a major achievement, the broadcast had serious problems. The dim lighting meant that figures and details could not be discerned with sufficient clarity. An excessive number of long shots reduced the size of people on television screens, which were very small. Critics also observed that the timing and placement of shots were poorly synchronized with music and action. Despite the shortcomings, however, the telecast augured well for the future. Opening nights at the Met returned to television the next two years, but these would be the last of the series because of high costs for ABC and the Met's decision to pursue closed-circuit broadcasting.

Impressed by the impact of ABC's telecasts, the other two networks became involved in opera on television. NBC assumed the lead with its NBC Opera Theatre, which lasted for fifteen seasons, from 1949 to 1964. The venture was imaginative and of high quality. It was also courageous given the paucity of financial support. Although initially reluctant, chief executive David Sarnoff and later son Robert saw themselves as musical patrons for the public through their network. In the later years the Sarnoffs themselves paid the lion's share of expenses for many productions. They worked closely with music director Samuel Chotzinoff, a former music critic, and hired talented producers and directors—none more so than Adler, who would lead the Opera Theatre.

A Czech-Jewish conductor and student of Alexander Zemlinsky, Adler was an ardent supporter of television opera. In a piece in *Musical America*, Adler wrote in 1951 that television could rejuvenate opera in the United States. He said it would "bridge the gap between the mass audience and the opera house" and "develop a new kind of opera."[50] Under Adler's leadership the NBC Opera Theatre was an artistic success, although his grand vision for opera in America did not materialize. In these years several works were commissioned for the series, which include Menotti's *Amahl and the Night Visitors* (1951) and *Labyrinth* (1963), and Lukas Foss's *Griffelkin* (1955). *Amahl* was very well received and became a holiday favorite. As gauged by Olin Downes's review on the front page of *The New York Times*, the premiere marked a recognition of the arrival of opera on television.[51] Unlike most studio productions, *Amahl* found sponsors for most of its broadcasts. The artistic and commercial success of *Amahl* in the United States inspired producers in other countries to commission and broadcast operas for television.[52]

The NBC Opera Theatre also presented standard works but most were modified to suit the medium, the audience, and the time-slot (usually one hour). For example, an early *Carmen* created a condensed framework by returning to the literary source. Like much of the Mérimée, it is constructed as a flashback and omits Micaela. Naturally, it is in English.[53] Some large-scale works were attempted, as in 1953 when a three-hour *Der Rosenkavalier* appeared in two installments on successive Sundays. Although great care was expended on the production, the lavish opera proved unsuitable to the intimacy of television.[54] NBC Opera Theatre also introduced America to new operas composed abroad, as in its production of Benjamin Britten's *Billy Budd*. Premiering in London in December 1951, the opera was telecast in October 1952 and was the first Britten opera to be aired on television.[55]

NBC Opera Theatre did not shy away from controversy. In 1954 it offered a complete *Salome*, with actors lip-synching some of the roles. A year later black soprano Leontyne Price appeared in the company's *Tosca*, her first full-length opera in any venue, and several Southern affiliate stations dropped out of the broadcast.[56] As the series matured it benefited from the talents of television director Kirk Browning and from an innovation that placed the orchestra in a separate space. This allowed the camera unrestricted movement in the studio.

CBS also promoted opera in these early years but its involvement was limited. In December 1948 the network televised *The Medium*, with Marie Powers, on its Studio One series (NBC had broadcast the opera a month before). The 1949–50 season introduced CBS's Opera Television Theater, headed by Lawrence Tibbett and Henry Souvaine, which lasted only that year. It opened with a successful *Carmen,* sung in French and directed by Boris Goldovsky and Byron Paul. But without sponsors the series folded. The network's next foray into opera, in 1953, was part of *Omnibus,* a Sunday afternoon series that offered imaginative cultural fare. With support from the Ford Foundation rather than commercial sponsors, the program promoted experimentation. Over the next few years a variety of opera telecasts were presented. Notable was Graf's 1953 production of *Die Fledermaus* by the Metropolitan Opera company, and performances in later years of American works by William Schuman and Douglas Moore.

In 1959 a significant impetus to televised opera on the international level was initiated: the Salzburg Prize, an award given every three years for the best new opera written for television. In addition to a cash prize, winners were assured of a televised performance. They include Paul Angerer's *Passkontrolle,* performed in 1959 on Oesterreichischer Rundfunk, and Ingvar Lidholm's *Holländarn,* on Sveriges Radio Television in 1967.

Later History

Subsequent history was shaped less by idealism than by economics. The costs of studio productions became exorbitant, and without creative solutions the future of television opera was in jeopardy. The United States imported many productions from Europe and relied increasingly on public television and "niche" cable networks to broadcast opera. The relay became the main format. In Europe television stations joined forces to co-produce operas. In ventures with private European companies, like the Munich-based Unitel and Mediascope, consortia produced studio films for television. Eventually that support declined, and by the late 1980s the relay was favored in Europe as well. For major houses in particular, the preference for the relay has been driven by the home-video market and a desire to create a record of their productions. Despite its economic advantages, however, many consider the relay regressive because it marks a return to the early years of television and scarcely capitalizes on the capabilities of television as a medium. Scattered support for new operas has surfaced in the 1990s, especially from Britain's bold Channel 4, which has commissioned and broadcast several new works.[57]

In the United States, commercial stations withdrew opera from their programming after the demise of the NBC Opera Theatre and noncommercial outlets became televised opera's main venue. In the mid 1960s the Ford Foundation asked Adler to draft recommendations for opera on noncommercial television. The main result was the NET Opera Company, a sequel to the NBC venture. Kirk Browning, another veteran of the earlier company, came on board. Leos Janacek's *From the House of the Dead* inaugurated the series in 1969 and was substantially reworked for television. In the 1970–71 season the network turned to foreign stations for joint sponsorship. An important work was Britten's new opera for television, *Owen Wingrave,* which bowed on 16 May 1971 in Britain, Canada, and the United States.[58] Commissioned by the BBC in 1966, the opera was prerecorded in November 1970. It would also be presented at the opera house a few years later, but it has not seen many performances in either medium since.[59] In 1974 a highly publicized premiere by Hans Werner Henze, *Rachel, La Cubana,* took place. Unfortunately high costs and unconventional dramaturgy alienated many affiliates, and as a result the series could not sustain its support and within a few years it ended. But before the demise it had imported several fine productions, like Leonard Bernstein's *Trouble in Tahiti* from Britain. Beginning in the 1980s, European productions of all types found their most accommodating American venue on cable stations devoted to the arts, especially Bravo and the Arts & Entertainment network (mergers and name changes notwithstanding).

In the late 1970s the relay became more feasible because of technological advances in cameras and lighting. The financial situation improved as well: production costs were lower because no new staging or opera was required and the television producer shared expenses with the opera house. Video distribution, which became common after 1985, also supported the production. In the United States the PBS umbrella series Great Performances turned to relays in the late 1970s. Douglas Moore's *The Ballad of Baby Doe,* from the stage of the New York City

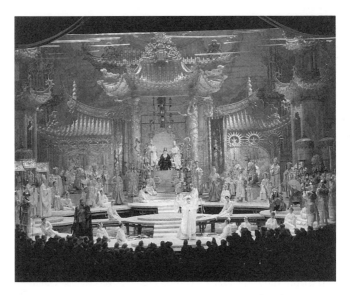

Fig. 2.5 Plácido Domingo and Eva Marton in *Turandot* (1987),
Metropolitan Opera. Directed by Franco Zeffirelli. (Courtesy
Metropolitan Opera. Photo by Winnie Klotz)

Opera, inaugurated the "Live from Lincoln Center" series in
spring 1976; Browning served as television director. The selection of an American work for the first broadcast suggests a
populist aim, much in the spirit of predecessors at NBC and
NET. "Live from the Met" commenced a year later, with *La
Bohème*, a popular work, to be sure, but still a European opera
that required subtitles. Browning directed, Pavarotti and Scotto
drew a large audience, and Texaco served as sponsor. Over the
next few years, British director Brian Large also directed Met
telecasts. In the 1979–80 season "Live from the Met" used some
tape-delayed relays, a practice that became standard in most
houses in the next decade. Eventually the Met telecasts appeared under the rubric "Great Performances."

A Met telecast of *Turandot*, from 1987, demonstrates the level of sophistication in the relay by this time (fig. 2.5). Directed for television by veteran Browning, the lavish Zeffirelli production received a nuanced and idiomatic interpretation for the small screen. Camera angles and composition are rich and varied, although Browning prefers the close-up.[60] His attention to detail seems tailored to the exuberance of Zeffirelli's overdecorated sets. In Act I, for example, skulls of previous suitors, an insignificant detail when seen in the opera house, fill the screen at times; in the court scene of Act II Chinese icons are highlighted. Browning intercuts such images with close-up shots of the main story and players. The camerawork favors relatively quick cutting, varied angles, and frequent zooms. These accord well with the musical drama because they are often tempered by another device: the use of dissolve between cuts. The dissolve promotes continuity and suggests a cinematic style in the way video's "hard edges" are softened to approach film. The device works well in this cinematic opera, whose instrumental continuity, unifying motives, and melodramatic narrative recall many a movie score. The telecast also features typical trappings of the relay. Viewers feel the sense of occasion in sharing a night at the opera house, seeing first a lengthy exterior view of the Met and the fountain on the plaza. *Turandot*, cast and conductor, and Zeffirelli-Browning may appear to be the stars; but the Metropolitan Opera as a mecca of high culture is celebrated as well.

In Europe the relay also became the favored format. The Chéreau-Large-Boulez *Ring* cycle of circa 1980, recorded in an empty hall, marked a major event. Unlike the American return to the relay, the European return continued its engagement with televised opera in film and studio formats. Many leading directors and conductors made these treatments. While the productions were tailored to television, they needed fewer adjustments than Adler and others had to make for American audiences. Europeans are more willing than Americans to accept the conventions of opera; matters of length, language, and performance style pose fewer problems for Europeans. Governmental support has also freed stations from concerns over viewership. The state, for its part, has viewed cultural preservation as part of its mission. The televised films may reflect an interest that also found expression in full-length motion-picture opera, or what I call film-opera. Although film-opera flourished in Europe in the 1980s, it was noticeably absent in America.

Films for Television

As discussed earlier, Von Karajan conducted the Salzburg production of *Der Rosenkavalier* that was memorialized in a movie directed by Czinner. This conductor became a central figure in operas filmed for television and sometimes served as director. These projects are characterized by a convergence of media; a film was linked with a prior stage production and music recording, and a video was issued later. Rolf Liebermann, director of the Hamburg State Opera and Paris Opera, reports that Von Karajan required these outlets be guaranteed before he would direct a stage production; he also controlled a substantial share of the future rights of the properties.[61]

A treatment of *La Bohème* from 1967 typifies an early example. Produced by DGG and Unitel, *Bohème* re-creates a famous La Scala production directed by Zeffirelli in 1963, his first for the house. Although shot at La Scala, no audience is present. In the opera proper we never see the proscenium or other traces of the opera house. Yet La Scala as icon is instilled during the opening credits through a fixed image of the hall as viewed from the stage. Von Karajan insinuates himself as icon during an extended shot of the conductor in tails at the start of the overture. While reminiscent of *Rosenkavalier*, it occurs only once in the film (thankfully). The opera house does not reappear, and from this point *Bohème* has the feel of a studio production. The glory of the film is the music. With fine performances by Mirella Freni and Gianni Raimondi, the singing is first-rate, and the orchestral sound and general pacing under Von Karajan merit high marks. The recording from DGG is obviously a major addition to the *Bohème* catalogue on disk. Visually, however, the film is not as interesting. The camera is static and unimaginative, and the plane of the front of the stage is preserved as the principal vantage point—another indication of its provenance. With a few exceptions, one keenly senses the scenic and spatial limitations of a stage production. The singers affect stylized gestures rather than a more natural style suited to television. The film's main function is to supply visual accompaniment to a musical performance. It substitutes for those who could not experience the opera first-hand and offers a visual account of an error-free musical interpretation. The film also reveals the success of *Bohème* on the small screen. Puccini's emotional music has an affinity for the intimacy of the televisual experience. Frequent climaxes in the music call for close shots and these draw us into the drama.

Other major projects came from DGG and Unitel. One of the more interesting films is *Otello*, of 1974, directed and conducted by Von Karajan. Freni portrays Desdemona, with Jon Vickers as Otello and Peter Glossop as Iago. As in *Bohème*, this *Otello* is intended as visual enhancement of a definitive musical performance. Although the musical aspects are not entirely successful—the pacing is more Wagnerian than Verdian—the film has more to offer visually. Capitalizing on the expanded spaces of a studio, *Otello* uses several sets, even within a scene. Some sets suggest the outdoors, some scenes move from one interior space to another. Dissolves link shots in sensitive places, as in seams between sections of the Act I Love Duet or in changes of angle in Desdemona's scena at the start of Act IV. Emotional inflection also comes from the occasional juxtaposition of soft- and hard-focus. While the camera is more mobile than it is in *Bohème,* most scenes retain a point or plane that organizes shots. Stylized gestures, especially of Vickers, and static crowd scenes recall the stage. Freni's impassive face plays poorly before the probing eye of the camera.

In the same period Liebermann organized more than a dozen television films that were intended to enhance the reputation of the Hamburg State Opera and increase its audience.[62] Joachim Hess was chosen to direct twelve productions between 1967 and 1972. The series was planned originally as relays from the opera house, but Von Karajan's activity in media apparently persuaded Liebermann to do films instead. Expenses were shared between the opera house and the production company.[63] German works, from Lortzing's *Zar and Zimmermann* to *Fidelio, Flute, Freischütz,* and *Wozzeck,* make up the bulk of the repertoire. *Wozzeck* (1971) was shot on location in southern Germany and represents one of the highlights. Liebermann's television films might be considered a precursor to the fully cinematic film *Don Giovanni* (1979) directed by Joseph Losey, another project instigated by Liebermann.

Opera director Jean-Pierre Ponnelle produced sixteen opera films for television before his death in 1988. A designer turned director, Ponnelle paid much attention to the visual appearance of a production. His stage interpretations have also become famous for their innovation and vision. The sense of daring carried over to his films. An activist behind the camera, Ponnelle exploited a wide range of visual effects and produced a style that is flamboyant and strongly cinematic. He claimed that there was little difference between a film for television and for cinema, except that the latter was shot in the outdoors and made playback recording problematic.[64] He saw himself as a composer with the camera: an artist tailoring the rhythms, movements, and colors of the visual apparatus with the rhythms, dynamics, and harmonies of the musical score. "For me the language of the camera is like additional lines in the score," said Ponnelle, a striking statement when one considers that Ponnelle knew the orchestral score of every opera he directed. He does not necessarily mean that music and image move in a parallel relationship. While music is the primary element, the image can relate to it in endless forms, including those that question, challenge, or bring out ambiguity in the narrative. For Ponnelle such representations can result in a separation of music and image, as when a character sings but no lips move. Such inner monologue serves to probe psychological conflict in a character or reveal dramatic irony in a group. Used in such an effective manner, the device helps to explain the director's favorable opinion of the "playback method" of creating an opera film, which allows singers to concentrate on their acting. Indeed, Ponnelle requires singers to be physically active, expressive and nuanced with their faces, and free of artificial gestures. Above all, Ponnelle's love affair with the camera is guided by the knowledge that it can bring out many more details and expand his creative reach for interpreting traditional works.[65]

Madama Butterfly of 1974, Ponnelle's second film, is an unforgettable rendition of the popular opera.[66] Freni and Domingo excel vocally and give fine acting performances under Ponnelle's direction. As in most productions of *Butterfly* Ponnelle stresses the conflict between East and West. He personalizes the gap as the clash between two fantasies: Pinkerton's dream of possessing a young girl, ripe for the plucking, without any personal responsibility on his part; and Butterfly's wish of being possessed by a Romantic vision of love, made more seductive by the nobility of becoming a Westerner. Through a bevy of effects—filters, sepia contrast, soft focus, lap dissolves, slow motion, freeze frame, fast pans and zooms—the camera evokes the dream world the characters inhabit psychologically.

A violent gesture at the beginning brings reality and fantasy into sharp relief: Pinkerton breaks through a paper wall in slow motion, in washed-out color; anguished, he runs down a path. It is an intriguing re-interpretation of the fugal introductory music. Next his face dissolves out-of-focus and a new scene, in full color, presents a smiling Pinkerton as he arrives with the broker. This begins the story proper, a flashback in Pinkerton's mind of the events leading to his return and Butterfly's suicide. The suicide is staged with Pinkerton present, who then proceeds to back away and crash through the wall. This image is frozen at the end; its continuation opens the film. The breaking through physicalizes the libretto's themes of fragility and impermanence. For Pinkerton it suggests an obsessive need to break free of his guilt and the psychological drives that led to the tragedy. It also symbolizes a kind of reverse sexual penetration of Butterfly and her culture. In any event, Ponnelle's circular construction implies that escape is not possible and Pinkerton is trapped.

In this film, Ponnelle uses the camera to convey a sense of American culture and imperialism: one of the first shots is of a gum-chewing Pinkerton whose body language exudes the ease and confidence of someone from the West. Pinkerton first sees Butterfly amid a heavy mist over the hill from which the voices of young women rise ethereally. Early in Act II we see a telling split shot: on one side Butterfly is wearing Western clothing and praying to Catholic icons; on the other side Suzuki is dressed in traditional garb and praying to Japanese gods. Later, Butterfly's horrified reaction to Sharpless's question about her future should Pinkerton never return is marked by a fast zoom to her face. The camera creates a sense of rhapsody in the flower scene: mixed focus as the women pick the blooms, and then a mix of freeze frame and slow motion as the petals are scattered. Here the languorous tempo of Von Karajan as the women sing in close duet is paralleled by the image. During the instrumental music of the Vigil Scene, the passage of day into night is marked by time-lapse photography of the outside of the house. And, of course, the dream sequence of Butterfly is ideal for film. More than seven minutes long, the images of a happy past and fantasized future appear before us. The scene culminates in a fast pan among the images. After this recapitulation the morning, and reality, arrives.

Two years later Ponnelle filmed *Le Nozze di Figaro,* another major achievement. With a stellar cast consisting of Hermann Prey, Dietrich Fischer-Dieskau, Maria Ewing, and Kiri Te Kanawa in addition to Freni (as Susanna), this *Figaro* stresses personal relationships. The struggle for power between Figaro and the Count becomes a major theme, but more as a matter of personality than of class or ideology. The camera functions as a sensitive barometer of character. More often than in *Butterfly,* Ponnelle allows image to interact with music without a "seen" voice—a heard voice that is uttered by moving lips.[67] This occurs in several arias, including Cherubino's "Non so più" and the Count's "Vedrò mentr' io sospiro." In "Vedrò" the music becomes outer accompaniment to the reflexive text of how the Count is being bested by inferiors. Ponnelle has us focus on the nuanced expressions of Fischer-Dieskau and the resolve in his eyes, which are juxtaposed with determined looks on Figaro's face. The confrontation occurs in a courtroom with the Count as judge—an allusion to the omitted trial scene from Beaumarchais's play. Interiorized music is also put to good use in ensembles. In the trio "Cosa sento" in Act I,

Susanna's first reactions to the confusion are uttered to herself. In the Sextet of recognition the reactions of each character after Susanna slaps Figaro are internal. They are heard against a freeze-frame image of the group, whose inertness reflects their confused feelings.

Three arias illustrate the imaginative use of the camera. In "Non so più" Cherubino's aimlessness is captured by a circling motion of the camera in much of the number. Near the end he is trapped against a wall, caught in the net of his own confusion. Before that we see much of the aria through his eyes: the kindly face of Susanna, and the unsteady glances at others as projections of what he sees on their faces. We also see him as if he were looking at himself, with herky-jerky motions suggestive of a hand-held camera. The lack of visual control tells us that Cherubino cannot master himself or his environment. In a second aria, the retrospective "Dove sono," the Countess muses internally on her happy past with a sepia-tinted flashback of their courtship. Idealized dress and slow motion add to the nostalgia. At the allegro section the Countess returns to visible voice as she resolves to save her marriage.

The third example forms the most sensational element of the film: presentation of a split persona. Figaro's diatribe in Act IV against women, "Aprite un po' quegli occhi," shows us two Figaros. Figaro-bridegroom sits dejected on a bench, mute, while another Figaro, in servant's garb, gives voice to the feisty Figaro seen earlier. The split also depicts an argument between reason and feeling, a lively debate in the Enlightenment. At one point the two personas argue musically. Technically the split is achieved through a film projected within the film—the bridegroom fuzzy while rational Figaro looks fresh and clean. The device creates multiple agents between characters, singers, and viewers, and it raises fascinating issues about who is hearing whom or what.

Fig. 2.6 The Three Boys in *The Magic Flute* (1975). Directed by Ingmar Bergman. (Courtesy British Film Institute)

Ingmar Bergman's *Magic Flute* of 1975, a television film shown widely in movie theaters, represents a landmark of filmed opera (fig. 2.6).[68] One major concern is the interaction between onscreen audience and work. The film is structured as a play-within-a-movie and returns to the face of a young girl (Bergman's daughter) who represents an ideal viewer and registers our emotions on her face. This universalism underlies the project as a whole, which resulted from a commission by Swedish Television for its fiftieth anniversary. Shown on New Year's Day 1975 and later by other stations on Christmas Day and other holidays, the film assumed a function as family fare entertainment similar to that of *Amahl* in early television. Nonetheless, despite criticism of its "culinary" idealism,[69] Bergman's film is a joyous yet serious rendition of Mozart's late work. It manages to delight in childlike naiveté as it plumbs psychological depth. One way this is accomplished is through the removal of Masonic text and imagery, which makes Sarastro and his followers more generalized. Sarastro's paternal demeanor approaches archetype, and Bergman even makes him Pamina's father. As a result the film explores a parental struggle for the daughter and depicts the maternal as a hellish force that must yield to the wisdom of the father.[70] While disturbing, the conceit raises an important social issue.

Flute is similar to other Bergman works. Like *Flute*, many films are concerned with ethical quest. The director describes the light touch of his *Smiles of a Summer Night* (1955) as "a bit of Mozart," while *The Seventh Seal* (1956) offers a romantic fairy tale along the lines of *Flute*. The most obvious likeness to *Flute*, however, is *Hour of the Wolf* (1968), which explores a quest and the contrast between day and night. It even contains a scene from *Flute* that is performed by puppets: "O ew'ge Nacht," the moment of Tamino's ethical crisis.[71] In *Flute* the scene forms the psychological core of the film and departs farthest from the frame of the opera house. In fact, with a black background behind a facial close-up, the shot has no specific location other than Tamino's mind. After his conversion he returns to the stage, reconnects with the contrived audience, and the story continues.

Other features of *Flute* bring a smile to the face. There are the self-mocking placards of serendipitous texts, the grinding simplicity of the stage machinery, the cherubic boys who descend in a balloon. In what Pauline Kael calls "the story of the performance"[72] Bergman offers a glimpse of backstage activity. At intermission, for example, Tamino and Pamina play chess, the Queen drags on a cigarette under a "No Smoking" sign, a minion of Monostatos pores over a comic book, and Sarastro studies the score of *Parsifal,* the opera that culminates the ethical quest and German Romantic tradition begun in *Flute*.[73] The film pays homage to the theatrical origin of opera yet becomes a convincing cinematic portrayal that juxtaposes multiple dramatic levels. *Flute* remains one of the few opera films that has great appeal to audiences, on television, in cinema, and on video.

THE MODERN FILM-OPERA

The economic exuberance of the 1980s is largely responsible for a renaissance in motion-picture versions of opera. The producers of Zeffirelli's *Otello* (1986) typify the heady climate. Menachem Golan and Yoran Globus of the Cannon Group, venture capitalists known for making adventure films, decided to invest in high culture and provide generous support for a movie of an opera. The renewed interest in opera films was of a certain kind. Most earlier films cut and arranged at will; many created a new story on operatic themes or only used operatic excerpts. The typical film was one of many possible representations centered around the concept "opera." But in the late 1970s and 1980s many versions that stay closer to the original were made, and they fully exploited cinematic techniques and possibilities.[74] In this book, I examine four films from this period: Zeffirelli's *Otello*, Syberberg's *Parsifal*, Rosi's *Carmen*, and Losey's *Don Giovanni*.

Other incentives made the period attractive to filmmakers, producers, and investors. Video distribution helped recoup the huge sums needed for a motion picture, and potential sales of the "soundtrack" drew recording companies into the project. As in the relay and television film a consortium of interests was required. Despite these possibilities Hollywood continued to avoid opera on film, especially as film-opera.

Aesthetic conditions seemed to favor the genre during this era. Arguably directors turned to motion pictures because of their disappointment with the relay and the future of opera on television. Ironically, it was cinema, where screen opera began, that again provided fertile ground for renewed interest in the genre. Liebermann, the impetus behind the self-proclaimed first film-opera, Losey's *Don Giovanni*,[75] epitomizes the shift from television to cinema. But to focus on the failure of opera on television may be to deny the seductive appeal of cinema. Motion pictures are grand affairs, like operas, and their combination captures the exuberance of the era: a time of big spending, corporate take-overs, and risky bank deals. Many film-operas of this period are influenced by social context. Rosi and Losey censure the powerful, while Syberberg takes aim at rightist tendencies in German culture. Zeffirelli, however, seems to affirm the *Zeitgeist* by stressing opulence and avoiding social critique.

These interpretations underscore the openness of opera as a text for personal expression. For these figures, almost all experienced film directors, an opera movie represented a challenge. Losey, for example, knew little about opera and was unfamiliar with Mozart's work. His willingness to do the project suggests that he recognized opera's ability to interrogate social issues. This attitude is consistent with the auteur tradition that was prevalent in Europe after the 1950s. Moreover, many directors attached great importance to the operatic project. Syberberg, for example, authored a book on his *Parsifal*—a tract that approaches Wagner in its complexities of symbol and syntax. He joins the company of Bergman, Losey, and Rosi as famous exponents of the tradition. Within their oeuvre the film-operas do not stand alone but share themes with other films, creating a kind of musicalized intertextuality. Although Zeffirelli lacks credentials as cinéaste, his unmistakable style renders him a major authorial presence nonetheless.

Don Giovanni, produced by the French firm Gaumont, is striking for its length—essentially a complete version of the

Mozart masterpiece.[76] Syberberg's *Parsifal,* another product of Gaumont, also presents the complete opera, which lasts more than four hours. These represent remarkable films given the two-hour length of most movies. As discussed in chapter 4, the extended length of *Parsifal* recalls Syberberg's earlier films, which are also very long and focus on Wagnerism and German guilt. Most other film-operas, including Claude D'Anna's *Macbeth* (1987) and Frederic Mitterand's *Madama Butterfly* (1996), run two to two-and-a-half hours. Rosi's *Carmen* belongs to a group of *Carmen* films released in 1983–84, an outpouring attributable to the score's recent entry into the public domain. While the others show nominal ties to the Bizet, the Rosi film presents the opera essentially intact and proffers critique. The public greeted the film enthusiastically, and many consider it the best movie of an opera.

Distributed worldwide, Zeffirelli's *La Traviata* (1982) garnered great success at the box office. In the United States the movie appeared in regular theaters as well as art houses. A costume drama of nineteenth-century Paris, the opera *La Traviata* is tailored to Zeffirelli's lavish style (fig. 2.7). The director served up a visual feast that was capped by Teresa Stratas's sensitive portrayal of Violetta. Zeffirelli also made fine use of flashback as a structural device. As the male lead in *La Traviata,* Domingo added to his list of screen credits (he also starred in Rosi's *Carmen*) and his growing celebrity. As the doomed Moor of *Otello,* Zeffirelli's next film-opera, Domingo excelled in a role he has defined on the stage since the early 1980s. Critics and audiences, however, did not like *Otello* as much as *La Traviata.* Despite fine performances and stunning locations *Otello* remains a problematic film.

Nineteen eighty-seven marked a high-point for film-opera. Critical attention was keen, especially in France. Two major journals, *L'Avant-Scène Opéra* and *Revue du Cinéma,* devoted

Fig. 2.7 Teresa Stratas in *La Traviata* (1982). Directed by Franco Zeffirelli. (Courtesy British Film Institute)

special issues to the genre and to the general area of opera on film. A special session on opera and film also took place at the 40th Cannes Festival.[77] In spite of the interest, however, only a few scattered film-operas have appeared since, for example, Luigi Comencini's *La Bohème* (1988). The economic situation has forced corporations to pay heed to the bottom line. Television, a more cost-effective medium, has emerged as the main beneficiary. The relay has become the main format for screen opera and modest films for television are being made—for example, a *Dido and Aeneas* from the BBC (1995), under an hour in length. Generational change could also account for the decline in motion-picture opera, as classic European cinéastes are passing away and younger audiences, a major target of film demographics, have less interest in opera than their predecessors.

Opera has nonetheless continued to appear in film, on both sides of the Atlantic. In *Pretty Woman* (1990), for example, a fantasy of the bad-girl-turned-good, corporate raider Richard Gere takes call-girl Julia Roberts to the opera. They see *La Traviata*, a story with obvious similarities to their own situation. In *The Age of Innocence* (1993), the opera house functions as a signifier of class, and the protagonist first sees the intriguing Countess Olenska at the opera house. The opera onstage, *Faust*, re-enacts his own search for beauty and knowledge. In the popular movie *Moonstruck* (1987) opera, namely, *La Bohème*, functions in several ways. An operatic tone colors plot, dialogue, and character. More specifically, excerpts from *Bohème* are used as underscoring at key emotional moments. Their function may change from diegetic to non-diegetic. For example, at the start of one scene Ronnie, the male lead (Nicolas Cage), plays a number from *Bohème* on his turntable. At the musical climax, just as the scene cuts away sharply to a street scene, the music becomes non-diegetic as it accompanies his lover Loretta (Cher) during a walk in the early morning.[78] *Bohème* becomes most prominent when Ronnie and Loretta attend a performance of the work at the Metropolitan Opera. More in the spirit of opera buffa than verismo, the opera house hosts familial confrontation. Loretta's "I don't get it" reaction to opera may be a way of distancing her from the spectacle and allowing the average viewer to continue to identify with her.

Films about opera singers continue to be made. Many use a singer as point of departure for a complex narrative, as in Werner Schroeter's *Death of Maria Malibran* (1971) or Jean-

Jacques Beineix's *Diva* (1982).[79] These examples suggest that in spite of increasing unfamiliarity with individual operas, audiences still recognize the cultural position of opera and respond to it accordingly.

RECENT YEARS

As noted, television has emerged as the main medium for screened opera. But recent years have seen fascinating experiments, and some encourage comparison with the heady innovation in the early days of cinema and television. If there is any common theme among recent examples of screen opera it would be the crossover among media and formats. We also find a curiosity and excitement about new ways of applying technology to the representation of opera.

The most spectacular production of the 1990s is the *Tosca* aired in July 1992, a live transmission broadcast at the designated times of day from the designated places in Rome. Produced by RAI and co-sponsored by more than one hundred stations around the world (many of which could not broadcast live given the differences in time), the project represents a major feat. In order to allow the cameras complete freedom of movement, the orchestra was placed in a remote location. The singers and conductor Zubin Mehta used television monitors to coordinate with each other, and singers' voices were picked up by body microphones linked to a special form of transmission, via microwave. The singers also faced the challenge of lengthy separations between acts, which occurred in early afternoon, evening, and dawn the next day. They had to stay awake during the night and sing in the early morning, always difficult for singers. They were not only tired but they had the challenge of sustaining excitement from the night before.

The video version robs the project of some of its vitality.

Liner notes reveal that a small portion of the videotape has "corrected" passages, for instance, the elimination of a minor fall of Domingo. But as a whole the project, dubbed a "live film," has fascinating implications. It creates a new operatic ritual for a viewer in Europe and nearby time zones. One has to tune in to the event at three different times in a twenty-four-hour period. Unless one can time-shift by way of videotape, one must organize the day's schedule around it. Furthermore, the experiencing of the diurnal cycle in tandem with a dramatic event creates a special bond that is absent from staged opera, where time and light are manipulated theatrically. Even cinema, with its possibilities for exterior scenery, compresses opera into a few hours that are digested in a dark interior space.

This *Tosca* stresses liveness in other ways. At the start and between acts we see Rome from a helicopter whose noise is so loud that we must be inside the craft. This suggests *reportage* as in a live news report. The emphasis on the machine sets the stage for the notion of a high-tech transmission, counterpointed against an old work in old buildings. In this regard Jonathan White has discerned the travelogue aspect of the production.[80] Three magnificent locations—church, villa, and castle—exalt the eternal city as a mecca of civilization. In addition, the global reach of the "live" telecast takes on the worldly significance of an Olympics or some other international meet. And at the heart of this munificence stands Rome, and by extension Italy, the birthplace of opera.

The replication of the temporal plan is an attempt to create realistic conditions within the boundaries of the story. If one has the experience through real-time television, then there are only the conventions of television as an electronic mediation and the knowledge that this is a "staged" dramatic work to act as a buffer between you and the work—a desirable buffer, as art should be approached as a representation rather than the "real thing." But if one experiences the telecast in a remote time zone or through video playback, then the pretensions of "liveness" become confused. One knows the performance is an electronic reproduction that places distance between you and the work; yet the stress on a live event causes confusion. What is real and what is not, especially in relation to time? What do we get out of a version whose raison d'être is the experiencing of the work simultaneously with the performers? And does this mean that the best way to view the work after-the-fact is to see the acts at their designated times within a twenty-four-hour cycle? What I suggest is that the promotion of literal liveness within mediated patterns of reproduction is problematic.

Nonetheless, this imaginative *Tosca*, directed by Giuseppe Griffi and prepared for television and video by Brian Large, has a great deal to offer. The settings are magnificent,[81] and the characters move through them freely. We are treated to full perspective (360 degrees) but have live singing instead of playback—a rare combination in screen opera. As in the relay we encounter a wonderful sense of embodied singing. But here the vocalized physicality becomes part of the larger physicality made possible by cinematic perspective, movement, and camerawork.

Other projects scuff the veneer of opera, either through updated settings or large doses of popular culture. Peter Sellars's four telecast productions of the early 1990s—three operas by Mozart and one by Handel—deploy both in an Americanization of standard works. A radical who is traditional in some respects, Sellars takes pleasure in creating a dual vision in his productions. He hopes that the space between the two tracks will be filled with new thinking about the work. He draws on a variety of popular discourses, including soap opera and MTV.

Popular culture plays a central role in another novel venture, the film *Aria* (1987). With backing from RCA and MTV, Don Boyd produced an anthology of ten-minute segments by ten directors, each based on a different opera.[82] The interpretive range is wide and free-wheeling: from Jean-Baptiste Lully to Erich Korngold, from straight musical number to fragmented mix, from kinky acts to death fantasies. Ken Russell, known for such controversial biopics as *The Music Lovers* (1971, on Tchaikovsky) and *Lisztomania* (1975), sets "Nessun dorma" from *Turandot* as a hallucinatory struggle with death by a car-accident victim. Franc Roddam shoots the "Liebestod" from *Tristan und Isolde* in Las Vegas, which becomes the couple's haven for a slow suicide. And in another interesting segment, Jean-Luc Godard transposes Lully's *Armide* to a gym in Paris. Boyd claimed that the film attracted a young audience and those unfamiliar with music; the soundtrack, comprised of RCA excerpts and artists such as Leontyne Price and Jussi Bjoerling, sold well. Although the film's construction seems conducive to a division into segments, for MTV, it was intended to be shown as a whole. But the basic unit of construction, the fragment, affirms *Aria's* postmodernist tone. Like Sellars's postmodernist readings, this film asks us to reconsider the meanings of a venerable art form in a media-saturated age.[83]

Finally, there is the new kind of film musical. *Evita,* the 1996 movie of Andrew Lloyd Webber's hit show, amounts to a postmodernist *Umbrellas of Cherbourg:* a rock-saturated *Gesamtkunstwerk* that might be called a rock-opera film-musical. *Evita* has predecessors, of course, like *Jesus Christ Superstar* and *Tommy,* both from the 1970s. With continuous music and near-continuous singing the genre approaches the ideal that was envisioned in the early sound era for a new kind of screen opera, even though the rock films are based on pre-existent works. I hope to see more of these films. As of this writing, for example, plans are underway for a film of the Broadway rock-opera *Rent*, itself an updated *Bohème*. In this way Hollywood might create its own brand of opera film and revive a genre that it did so well, the musical. Thus the future of screen opera suggests a further expansion of the content and meaning of opera—a prediction that augurs well for the longevity and vitality of opera as a medium.

3

A Matter of Belief:
Otello on Film and Television

Verdi's *Otello* has captivated audiences and performers since its premiere in 1887. This late work of Italy's musical hero is a magnificent musico-dramatic achievement; many consider it one of the finest operas ever written.[1] Some critics recognize its sophisticated dramaturgy but lament how it further flattens Shakespeare's gullible hero and hinders our ability to believe in his slide into destruction. Even so, the composer's control of dramatic pace through a continuous musical score is masterful, and in its focus on the psychological dynamics of the characters *Otello* works well on the stage.

Given this fit it is interesting to see what happens when *Otello* finds expression in other media—what happens when the camera becomes a major force in shaping narrative and representation. What happens to our belief in the tragedy played out before us when our eyes are guided by the eyes of the camera and the director behind the camera? In establishing this framework I am not implying that the original opera is perfect and inevitably sullied in another medium. What I hope to show through a comparative approach of two treatments of *Otello*, one for cinema and one for television, are the ways in which medium structures interpretation.

Otello has been presented on film and on numerous telecasts. Franco Zeffirelli's movie of 1986 is probably the most famous version for cinema, and it achieved widespread distribution. The cast includes Plácido Domingo as Otello, Katia Ricciarelli

Fig. 3.1 Sergei Leiferkus (left) and Plácido Domingo in *Otello* (1992), Royal Opera House, Covent Garden. Directed by Elijah Moshinsky. (Photo by Zoë Dominic)

as Desdemona, and Justino Diaz as Iago; Lorin Maazel is conductor. On television, Verdi's opera marked the first broadcast from the stage of the Metropolitan Opera, on opening night in 1948. Herbert von Karajan produced a well-known studio film in 1974, with Jon Vickers and Mirella Freni.[2] In the early 1980s the Arena di Verona became the site of an outdoor performance that was telecast and distributed on video. Among more recent relays is a performance in 1992 from the Royal Opera House, Covent Garden, which has also been distributed on video. Directed for the stage by Elijah Moshinsky, for television by Brian Large, and conducted by Georg Solti, it too features Domingo in the title role—a part he has defined for nearly two decades—and includes Kiri Te Kanawa as Desdemona and Sergei Leiferkus as Iago (figs. 3.1, 3.2).

Fig. 3.2 Justino Diaz (left) and Plácido Domingo in *Otello* (1986).
Directed by Franco Zeffirelli. (Courtesy British Film Institute)

Zeffirelli is notable among directors of film-opera in his
eclectic background. He has strong credentials as a designer and
director of opera and theater as well as substantial experience
in film. His fondness for Shakespeare has led to Hollywood
films, including *Taming of the Shrew* (1967), *Romeo and Juliet*
(1968), and *Hamlet* (1990), as well as productions at Stratford-
on-Avon. His career in opera has taken him to the leading
houses of the world, and many of his productions have been
taped for television.[3] Ever since the 1950s he has been interested in combining opera and film. After two failed projects (an
Aida to be filmed in Egypt and a *Traviata* with Maria Callas),
studio films of *Pagliacci* and *Cavalleria Rusticana* were made
in the early 1980s. In 1982 his goal of a full-fledged film was
realized in *La Traviata*. With wonderful acting from Teresa
Stratas and an Alfredo played by Domingo, the movie achieved
popular and critical acclaim.[4]

A well-financed *Otello* followed a few years later. Although

Otello was less successful commercially than its predecessor, Zeffirelli considers it a high-point in his career.[5] Visually, *Otello* typifies Zeffirelli's affinity for lavish and ornate productions. Indeed, the director contends that his main aim in *Otello* was to provide the viewer with an experience of great beauty.[6] The Moshinsky-Large *Otello*, in contrast, displays notable restraint in its visual appearance. Sets (Timothy O'Brien) and costumes (Peter J. Hall) show a classical simplicity of dignity and understatement. As we will see, these basic differences have meaningful implications for their respective dramatic conception.

Even though the Zeffirelli and the Moshinsky-Large treatments are both examples of screen opera, they are obviously two separate productions, for two different media. This can mean that one may be of higher quality than the other, or that one is more successful artistically than the other. It can imply that one medium is "better" than the other for screen opera. As much as possible I ignore exploration of these issues in and of themselves. They do matter a great deal, however, with respect to the ways the medium shapes the given interpretation. In other words, one of the treatments may be more successful than the other in responding to affinities of its medium for a given technique or procedure, or both may find successful but different ways of handling those characteristics. Nonetheless, one should keep in mind that, independent of medium, the two productions offer very different readings of Verdi's opera.

The main issues of this chapter grow out of the distinctive characteristics of the two productions and their importance in highlighting ways in which cinema and television can affect screen opera. Musical organization forms the focus of the first section, which discusses the effect of medium on the presence and function of the operatic score. The next section investigates the workings of camera and image in these productions and their relationship with drama, representation, and spectatorship. In the third and last major section we concentrate on regression, psychological and dramatic, and its impact on how we view Verdi's opera, which itself exhibits regressive features. And finally, in the spirit of a coda, a concluding section engages the larger aesthetic issues of the leveling effects of video and the success of these two versions of *Otello*.

MUSICAL ORGANIZATION

The Moshinsky-Large relay of *Otello* is crafted for television and shaped by the characteristics of the medium. One of the prominent features of television is its affinity for presence. While this has several meanings (see also below), presence in terms of the viewing experience concerns us here for its suggestive relationship with the musical organization of the relay. Television is ever-present, as media theorist John Ellis observes.[7] Whether or not we turn it on we know that networks are filling their stations with programming, much of it around-the-clock. It exists without our having to attend to it. When television is attended to, that is, when we turn on the set, we may pay it less sustained attention than we do film at the cinema. It often becomes a casual activity and competes with other domestic activities for our attention. We might have the television on as background noise while preparing dinner or reading the paper or talking on the phone. In these situations television's sound is more constant than its image. Television's sound radiates in all directions and pervades greater areas of space, whereas image is aimed in one direction. As Ellis describes their relationship, "Sound carries the fiction or the documentary; the image has a more illustrative function." Michel Chion goes further, calling television "illustrated radio."[8]

While these writers tip the scales too far toward sound, their theories are pertinent to the Royal Opera House telecast. This *Otello* offers a continued aural presence through the completeness of the Verdi score. Moreover, the continuous musical score and its lack of pauses contribute to the steady stream of sound. As interpreted by Solti, this is a fast-paced rendition of a score with a strong drive to resolution. This sounds like an obvious description of the opera, but Zeffirelli's film shows that *Otello* can be organized differently. It presents a work that is comprised of heightened moments that are separated by pauses.

"Music as handmaiden to the camera" characterizes the fundamental aesthetic premise of Zeffirelli's film: music as subservient to visual and other cinematic elements. As a result, the musical organization differs significantly from the opera. The principal changes come from cutting (ca. 35 minutes from the score), re-ordering, recomposition, fragmentation, and insertion of pauses. Despite Zeffirelli's statement that movie audiences cannot sit through the complete opera, commercial factors seem to be responsible for the shortened length, which is just under two hours. The film sustains the most cuts of the major film-operas of the period.[9] Zeffirelli anticipated criticism over the changes. Not only did he assert that this is a film and not an opera,[10] but he barred music critics from press screenings in New York.[11] Perhaps Carlos Kleiber, the original conductor, dropped out of the project because he was unwilling to make the changes; Maazel, his replacement, was fully cooperative.[12]

In many respects the model of the musical score for the standard Hollywood film applies to the process of adaptation followed in Zeffirelli's *Otello*. In this classical model, cinematic considerations are primary, and the score has to fit in precisely with the director's wishes on placement and mood. Towards that end detailed time-sheets, down to tenths of seconds, are prepared. In those places where quick musical changes must be synchronized with fast cinematic action, a device called a click track may be used. Editing is generally completed before the score is done, but sometimes last-minute cutting ruins the logic and flow of a musical segment.[13] For that reason, composers are advised in Leonid Sabaneev's classic manual of film composition (1935) to write in a language that can accommodate cuts or insertions with a minimum of musical damage. The author recommends occasional pauses, sequences, and short phrases for such purposes.[14] Music with discrete, removable blocks is most appropriate.

Although it is unclear whether these timing devices were utilized for *Otello*, it seems as if the essential components of the cinema-music relationship were retained. Maazel, for instance, refers to the operatic music as a "soundtrack," and was willing to tailor the music to the needs of filmmaking. As he observed, "You can't make a film soundtrack, as it were, for a film without having spoken first to the director, . . . been given a fairly clear idea of what he wants for each scene—very specifically in certain cases in terms of tempo and phrasing."[15] The two worked in a spirit of cooperation. Zeffirelli would hear a recorded version, suggest changes, and request that certain passages be recorded differently. Maazel would be responsive, offer his own suggestions, and even record several versions of a passage. Moreover, the conductor was sympathetic to making cuts, inserting bridge passages, and orchestrating and re-ordering material.[16] The documentary on the making of the film shows that musical decisions were made throughout the filming process and up to the final editing.

What is the nature of the transformation? The most obvious change is the elimination of some major numbers: the "Fuoco di gioia" chorus in Act I, the Concerted Finale of Act III, and the "Willow Song" of Act IV (Zeffirelli finds it "boring," even on the stage[17]). In addition, major sections in individual numbers are cut: a few pages of the "Vittoria" chorus (Act I), the second stanza of the Drinking Song (I), a large portion of the final stanza of "Si pel ciel" (II), and various passages in the Duet between Otello and Desdemona (III). There are also many small cuts in the semi-declamatory syntax that pervades the work. While some seem random, most derive from the director's emphasis on the good-evil struggle as thematized through Catholicism. As a result, Otello's jealousy erupts even earlier and more irrationally. For example, Iago's "Temete, signor, la gelosia!," a prelude to Otello's first real outburst, loses five pages of preparatory innuendo about Desdemona and Cassio. Calling such passages "anti-cinematic," Zeffirelli believes that "in film, one shows—one is not supposed to announce in advance what is going to be shown."[18]

Awkward seams may result from the changes. One such example occurs at the end of the "Credo." The music comes to a complete halt two bars after the high F of "ciel," for a blackout; the transitional four bars are cut entirely. Now, as accompaniment to Desdemona, Cassio, and Emilia walking outdoors, the music reverts to some of the instrumental music that opened the act. Then we pick up where we left off, four bars after the Credo, with semi-declamatory music that grows out of the end of the Credo (although that, itself, grew out of the introductory instrumental music to the act). The new organization affects our sense of Iago, who now seems more leisurely and casual. Characterization can be affected in other ways. In the Quartet of Act II, for example, the rearranged vocal lines create different relationships among the characters. And the sharply curtailed musical role of Roderigo throughout the opera has Iago acting more directly on his own.

The most serious rearrangement occurs at the start of Act IV, where the changes amount to recomposition. The act now begins with the instrumental music that follows the "Willow

Song" (itself cut), eight bars after letter "P." Then the music stitches together fragments from widely spaced places. It ends with the same instrumental passage that began the act in the new version. Thus a closed musical form emerges for the first half of Act IV—an unusual scheme in the context of the whole. I have not detected any visual reason for this organization.

A need for greater visual time is responsible for other kinds of revision, as in the repeat of a ritornello passage in the Duet in Act III, or the extension of a transitional vamp before the Drinking Song in Act I. The film also contains a few full-scale additions. In Act I, various strains of the Arabian Dance, one of several numbers composed by Verdi for Act III of the Paris production (1894), are inserted. The excerpts accompany entertainers at the lavish party that is added to celebrate Otello's victory, a scene that replaces the less spectacular "Fuoco di gioia." The Greek Dance of the Paris additions appears in the public ensemble scene in Act III.[19] Such examples of new material serve as one of the ways in which the film score, ironically, *adds* length. Many numbers are performed with extremely slow tempos, and the film inserts pauses fairly often. Additional time for visual effects accounts for most of these places.

The result of these cuts and changes bears a strong resemblance to the organization of a classic Hollywood film score.[20] Such a score consists of discrete passages that are separated by stretches without music. While these episodes may be related by theme or some other musical feature, for example, Leitmotif technique, they do not form a continuous narrative, at least not in the usual sense of continuous. In isolation, any one might seem like an excerpt from a larger work, or at most a short movement from a suite of incidental music.[21] ("Theme song" music over opening credits would be an exception.)

These traits characterize non-diegetic film music: music that

Fig. 3.3 Katia Ricciarelli and Plácido Domingo in *Otello* (1986). Directed by Franco Zeffirelli. (Courtesy British Film Institute)

exists outside the world of the film. This type of discourse enhances the emotional content of a story and breaks down potential defense mechanisms in the spectator against the illusion and the willingness to indulge in fantasy.[22] Sometimes called "sourceless music," non-diegetic music seems disembodied because its source is generally absent from spectators' view. It also serves as a compensatory factor for the technical discontinuities that make up film. If one views a film without sound, for example, its technical basis is more apparent. One becomes aware of the artificial means by which a story is put together visually, for example, the non-congruities of successive shots.[23]

I find a curious inversion in Zeffirelli's *Otello*, however. Whereas non-diegetic film music generally obscures technical or visual ruptures, in *Otello* the visual may obscure the musical ruptures. I am aware, of course, that the musical fragmentation in the film resulted largely from visual considerations. Still, once the musical accommodation has been made, the visual attempts to compensate for it. The strategy is not entirely successful, however, especially for the musically knowledgeable viewer. Another way to describe the relationship would be to say that non-diegetic film music "completes" the cinematic text; it fills in what would otherwise be a lack. In the Zeffirelli, however, the visual attempts to complete the musical lack or deficiency. One difficulty, however, is that Verdi's continuous score does not lend itself to fragmentation. Thus it can be challenging, even (or especially) in Zeffirelli's sumptuous treatment, for the apparatus of cinema to find ways of filling in the musical holes. In any event, we should keep in mind throughout these discussions that the diegetic/non-diegetic model is most appropriate to ordinary films, where speech is the main discourse. It serves as a useful comparative framework for film-opera but does not describe literally how music behaves in the genre.

Another pertinent aspect of the relationship between film music and visuality is that non-diegetic music adds depth and three-dimensionality to visual images. It rounds out and humanizes what are only flat images on the screen. This function is one of the reasons why music has participated in commercial cinema.[24] In Zeffirelli's *Otello* we find interesting aspects of this relationship. Although the general disposition of the score resembles the (non-diegetic) Hollywood film score, that score is constituted by a range of musical behavior, and it has a varied effect on space. Toward one end of the scale lies background or transitional music, typically instrumental, and similar to regular film music. One example is the instrumental music that opens Act II, where a musing Cassio appears against a rich panorama of harbor and castle. The long- and medium-shots, the intervening zooms, and the exterior setting help to articulate depth. But the background music lends credence to the reality of the space. Not only are spatial planes defined in relation to each other, but they are linked as well: an illustration of Claudia Gorbman's thesis that "film music is a gel" and a device that "bonds" shot to shot and audience to narrative.[25]

Music that is foregrounded qua music occupies the other end of the spectrum. Examples are the "Credo," the Love Duet, Otello's "Dio, mi potevi scagliar," or any of the other discrete lyric numbers of the score. With these more formal operatic pieces, the spatial functions of the music tend to lessen. Perhaps this is because our attention is closely fixed on the singers—the apparent producers of the sound—and considerations of space yield to those of emotion and expression. In Zeffirelli this interest is further encouraged by extensive use of close-up. Perhaps one would expect this style of shooting given that the texts in these numbers are more personal. Yet a comparison with another film-opera, Rosi's *Bizet's Carmen*, shows that this need not be the case. Rosi's film is striking in its frequent use of medium- and long-shot during an aria or duet of a personal nature. This creates a gap between audience and character that allows the drama to be viewed more dispassionately (see chapter 5). While it is only an incidental effect, the music involved in such shots helps to articulate spatial depth.

This aspect of Rosi's technique underscores a general problem in film-opera. Because the music is prerecorded, the soundtrack does not make distinctions in volume to reflect distances in the filmed space. In Zeffirelli's *Otello*, the heavy use of close-up lessens the problem, for distance remains relatively constant in a close-up.[26] For opera on television, depth does not become such a major concern because the action occurs in an interior location and television generally focuses on details rather than expanses of space. Distinctions in space do occur on the stage of the telecast relay. Because there is no prerecorded soundtrack, such differences are articulated by greater variations in volume than occur in film-opera. In the Moshinsky-Large relay, for example, Otello's forceful line "Abbasso le spade" (Down with your swords), at his reappearance after the fight in Act I, is sung further back on stage and is not as loud as the usual volume level. Despite such occurrences in this telecast, electronic manipulation of a relay's sound through multiple miking can efface such differences. Only attendance at a live performance in the opera house assures that these distinctions are heard (assuming, that is, no special electronic manipulation in the stage production).

Another useful aspect of diegesis involves diegetic sound effects, and there are many in the *Otello* film. We hear such sounds as the rushing water of the storm and confused crowd noise at the opening, and the loud clanging of doors throughout the film. These noises are superimposed on the music or appear where there is none, but in either case are prominent.[27] They impose a frame of reality—as if the sounds are marking events in real time and space. In this manner they provide contrast with the illusionism of film and with non-diegetic music, both of which tend toward atemporality. Sound effects can assert a naturalism that counterbalances the fragmented score and the aesthetic nature of music itself. As for the Moshinsky-Large relay, the sound effects, which include noises entailed in movement and props, result from actual noises that are produced at the same time that the music is being performed. Unlike film, where the music track and noise track are separate, here there is no layering or superimposition. This makes the music seem more integrated into the dramatic apparatus that marks off real events on the stage. On the other hand, when music is being sung in the Moshinsky-Large relay the volume is so loud that sound effects are not easily heard. On the whole, their use in this telecast is more limited than in the Zeffirelli film, where they have an important function in the mediation of reality and illusion.

The film musical becomes pertinent to our discussion in light of Zeffirelli's belief that film-opera represents the logical successor to Hollywood's lavish musicals of the past.[28] His fragmented *Otello* in fact resembles the musical in its focus on heightened, emotional moments that are separated by transitional kinds of discourse.[29] This places emphasis on the sheer sound of the music and brings the organization closer to that of number opera. Of course, Verdi's original bears traces of this kind of construction. But it also displays a linearity and horizontality that shape the narrative drive of the drama. In Zeffirelli's film, however, the horizontal connections have been severed and replaced with a verticality that recalls the musical. What this means is a luxuriating in the moment: an aesthetic that ties in well with the filmmaker's propensity for the visual.

Ironically, the presence of the complete score in the Moshinsky-Large relay production can detract from the music's importance. What I mean is that, unlike the Zeffirelli, its seamless construction does not call attention to itself. It seems natural and unexceptional. The absence of sumptuous image plays down any complicit role that music might have in highlighting brilliant image. The result is a balance between sound and image—not a balance of luxury, as in the Zeffirelli, but one of moderation that is well equipped to convey the presence that is a characteristic feature of television.

CAMERA AND IMAGE

Presence in the relay broadcast is furthered by the use of videotape, which produces an image that looks closer to reality than film.[30] It lacks the idealizing qualities of film stock and feels familiar because of the widespread use of the home video camera. Videotape offers a practical means of recording events because it is flexible and inexpensive, and unlike film it does not have to be processed. Its nearly "real-time" existence renders it the ability to be reviewed, altered, and reedited, in close temporal proximity to the original taping. A sense that videotape conveys real events is key to promoting the illusion of our attendance at a live event, as in the relay. It helps us to experience the presence of an actual theater, and audience, orchestra, and conductor as well. What we see becomes a situated act, with a knowable source, and one that can be easily identified by the viewer.

The relay offers live singing instead of the dubbed sound of film ("live," a relative concept, will be discussed below). This makes the music embodied—there is an actual presence emitting the sounds—and underscores the bodily exertion of the production of that sound. Many television directors, such as Large, practice restraint so as not to emphasize unpleasant physical exertions. (Sometimes they are not avoided, as in close-ups of Domingo with sweat pouring down his face.) Is this a deceptive means of glossing over the physical labor that is needed to produce art?[31] I think not, for people in the hall do not discern such exertions. The analogy is limited, of course, since audiences do not have a mediating camera that selects what they see. The example indicates the tremendous power of the television director and his or her affinity with a film director. Both produce constructions—virtually new works—fashioned by the camera.

The relay operates in one interior location, even if varied shots of house and sets deflect a sense of monotony and confinement. Cinema, however, offers unlimited scenic potential, and that includes interior and exterior locations as well as virtual or animated images. The feeling of rootedness that is encouraged by the relay also comes from the knowledge that we are seeing a one-time event that actually happened. We share in the "sense of occasion" that is conveyed by the telecast—a sense furthered by the ritual and elitism that attend a visit to the opera house. This *Otello* has the added prestige of coming from a "royal opera house." We not only have the pleasure of seeing the royal crest on the main curtain but royals themselves (as the British call their royalty), in none other than Prince Charles and Princess Diana a few years before their divorce. Shown applauding at the end of the performance, the couple provides a fascinating contemporaneity for the proceedings, not to mention titillation. Considering the entire broadcast as a text, might we not see parallels between the star-crossed lovers on stage and those in the box? That like Otello and Desdemona, their union held the seeds of its own destruction? And that like Desdemona, Diana is doomed to die young? These may be fanciful comparisons, but the symbolism seems apt.[32]

The relay organizes most of its shots from the perspective of an audience member or rather from a spectator in six to eight choice seats in the house. Essentially it preserves the plane of the front of the stage as the perspective to which stage action is geared. Cinema, in contrast, has the possibility of multiple perspectives and the ability to capture swift movement and juxtapose different locations. Time and place need not coincide. One practical limitation on what the relay can do is the presence of an audience at the performance that is being taped. This means that cameras cannot block sight lines and intrude unduly on the stage action. It also means that the cameras have to remain stationary, and this precludes a host of interesting effects, for example, the tracking shot or dolly shot. Other cinematic effects, such as flashback or animation, are also not possible in the relay. Reconfigurations of the sound-image relationship, such as voice-off or mime, are generally avoided as well. Of course, if the stage version itself includes unusual effects, such as a filmed segment or rear projection, they will be captured on the relay. But to date, the typical relay does not add much in the way of visual gadgetry to what is offered in the hall.

In spite of differences, the gap between the two formats has narrowed considerably. Many kinds of cinematic adjustments are made for the television camera. The exaggerated gestures and makeup that are called for in a large hall are inappropriate to the close-in shots for television. A more naturalistic, less theatrical style is needed. Blocking is also modified for the camera. In the expectation that much of the stage will be excluded from a given shot, action is geared toward the composition and angle of the intended shot. Cinema also has a great influence on the camerawork. Even though television cameras are fixed and are situated in front of the plane of the stage, pacing, angles, and cutting often approach a cinematic ideal. For example, zooms and pans create motion. Wide-angle shots, especially for "establishing shots" of the stage, lend a sense of monumentality. The four or so cameras in the corners and center of the front row seats of the orchestra, used for close-in shots, angle up to the stage and create a monumentalized view of the singers: a dramatic effect that nonetheless has become so common that it hardly stands out as special.[33] The two corner cameras from the front row create a very sharp angle with the stage and are often used for a medium group-shot. The extreme angle can make the cameras seem parallel with the stage action—as if they are situated on the side of the action. When used sensitively they can impart a feeling of three-dimensional perspective.

What these adjustments show is that the relay is a carefully crafted construction that is distinct from the performance it is recording. It also differs from that performance by not being live. Since the late 1980s relay telecasts have shunned simultaneous transmission, and economics is probably the main reason. A costly endeavor, the relay has welcomed the support of record companies, who create a video version of the telecast.[34] But since video creates a permanent document, there is a desire for high quality in production and performance. Live performance, however, carries the potential for error; a delayed broadcast provides an opportunity for correction and improvement. Thus an editing process takes place after the taping of the main performance. Passages from camera rehearsals supply most of the footage for substitutions. Although relatively few insertions are actually made, the practice reveals "live" to be a blurry concept and suggests that videotape relays have been influenced by the practices of cinema (and of much television work as well). In any case, even when transmission is simultaneous with the event, "live" entails a technological manipulation of sound and image and means a manufactured representation of the event.

The Moshinsky-Large Relay

This telecast offers a visual simplicity that is notable, even for television (fig. 3.4).[35] Television in general avoids detail and fussiness in favor of a foregrounded element or group. The small screen provides an obvious reason for this configuration in scale, but a desire for directness and currency is also responsible.[36] Devoid of detail, the sets in the Moshinsky-Large production are simple and geometric, especially in Act II. Most are dark and barely tinted, and variations of black, grey, and olive form the prevailing color scheme. The background for much of the opera consists of a solid color. The lighting, although brightened for television recording,[37] seems subdued and almost somber. This understated visual vocabulary allows us to focus attention on

Fig. 3.4 The set for Act II of *Otello* (1992), Royal Opera House, Covent Garden. Directed by Elijah Moshinsky. (Photo by Zoë Dominic)

critical elements of narrative, especially music and psychology. Large's restrained camerawork also contributes to this simplified style of representation.

In what might be called a "northern" portrayal, Otello approaches a tragic figure in this telecast. Thoughtful and deliberate, he is guided by intellect as much as by emotion. This means he has a lesser need to run and gesture wildly in order to express emotion. In fact, Domingo's gestures (and those of the other singers) are subdued, and the tone accords with Large's view that gestures must be purposeful and natural for television.[38] For his performance in the movie, Domingo has said that Zeffirelli did not restrain him from using broad gestures of the stage, and that he found this a welcome change from the physical constraints that Rosi placed on him in the film *Carmen*.[39] Zeffirelli's Otello is physically active and suits the director's (hyper-)active camera. In this regard it is interesting that a telecast of a stage production calls for physical restraint in actors, and that some films, especially the Zeffirelli, encourage a broad physical language that is characteristic of the stage.

Large has the camera trace the nuances of Otello's disintegration. Typical of his style, Large uses close-ups sparingly and saves them for special moments.[40] One is a very tight shot of Otello's face, the closest used so far, in the middle of his monologue "Dio, mi potevi scagliar." Well into the workings of Iago's poison, the number occurs in Act III after the shattering duet in which he calls Desdemona a whore. Large aims the camera inward at the dramatic turning point, where the music resolves into a new key and embarks on a new text. Otello speaks in anguished metaphor of what the loss of Desdemona means. The very tight shot marks a climax in his disintegration. Another place in which the camera registers Otello's psychological state is at Iago's narration of Cassio's dream, "Era la notte." Whereas Zeffirelli's Otello shows wide-eyed horror, this Otello bears intense sorrow and almost weeps.

In the duet "Si pel ciel" at the end of Act II we see a different Otello. Large exploits television's power of direct address by having Otello look squarely at the camera as he sings of revenge.[41] The first such view of Otello in the telecast, the shot promotes a special bond of intimacy with the viewer and underlines the force of Otello's determination at this climactic point in the middle of the opera. Zeffirelli, in contrast, had Otello sing the number with Iago with their hands raised to a crucifix in a cavernous room. Justino Diaz, who plays Iago in the movie, offers a telling remark on differences between film and television when he notes that in film the singer is not to look directly at the camera but at best slightly away from it.[42] In cinema a direct look is unsettling and can shatter the illusion of the medium. In television it affirms co-presence and familiarity.

Other aspects of the camerawork in the relay are appropriate to the opera. Large favors well-composed shots. He is interested in beauty, but a dignified rather than lavish beauty. At the start of Act II, for example, we see massive classical columns that frame an architectural space with a Vermeer-like floor. The background is plain, consisting of a solid color. Figures appear small against the vast space above them. In general a sensitivity to music informs Large's visual choices and explains why he is the most sought-after director of televised opera. The start of *Otello* offers a good example. Here a variety of shots captures the restless storm and its changeable music. When the music finally becomes stable, at the tutti section in a minor, the camera offers a "tutti" view to match: a long shot of the entire stage, with chorus massed and singing together. The visual cut to this view occurs precisely when the harmony sounds the brilliant a-minor resolution.

Although Large's style is generally restrained, it can respond to individual circumstances as needed. Before the Drinking Song, for example, the camerawork becomes more active. Iago is at work, manipulating Cassio and Roderigo to do his bidding. The camera captures Iago's duplicity as it accelerates in rhythm and shifts quickly from his exchanges with one and then the other. Large also uses dissolves at special moments. During the transition to the Love Duet, Desdemona's descent from the balcony is lyricized by a gentle dissolve between shots. The visual effect accords with the intimate chamber-music texture (four cellos) of the passage. Later, in the "Ave Maria," dissolves mark the transition to the return of the A section and to the climactic "Ave" at the end. Both examples feature subtle musical coloring: both have muted strings, and both lie in subdued, chromatic flat keys (Db/Gb in the first, Ab in the second). The dissolves act as a softening device in these reflective moments and help to create a feminine tone. The "Ave Maria" is further softened through an orange tint in the lighting. While the effect might seem Zeffirellian, it lacks the excessive backlighting and other high contrasts that occur at the comparable place in his version.

Visual Excess and Catholicism in the Zeffirelli

Zeffirelli faced the challenge of transferring a psychological drama—an opera centered on jealousy—to the large screen. Given his thorough familiarity with the music, the play, and the medium of cinema, it would be surprising if Zeffirelli had not considered the matter. The issue is not new with adaptation to film, however; concerns were raised at the prospect of operatic adaptation of the play. In a review of an early performance of the Verdi/Boito work, for example, Eduard Hanslick expressed doubts about basing an opera on Shakespeare's *Othello*. "Among all tragic passions, jealousy is the least ideal, the least musical one;" it cannot be represented easily in music.[43] The connection between play and opera has been characterized in other ways. George Bernard Shaw, for his part, likened the exaggerated characters and insufficient motivation in the play to Italian opera.[44] Many Shakespearean scholars also consider motivation a major weakness of *Othello*.

In Zeffirelli's reading, psychology is bypassed in favor of a more diffuse focus, one that is conducive to visual treatment. But there is a problem. Aside from the storm scene at the start and the arrival of the Venetians in Act III, the opera is not especially visual. It features few set changes (one set per act), and most scenes involve only a few individuals rather than large numbers of people who can be deployed in novel ways. The problem is solved through the imposition of a dramatic theme with good visual possibilities: Catholicism. "My *Otello* is a very

Catholic affair," asserts Zeffirelli. "Otello's struggle is in a very real sense a religious one."[45] While "Catholic" has many meanings, the director stresses in the film "the monumental conflict between good and evil. It is the devil himself who dons the costume of Iago in order to undermine happiness and destroy love."[46] Human struggle is displaced by symbolic conflict.

The symbols assume concrete form as Catholic icons and rituals that make dramatic appearances at several places. The most arresting image is the tall crucifix at one end of a subterranean chamber. No ordinary room, the cavernous space has walls and ceiling that join in a continuous curve, like an igloo, and contains an opening in the ceiling that admits a shaft of light. The setting becomes a confessional to key emotional moments. Circling and raging, Iago vents his "Credo" to the inert figure, and also to us as the camera/audience assumes the vantage point of Christ. It is not enough for Iago to intone his nihilistic message. Zeffirelli wants us to understand that here is someone outside the moral order. Our complicity in this arrangement is assured by the sequence of shots that installs us as the object of Iago's blasphemy. We become the moral order. Once the internalization is accomplished, we will believe in Iago's almost supernatural power to wreak havoc on Otello. The crucifix reappears at the end of the act for the melodramatic duet, "Si pel ciel." In this ritual of male bonding, which has homoerotic implications, Otello and Iago kneel in front of the cross and pledge fealty to their common mission of revenge.

The context of the scene also has bearing on Otello's character. Increasingly agitated, Otello has been running through tunnels, the music growing more fragmented and intense. At the climax—the V-I resolution into A major—Otello pushes open swinging doors with a cross on them and explodes into the blinding light of the cavern. It is quite a moment. Before the crucifix he finds his voice in the rational discourse of tonal, melodic, and harmonic stability, although the best he can do at first is utter a static countermelody (largely on E) against the theme in the orchestra. Only with the Church as crutch can he articulate a plan of action. The presence of Iago, who follows him there, is ironic: this is the very same setting for the mocking "Credo" some fifteen minutes earlier. The crucifix in this cavern will appear again, in Act III, for the cathartic second half of his soliloquy, "Dio, mi potevi scagliar" (see above for this passage in the relay).

Otello's need for Catholicism is affirmed by other touches. As the final catastrophe approaches, Zeffirelli offers two distressing images. In both Otello reverts to paganism: shedding the mantle of civilizing European religion and regressing to his African roots in magic.[47] When Catholicism is replaced by paganism there is no moral framework, and anything can happen. Both images of Otello are inserted into Desdemona's lyrical complex at the start of Act IV, which now has extensive musical rearrangement. After Desdemona's request to Emilia to put out her wedding dress, the scene shifts through dissolve to Otello. Accompanied by the woodwind choir from the instrumental introduction to the act (ca. m. 13), Otello sits on the floor in a red-orange glow, bare-chested, and conducts a ritual over candles and cauldron. He removes his cross and dangles it over the flames. As he drops it into the fire there is a quick cut to Desdemona's room, where she hears a noise. After she bids Emilia "addio," the scene returns to Otello, in the cavernous room with the beam of light. In a long shot he stands over the candles, and as he raises his arms he appears Christ-like in silhouette on the far wall. This image is accompanied by the transitional music to the "Ave Maria," and as it begins we return to Desdemona's room and see a painting of Madonna and child.

The striking sequence prompts the questions, Where does the Catholic interpretation come from? What purposes does it serve? Aesthetically the director needs a visual focus for a psychological drama. This use of Catholicism, however, seems to go beyond that. The film suggests that only Christianity can explain the motivations of the characters. It is true that the story has elicited disbelief over the years. How can Otello believe so easily that his wife is unfaithful? Unfortunately, Zeffirelli's solution accomplishes the opposite of his intentions: it acts to reduce motivation. It imposes simple explanations and robs characters of the complexities of human agency, in favor of some exterior force. It is excess that reduces.

Excess, of course, is defined in relation to cultural standards of normality. Furthermore, excess is not necessarily bad. Music as a discourse is often thought to constitute excess, and opera even more so. Italian culture often tends toward emotional excess, particularly late-nineteenth-century Italian opera. Zeffirelli, we may recall, is at home in this environment. Furthermore, he has made a conscious effort to thematize religion in his productions ever since a serious automobile accident in 1969.[48] But perhaps there exists stronger justification: perhaps the musico-historical context of the work suggests such a conception. Some, for instance, might point to the "Ave Maria" and the "Credo" as supporting evidence. Newly penned by Boito, the "Ave Maria" text is a personal supplication to the Virgin. In Shakespeare the only basis for this prayer scene is Othello's question to Desdemona in Act V scene 2 as to whether she has said her prayers. Thus Verdi's conception already represents a nod to Catholicism. But this must be considered in a broader context. Verdi often included a prayer or prayer-like lyrical number ("preghiera") for the heroine in the final act. A standard set-piece,[49] by the time of *Otello* audiences may have expected it, especially since Rossini composed one for Desdemona in the last act of his popular *Otello* (1816). The Verdian *preghiera* did not signal a Catholic interpretation for the entire opera; it was more like a familiar gesture.

The "Credo" is also an addition by Boito. Structurally important because so many Shakespearean monologues of Iago are omitted, the piece has been subject to diverse interpretation.[50] Like Zeffirelli, some see it as proof that Iago is Satan, not human. For others, the number shows Iago more as nihilist— a cunning human set on destruction. He defies God rhetorically, not theologically. He may be an agent of evil, but evil as more of a metaphysical than religious idea. Verdi considered the text "Shakespearean in every way," perhaps thinking of the nihilistic passage "Life's but a walking shadow . . ." from *Macbeth*, which he included in his earlier opera.[51] Diaz's portrayal of Iago in the film seems to contradict or at least problematize the director's more symbolic conception. Subtle facial expressions indicate a rational mind—not one manipulated by some abstract evil force. Such an interpretation conforms with the advice of composer and librettist in the Production Book: "The grossest error, the most vulgar error an artist attempting to interpret this character could commit would be to represent him as a kind of human demon, to put a Mephistophelian sneer on his face, and to give him Satanic eyes. Such an artist would show that he had neither understood Shakespeare nor the opera we are discussing here."[52]

Can we learn anything more from composer or librettist about a Catholic interpretation? Verdi was deeply spiritual but had little use for Catholic theology or Catholicism as an organized religion. As Boito recalled in 1910, "In the ideal moral and social sense he was a great Christian, but one should take care not to present him as a Catholic in the political and strictly theological sense of the word: *nothing could be further from the truth.*"[53] While personal beliefs do not necessarily translate into art works and author intentionality cannot serve as sole basis for valid interpretation, the aggregate of evidence in this case suggests that a Catholic interpretation is surprising and possibly troublesome.[54]

It could be argued that this assessment contradicts the notion of a film as an independent text that creates its own narrative position. A more productive framework is whether the theme and imagery work in the context of the film *Otello*. They "work" in the sense of providing a visual and moral focus, but they strip motivation even further and reduce the substance of the film. As it stands, Zeffirelli's interpretation shows the hand of a socially conservative maker,[55] from a Catholic culture.

The Moshinsky-Large version of *Otello* appears to be conservative at first glance. It offers an understated style in sets, movement, and camerawork and eschews fancy visual effects. The very fact that it celebrates the opera house, as relays typically do, and avoids ideological reinterpretation of the opera also render it implicitly a conservative example of screen opera.[56] Yet unlike Zeffirelli's film it refrains from imposing explicitly a conservative social agenda. It is true that we see Christian icons in this relay. A tall backdrop of a fallen Christ appears in the storm scene, and a 12-inch crucifix joins papers and books on a desktop in Act II. At the start and end of Act III the backdrop returns and offers a visual analogy of pity and sacrifice to Otello's slide in the story. Nonetheless, the religious images are not fetishized in this telecast. They do not receive much attention by the camera—the desktop icon is mostly ignored, and the backdrop image stands well above the prevailing focus on the singers and appears infrequently. Spectators in the hall are much more aware of the large image than we are at home. Moreover, individual characters do not interact with the religious imagery. Overall, the Moshinsky-Large relay uses Christian imagery as a decorative device to accompany a conventional reading of *Otello*. The Zeffirelli film deploys such imagery as a fundamental feature in shaping a highly individual, and Catholic, interpretation of *Otello*.

Regression

As we have seen, Zeffirelli's film offers abundant sensory pleasures to the spectator. Such pleasures tap into cinema's ability to evoke regressive longings for the pleasures of a prior time—indeed, make the spectator passive like a child and regress to an earlier stage. While this can also occur with live opera, certain conditions of cinema—the larger-than-life figures, the flattened illusion, the blackened house, and the technological control of our senses—make spectators more susceptible to such tendencies. A sense of something missing, namely, an absence of real figures on the screen, helps fuel the desire. Classic Hollywood film, in particular, can indulge spectators' fantasy such that they fuse more totally with the narrative on the screen. This effacement of the distinction between self and other can be accompanied by nostalgic yearnings for a better past. In psychoanalytic terms this means regression to the presymbolic or imaginary state: that idyllic stage of infantile development prior to the mirror stage of self-other differentiation and to the entry into structures of language. The imaginary stage has associations with a plenitude of pleasure and the adult will mourn the loss of that plenitude and attempt to have it restored. This is futile, of course, because the stage cannot be duplicated or restored once the child has moved past it.

These desires thrive in a medium that promotes a rapt atmosphere and takes place in a remote and ritualized venue. Television, however, operates rather differently. Television stresses presence rather than absence and this means fewer longings for something in a utopian past. Television unfolds in the home, a familiar venue, and takes on the trappings of daily living. When turned off, television blends in with objects and furniture and can be passed by rather easily. When turned on, its performance in an ordinary room, usually under ordinary lighting conditions, renders it an unlikely source for idealization. As noted earlier, television often accompanies or competes with other domestic activities, such as talking on the phone or preparing dinner. This creates an aesthetic of casual looking, of inadvertent rather than sustained attention: what Ellis calls an aesthetic of the glance as opposed to cinema's aesthetic of the gaze.[57] Television's small screen size in relation to viewer and to cinema further contributes to the unidealized nature of the viewing experience.

Television's size and venue foster a sense of intimacy and shared experience between the viewer and the actors on the screen. Describing the relationship as "a co-present intimacy," Ellis speaks of a "complicity of the institution of TV in the process of looking at dramatic events which increases their sense of co-presence with the viewer."[58] At the same time, the everyday conditions in which television is experienced promote a separation between viewer and narrative that blunts the potential for regressive urges. This separation minimizes voyeurism in the televisual experience; the viewer does not adopt a controlling gaze and thereby remains more distant from the narrative. Without such objectified looking, the televisual experience is better able to resist the fetishizing of objects and their later idealization as the basis of strong desires.

The relay displays some interesting practices with respect to these patterns. As in the Moshinsky-Large telecast, the relay typically includes a curtain call and this breaks the illusion of merged character-singer such as is found in film-opera. Suddenly it is Dame Kiri Te Kanawa who is taking a bow, and not Desdemona. This frames the fictional narrative within another level of reality—as do introductory commentary, intermission features, and views of house and conductor. Yet while the relay generally reveals its technical basis much more than cinema, it tries to mask the fact that it is recorded. It wants the viewer to think that he or she is witnessing a live event, indeed attending it: a concrete example of the co-presence that Ellis finds characteristic of television. The masking seems regressive because it wants to lull the viewer into experiencing opera as a live event. In this way it resembles cinema: it makes the viewer complicit in an illusion. This illusion, however, is still much tamer than the enveloping aura that attends cinema.

The Moshinsky-Large telecast *Otello* fits these patterns of televisual behavior. In comparison to the Zeffirelli, it promotes a more dispassionate viewing experience. We view story and characters more objectively. Figures appear smaller and closer to us, and the scale fosters an intimacy of shared experience. This quality is reinforced by the simplicity of sets and costumes, which focuses our attention on the characters. We watch the telecast in the home and the experience becomes less ritualized and separate—although, as noted, we are meant to believe at some level that we are in the hall and partaking of a ritual. We see establishing shots of the hall with closed curtain (with royal crest), medium shots of Solti and the orchestra as they begin each act, curtain calls, and final applause that includes the Prince and Princess of Wales. Yet the mundane trappings of home viewing mitigate against such ritualistic elements.

On the whole, excesses of representation and spectatorship have less of a role to play in the creation of meaning for this *Otello*. Potential desires for something missing do not have a chance to be activated because we operate on a more equal footing with the narrative before us. This Moshinsky-Large telecast produces a reading that emphasizes psychological disintegration, not visual spectacle, and without excessive idealization.

In this way it recalls the opera's roots as a Shakespearean play. At the risk of stating the obvious, we can claim that this relay telecast reinscribes the theatricality of the work.

The opera's direct roots, of course, lay in the late nineteenth century, when it originated. Not coincidentally, late Romantic music serves as the basis of the classic Hollywood score and acts as a powerful tool for regression in cinema. In general, as Caryl Flinn observes, the classic film score has the power to "restore an original quality or essence currently lacking."[59] Regressive desires are set in motion by the perception of a deficiency or something missing in the present. The subject wishes for something better, and it is the remote past—in this case psychic anteriority—that can provide it.

Verdi's opera has a fascinating relationship with these patterns of film spectatorship.[60] Its story, too, is predicated in the notion of a better past and the desire for its restoration; we hear a lot about past glory, past courtship, and past love. Arguably the *Otello* narrative concerns a quest, inevitably futile, for the restoration of a plenitude that is lost. As such, Zeffirelli's film has an obvious basis on which to engage nostalgic impulses of the spectator and evoke desires for the restoration of a lost plenitude. For the spectator, regression can provide a means of identifying with the characters. In this case, regressive desires also extend to a societal level: the wish for a utopian stage prior to racial consciousness or division. But a darker side of regression plays out in Zeffirelli's film as we see Otello's slide to a primitive state prior to the acquisition of Christianity. This interpretive strategy reinforces a Eurocentric hierarchy. Although Zeffirelli claims that the film was intended as a critique of such a structure,[61] it does not make that clear and actually affirms the racist status quo.

One technique that Zeffirelli utilizes to stress anteriority is the flashback, an idiomatic cinematic device. Four flashbacks occur in the Love Duet, and they sensitively pictorialize the reminiscences that substitute for Act I of the Shakespeare.[62] Three recapture the courtship and wedding in Venice, and we see an adoring Desdemona, a blissful wedding day, and a father's pain. The other flashback takes us further and exposes the agony of Otello's boyhood when he was wrested from his mother, branded, and sold into slavery.

These flashbacks in the film underscore the regressiveness of Otello's and Desdemona's love, a quality that is already present in Verdi's opera. Their relationship rests on—even depends on—the past, and regression into the utopia of the past is necessary for present happiness. This suggests a fragile relationship. Verdi's Duet not only relates the glories and intimacies of the past, but tells of how each told the other of events of the more distant past: a kind of doubled regression, almost a fetishizing of an idealized anteriority. Musically this is expressed by tonal wandering. It is also depicted by harmonic retrogression, notably in the backward circle of fifths when Desdemona first sings. The text moves from "Mio superbo guerrier" in the present to "Te ne rammenti!" and its evocation of the past ("My superb warrior" to "Do you remember"). Otello's section that begins on "Venga la morte" ("Let death come") features a melodic and harmonic retrogression in the bass—F, E-flat, and eventually D-flat—that evokes a meeting of the sublime and death in a manner that is reminiscent of Wagner.[63] The surfeit of feeling regresses to a kind of presymbolic time, prior to rational language. It is striking that the two characters do not sing together, except for the final gesture, when Desdemona utters "Otello" during his sustained "Venere splende." Even the self-indulgent Love Duet of *Tristan und Isolde* has the principals falling over each other musically, as they approach sexual union. But Otello and Desdemona are more involved in individual regression into Otello's past than in a present that they share.

His music, moreover, becomes increasingly irrational and offers a compressed version of his destabilization over the course of the opera, itself a kind of regressive process. Thus, while I am struck by the beauty and intensity of the Duet, I also believe it lays the foundation for the unraveling of their relationship.[64]

Regression in the film also entails a yearning for the lost maternal object. The maternal represents the site of blissful union prior to the self-other split. Music has the power to recall the pleasurable sensations of the time in the womb and imply a restoration of what was lost after the separation from the mother. Sound is apparently the first sensation that a human experiences, in the womb. Because of the connection between infantile pleasure and the sound stimulus, music heard later can hint at the pleasure of that state and trigger desire for it. Julia Kristeva has suggested that it is the voice that stimulates the infant, and particularly the female voice in the maternal bond. Thus the female operatic voice holds special significance.[65] Moreover, the functioning of the female body as the desired site of pleasure of the lost maternal object has important consequences. Because the pleasures of that close bonding cannot be recouped, disappointment over the loss can be displaced onto a woman in the form of her categorization in extreme terms: she is either idealized or debased.

In Zeffirelli's film the lost maternal object assumes concrete form in suggestive symbols. Caverns and passageways that appear frequently after Act I evoke a sense of the mysteries of the womb. The half-dome configuration of the room with the crucifix is particularly suggestive, and its brilliant shaft of light is obviously phallic. Does the placement of the crucifix in this room imply Christ's return to the true mother and by extension Otello's desire for his own maternal regression? It is interesting that Otello's regression to paganism takes place here: home to another facet of his cumulative process of regression.

Fig. 3.5 Katia Ricciarelli in *Otello* (1986).
Directed by Franco Zeffirelli. (Courtesy British
Film Institute)

Desdemona, expectedly, serves as the main embodiment of
the lost maternal object in the film. Highly idealized, she is
punished for her excesses, which include her role as symbol
of the sexual/maternal for Otello. Flinn's general statement
on woman in cinema is apt in this context: "The feminization of utopia requires the female term to operate as the
source of plenitude and unity for [the male] subject, although
at the same time, she is rejected for the goods she holds over
him. Woman—and her 'music'—are transformed into an empty
theoretical space, a discursively meaningless body." [66]

Visually Desdemona appears as purity incarnate for much
of the film (fig. 3.5). Her lighting tends toward softness and
golden tones, and her blonde tresses, typically backlit, resemble
an angel's halo. She often wears pure-white garments and her
skin is pale with little blemish. Zeffirelli presents a Desdemona

who conforms to the Romantic ideology of the "eternal feminine." Her idealization signifies body and threatens to evoke
male fears of the mysteries of the female body—fears that could
justify a violent end. But on the surface, at least, Desdemona
conjures up the pleasurable attributes of the feminine.

Zeffirelli's staging of her appearance in the Love Duet,
which differs from the opera's original instructions, illustrates
the point. We see Desdemona as the embodiment of female
passivity as she lies on the bed, angelically, with outstretched
arms, waiting for her "superbo guerrier." The perfect image
brings to mind Botticelli and the pose recalls Titian's reclin-
ing nudes, as in "The Venus of Urbino." While such stylization
suggests stability, the passivity signals a need for someone—
a man—to bring the artwork to life: another variation on the
Pygmalion myth. Otello fills the role when he arrives at the bed,
and Desdemona responds through facial and bodily gestures to
reminiscences of the past. Moreover, the very act of her waiting, which occurs several times in the film, exemplifies the trope
of the woman-who-waits that Mary Ann Doane has identified
in classic Hollywood film—a thematic element that acts to re-
structure dramatic rhythm away from progression and toward
eventlessness.[67] For Zeffirelli the device becomes another means
for promoting atemporality and ultimately inducing fantasy.

In Verdi we know little about Desdemona in her own right.
In Zeffirelli we know even less, and the character takes on an
aura of lack. Silenced through a large number of musical cuts,
Desdemona reinforces the Freudian stereotype of woman-as-
mystery and hence threat to the male order. The worst cut is
the "Willow Song." This music allows us to glimpse Desdemona's innermost emotions, when she is alone. It also provides
an opportunity for greater interaction between singer and character, even though the experience in film is diluted because of
the prerecorded music. The Moshinsky-Large relay, in contrast,

includes this number and also affords a more active and intimate relationship between the two personas because the music is being envoiced "live."[68]

The "Willow Song" is also significant, as Michal Grover-Friedlander contends, because it is at this moment that Desdemona turns to her mother,[69] even though direct reference is brief. Zeffirelli's excision of the maternal bears out Naomi Scheman's thesis on Hollywood cinema that for female characters the maternal is often ignored or denigrated. This leads to a covert affirmation of woman's location in a patriarchal rather than matriarchal order.[70] Zeffirelli does keep the "Ave Maria," which supports his Catholic theme. While we might be tempted to consider the number an affirmation of the maternal—of Mary—the mother is more of an exterior force than the personal presence of the "Willow Song."

In the opera Desdemona's downfall results from supposed sexual transgression.[71] In the film her role as representative of the lost maternal object also leads to her destruction. During the Love Duet, as noted, Zeffirelli has Otello reenact the moment when he was stolen from his mother. From his perspective the violent separation might feel like maternal abandonment. He displaces feelings of female rejection onto the obvious source of (female) pleasure-plenitude, his wife. In this view, Desdemona symbolizes the deceit of woman and deserves punishment.[72]

This type of displacement has suggestive ties with the workings of cinema itself. Cinema depends on a signifying system that attempts to recreate reality. But ultimately the medium amounts to a discourse of representation that substitutes for the real world.[73] As Kaja Silverman observes,

> this fundamental lack reveals a remarkable propensity for displacement. Sometimes the absence

which structures cinema would seem to be the fore-
closed real. At other times it is equated with the
concealed site of production. On yet other occasions, lack would appear to be inscribed into cinema
through the female body. Random as they seem,
these displacements follow a very specific trajec-
tory. The identification of woman with lack functions to cover over the absent real and the fore-
closed site of production—losses which are incompatible with the "phallic function" in relation to
which the male subject is defined.[74]

For Zeffirelli's film, Desdemona's inscription as lack is situated along the chain of displacement that not only aims to
reinstitute the authority of the cinematic text but proposes to
compensate for the lapses that inhibit Otello's acquisition of
full subjectivity—that is, his authority in the symbolic order,
which means mainstream society. The compensatory role of
woman's lack recalls the compensatory function of non-diegetic
music in film, discussed earlier. Both attempt to make up for
deficiencies in cinema, and both possess elements of excess.
Yet while both suggest regression, woman's lack has a much
more direct bearing on male subjectivity. In Zeffirelli's film it
buttresses an Otello who is vulnerable and who lacks full subjectivity.[75]

Whereas the "Willow Song" is an absent signifier in the
Zeffirelli that opens space for longings for its presence, the
situation is quite different in the Moshinsky-Large telecast.
Here Desdemona sings the number and indulges in the past
in front of our eyes. The very fact of her having a past lessens
the potential for her serving as an object of displacement for
Otello's fears. Moreover, the lesser illusionism of television as
a medium reduces the need for a chain of displacement such

as occurs in cinema. In this telecast, Desdemona's unidealized visual representation helps to stave off regressive urges toward some utopian plenitude of pleasure. She embodies presence rather than absence—absence as defined as something literally missing or as something desired because of idealization—and in this way contributes to an interpretation that focuses on human psychology and affirms one of the basic characteristics of the medium of television.

Final Considerations

Zeffirelli intended his film for mass-market distribution in the movie house, but it has achieved sustained life as a video. So has the Moshinsky-Large relay. This means that they are both experienced on television, and suggests that video may lessen differences between them. The Zeffirelli will reappear in movie houses from time to time but essentially it plays on television, in video form. How does this affect the meanings of the work? And how does it differ from the Moshinsky-Large relay, which was conceived for television from the beginning?

In the video version Zeffirelli's film loses its larger-than-life size and its towering command of the viewer. Figures shed some of their idealization on the small screen and the general tone becomes less monumental. Reformatted to fit the dimensions of the television screen, images are divested of some of their content and display new visual emphases. The experience of watching the film on video takes on qualities that apply to television viewing in general, and presence and casualness replace absence and rapt attention. Such conditions can undermine regressive tendencies of Zeffirelli's interpretation and affect its success in this format. It is interesting to consider that even though cinema's regressive tendencies make the spectator passive and many deem this a negative feature, the regressive tendencies of Zeffirelli's film tie in with the excessive visual apparatus of cinema. This includes viewing conditions such as the big screen and the darkened communal space. On television, however, Zeffirelli's treatment gives us only superficial trappings of excess—idealized backlit images, indulgent pauses and looks, and excessively slow tempos—and not the context in which they are meant to be experienced. The film probably seems more mannered because the discrepancies are more apparent on television. A treatment that is more consistent and accepts the excessive mechanisms of cinema and their particular functions may be preferable to one that highlights the disparities. In any case, we may welcome the chance to lose ourselves in the regressive pleasures of the film in the movie house, as this allows us to forget rational considerations such as the damage to Verdi's score. Distracting pleasures have distinct advantages in this situation. We might conclude that the video version of Zeffirelli's film approaches the classical balance of the Moshinsky-Large version. Successive viewing of both videos, however, reveals that a large gap remains between the two. Furthermore, the Zeffirelli still lacks the obvious intrusions of reality—house, applause, curtain calls—that anchor the relay to presence rather than absence.

The video version exerts additional leveling effects on the two treatments. Video in general narrows the gap between viewer and director/editor by according the viewer the ability to perform various manipulations on the work: stop and start, revisit and skip passages, proceed frame-by-frame, and so forth. This capacity has specific meaning for these treatments for it questions the notion of the integral musical work. *Otello* is reputedly a unified and linear opera but now, as with CD recordings, it can be fragmented by the respondent. This suggests an aesthetic that functions in accordance with the atemporality of Zeffirelli's film. The Moshinsky-Large version can also accommodate manipulation, but Zeffirelli's reorganization of the score makes it easier to disassemble on video.

This *a piacere* approach to video spectatorship bears some resemblance to televisual practices themselves. Television, we have seen, encourages familiarity, intimacy, co-presence, and intermittent viewing. With video, screened on the television monitor (now also the computer monitor), we control events with a casualness that is shaped by our familiarity with videos of all kinds and the VCR itself. One option in deploying an opera video (or any video) is to play it straight through. We might pause momentarily, perhaps at the end of an act, in a ritual that mimics intermission at a live performance. But in my hypothetical example, essentially the work would be played through. What I am proposing is that opera viewing on video elicits more sustained attention than occurs with television in general or other kinds of video. It is due as much to the type of viewer who watches opera videos as it is to the nature of opera. Those who rent or buy an opera video are probably already interested in opera, if not devoted to it. A special ritual for viewing might even take place—one with darkened room and planned intermission. In such circumstances, video mediates some of the differences in the experiencing of opera on cinema and television.

Regardless of the leveling tendencies of video, the two interpretations we have considered in this chapter offer different readings of Verdi's masterpiece. They ask us to believe in different conceptions of a canonic work as they add to an ongoing tradition of interpretive re-creations of the story. The Moshinsky-Large remains close to traditional interpretations, offering the most successful version of the opera to appear on video to date. Domingo gives a superb rendition of the Moor,

Solti's pacing is persuasive, and Large's camerawork is sensitive and moving. As I have argued, this relay is highly appropriate to its medium, television, and wears well in repeated viewings. In my opinion it ranks as one of the best relay versions of any opera.

Zeffirelli's film offers pleasures to the spectator and indulges many of our desires toward utopian fantasies. What are we to make of this beautiful but regressive film?[76] In addition to its visual opulence, Zeffirelli's conception asks us to accept a musical score with substantial revision. One can argue from an aesthetic standpoint that the rearranged score is not very successful—a judgment that is independent from a priori notions of fidelity. I offer the view while recognizing that the operatic newcomer might pay little heed to the music and not be disturbed by the musical ruptures. A more knowledgeable viewer, however, would notice them. Regardless of the difference, perhaps Zeffirelli and Maazel could have fashioned a better film by starting fresh: ignoring Verdi and creating a new score and scenario expressly for their cinematic *Ot(h)ello*.[77] Verdi's *Otello* was a poor choice for a film that indulges in luxurious image and leisurely pace. Indeed, Verdi's score used "straight" would place any movie director in a bind. Scenic motion would occur in tight bounds—bounds that are more appropriate to stage than cinema. Even hybrid types of filmed opera add time to accommodate the camera, for example, Peter Sellars's *Don Giovanni*. On the other hand, Von Karajan's studio film of *Otello* manages to inject a few cinematic features into a production that uses the score intact. But aesthetically it has more in common with a stage production than a full-fledged movie. It is a far cry from Zeffirelli's excessive yet cinematic style.

"Cinematic" can mean many things, of course. Continuous music is commonly considered cinematic because it implies motion, seamlessness, and linearity. Verdi's score, largely through-composed, is continuous. Yet an aesthetic problem arises when its supposedly "cinematic" music is used in a film version of the opera. It is well to recall Sabaneev's advice regarding composition for the movies: music with discrete blocks, repetitive and easily removable, works the best. This does not describe continuous music, or Verdi's *Otello*. Thus, ironically, continuous music is not always conducive to cinematic adaptation. The problem is compounded by Zeffirelli's rich visual style, which calls for a score that can be easily disassembled.

In fact, the director had found such a score for his first film-opera, *La Traviata*—a film much more successful artistically than *Otello*. *Traviata* works well because of the opera's roots in number opera and musical repetition. As such one could easily cut repetitive passages and entire numbers; it was suitable to lengthen pauses between numbers. Similarly, the success of Losey's *Don Giovanni* and Rosi's *Carmen*, both based on number opera, derives in part from the adaptability of the opera to the conditions of cinema. But before casting this as some kind of universal, we should note that some continuous scores lend themselves to cinema. Operas that are repetitive, leisurely, and rich in instrumental music, for example Puccini's operas, work well. Wagner's operas would also do well in this regard. In other ways his operas are difficult to adapt, especially if the films are intended for mass distribution. Syberberg's film *Parsifal*, a rarefied reading of a difficult work, solves the problem by relying on fantasy and conventions of theater—in other words, by ignoring many of the capabilities of cinema as a medium. In addition, ideology provides a thematic coherence that in Zeffirelli is taken up by visual excess.

Thus while the Moshinsky-Large *Otello* exemplifies the relay at its best, Zeffirelli's *Otello* exposes both the glories and pitfalls of film-opera. It suggests that few operas lend themselves to full cinematic treatment—a view shared by Zeffirelli, who nonetheless believed *Otello* a good choice because of its grand themes and Shakespearean story.[78] Ironically, the Moshinsky-Large is more successful in conveying the grandeur of *Otello* by virtue of the fact that it has limits—a condition that suits this very psychological opera.

4

Cinema and the Power of Fantasy: Powell and Pressburger's *Tales of Hoffmann* and Syberberg's *Parsifal*

In the early 1880s two operas appeared that capped the careers of their respective authors. In France, Jacques Offenbach was well along in the composition of *Les Contes d'Hoffmann* when he died in October 1880. Others completed the work and confusion arose among differing versions. Many of the basic elements of the opera, including the ordering of acts, the use of spoken dialogue or sung recitative, and the choice of single or multiple casting, were open to question. As a result, the work has developed a tradition of flexibility in staging and performance, and this is especially apt for a work subtitled "opéra fantastique."[1]

Offenbach wrote *Tales* as a more serious endeavor than his usual fare, which consisted mostly of fashionable parodies and divertissements for the Second Empire audience. He wanted to prove himself as a composer of significant works. The choice of German subject matter, in the form of reworked versions of E. T. A. Hoffmann, reflects Offenbach's serious intent and could be considered a return to his German roots. The theme is also of interest because German music was making inroads in France at the time, especially in the form of Wagner and Wagnerism.

Unlike Offenbach, Richard Wagner completed his last opera, *Parsifal*. A music drama of ethereal beauty, *Parsifal* is a challenging work and has been called "the most enigmatic and elusive work in the Wagner canon."[2] It has prompted a wide range

of interpretations, from studies of Christianity and Nordic my-
thology to explorations of more contentious terrain such as
anti-Semitism, homosexuality, psychoanalysis, and pathology.
Although it is risky to say that *Parsifal* is more serious than his
earlier efforts, one senses a hypnotic mysticism that seems more
intense than that of previous operas. The music is partly responsible. Economical in its motivic content and rich in orchestral color, the score reveals a mature composer at the height of
his powers. But the intensity has other sources. *Parsifal* represents Wagner's only opera composed after the formation of
the Reich, and it could be approached as a commentary on
the new German order. The earlier *Ring,* for example, exudes
an energy that paces out the journey toward that goal. *Parsifal,* in contrast, is static and suggests the sort of reflection
that occurs after a goal has been reached. Another factor is
Parsifal's intimate association with Bayreuth and the meanings
that surround Wagner's temple of art. In addition, some of
Wagner's personal concerns at the time of composition conspire to set a serious tone. The composer thought a great deal
about purity—of animals, food, body, race, and nation—and
this theme underlies much of the symbolic content of the opera.
And just as *Tales of Hoffmann* was intended as more serious fare
than the usual Offenbach opera, so *Parsifal* overlays ordinary
Wagnerian seriousness with a devoutness that mesmerizes.

What does it mean to be mesmerized? How can that effect
be achieved in art? One way is through fantasy. *Hoffmann* is a
"fantastic opera" that gives expression to the non sequiturs of
dream and imagination. Fantasy figures in many literary works,
as in E. T. A. Hoffmann's stories "The Sandman" and "Coun-
cillor Krespel," upon which much of the opera is based. Fantasy
has also found a congenial home on the movie screen. One need
think only of *Fantasia* or other Disney animated features, not to

mention horror movies, dream sequences in ordinary films, and exaggerated production numbers in musicals. We have already seen how cinema as a medium can cause spectators to indulge in fantasy. But the main concern here is on genre rather than subjectivity. With its vast resources and manufactured origin, film offers unlimited possibilities for the expression of fantasy. Thus it is not surprising that a successful film of *Tales of Hoffmann* should emerge, namely, the 1951 movie of Michael Powell and Emeric Pressburger, in English translation. It is, appropriately, a fantastical take on the opera and a bravura performance of the representational and expressive powers of cinema. As I will show, the film represents an ideal interpretation of the opera and, the dangers of absolute statements notwithstanding, perhaps *the* ideal rendition.

Parsifal is not a "fantastic opera," at least not in the *Hoffmann* sense. To be sure, as a Wagnerian music drama it trades in the language of symbols, both verbal and musical. But its high moral tone is so pervasive that it tends to render unremarkable any lapses from the everyday world. We are drawn into it hypnotically. The symbolism at the heart of the opera leaves it susceptible to imaginative interpretations, such as Hans-Jürgen Syberberg's film of 1982. This *Parsifal* strains the cinematic apparatus and the spectator as it mounts a critique of the ideologies upon which the opera and its reputation have been built. Fantasy plays a central role in its techniques of representation. I will argue that this controversial *Parsifal* offers an intriguing and original rendition of the opera but I will stop short of declaring it *the* ideal interpretation. For this writer it is futile to embark on a quest for the holy grail of interpretation. In spite of the critical nature of Syberberg's venture, my ambivalent relationship with the composer—just like Syberberg's—prevents absolute judgments, and these include ideal interpretations.

Thus these two films, some thirty years apart, marshall fantasy to create meaning. In the process, each depends on an interaction with certain thematic elements to shape narrative and mise en scène. For *Tales* they include an emphasis on performance, a separation of sound and image, and an affinity for parody. *Parsifal* is shaped by a stress on ideology, a tendency to promote separation, and a sensitivity toward memory and time. These themes help to stabilize the centrifugal tendencies of fantasy and organize spectators' subjectivity and desire. With a focus on the interaction between fantasy and thematic elements, the chapter aims to illuminate how and why these two films—so different in source and rationale—are yet alike in fashioning two of the most brilliant and original examples of film-opera.

A Tale of Two Movies

In 1948 the "Archers"—the British team of director Michael Powell and emigré writer Emeric Pressburger—scored a success with *The Red Shoes*, a modernized version of a fairy tale by Hans Christian Andersen. Although the film seems dated for the way it forces the aspiring ballerina to give up a dancing career or suffer fatal consequences, it broke new ground in its combination of fantasy, dance, and music. Vincente Minnelli's *An American in Paris* (1951), for example, owes a great debt to the movie. Powell later described *The Red Shoes* as a "sketch" for *Tales of Hoffmann*, which came out three years later.[3] The famous "Red Shoes" ballet sequence, some seventeen minutes long, became a source for fantastic effects in *Tales,* such as the woman jumping into an abyss (used in the Tale of Antonia). The earlier film can also be viewed as a feminine version of the masculine quest-narrative that we see in *Tales,* only in *Shoes* the evil threat comes from red toe shoes rather than a satanic rival. For the filmmakers, known for a wry juxtaposition of elements in their work,[4] the "composed" aspects of *Shoes*—dance and music—provided a liberating framework. Fantasy could emerge more readily without the need to coordinate speech and image track in much of the film.

A film of an opera was a logical successor, and the suggestion of Offenbach's opera came from Sir Thomas Beecham.[5] Built on the dance-music core of *Shoes*, *Tales* adds singing and continuous music to produce the "fully composed film:" a movie without dialogue, totally dependent on the prerecorded music. This makes possible a greater variety of filming techniques and Powell likened the process to that of shooting silent film, as in his early years. The absence of live sound also encouraged a physical easiness in cast and crew that led to experimentation and improvisation. The director's satisfaction with this manner of conceiving a film led him to call *Tales* the culmination of his career.

Like *Shoes*, *Tales* uses dancers in many principal roles and even many of the same players. For example, Moira Shearer, the lead in *Shoes*, here is Stella and Olympia, while Robert Helpmann, a ballet colleague in the earlier film, assumes the evil quartet of Lindorf, Coppelius, Dapertutto, and Dr. Miracle in *Tales*. We are also treated to a reprise of Léonide Massine, one of the great dancers of the century, as he frolics through the role of Spalanzani. He also plays Schlemil and (briefly) Franz in the other tales. Two of the main roles, Hoffmann and Antonia, are filled by actual singers and they are upstaged by the mimetic sophistication of the dancers. A new musical recording, in a new English translation (by Dennis Arundell), was made for the project. Claiming that he wanted "a performance, *not* a recording," Powell avoided operatic superstars and used singer-actors such as Bruce Dargavel (Coppelius, Dapertutto, Dr. Miracle) and Murray Dickie (Cochenille).[6] The other unseen voices include Dorothy Bond (Olympia),

Margherita Grandi (Giulietta), and Grahame Clifford (Spalanzani). Each screen character lip-syncs to the prerecorded track. The Archers retained another key figure from *Shoes,* the designer Hein Heckroth. His bold visual style draws heavily on surrealism, fauvism, and expressionism, and is crucial to the extravagant feel of the film. Another innovator, Frederick Ashton, served as choreographer for the project.

This combination of talent produced an eclectic film that eludes easy classification. *Tales* owes a debt to many traditions, notably ballet film (*Shoes* is the best example), film musical, silent film, horror film (especially German expressionism), and Walt Disney animation. The emphasis on ballet in the Tale of Olympia shows the influence of the stage ballet, *Coppélia,* which is also based on Hoffmann's story "The Sandman." Premiered in 1870, *Coppélia* had exerted influence on the libretto written for Offenbach. Through this connection with dance, the film not only reinscribes the opera's lineage but also affirms the Frenchness of *Tales of Hoffmann;* ballet, after all, has been a common feature of French opera. The mélange of art forms and national traditions, including English humor and language, produces a *Gesamtkunstwerk* that moves beyond the Germanic association of the concept.

The Wagnerian "total work of art" has obvious resonance for Syberberg's film, but its relationship to the concept is different. In *Tales* it is motivated largely from an urge to reshape meanings of cinema: as a medium of movement, irony, and social commentary. In *Parsifal* the concept is geared mainly toward ideology. Various devices, including puppets, death masks, and projections, reconfigure this key Wagnerian device and contribute to a critique of the ideology of Wagner and its role in German consciousness. The film *Parsifal* becomes Syberberg's way of uncovering the holy grail of Germanic history and exposing its shameful places against a professed ideology of purity.

Unlike *Tales, Parsifal* pays little attention to cinema itself. Its experimentation is deployed mainly in the service of ideology.

Parsifal displays an obvious relationship with earlier films of Syberberg. In 1972 he produced *Ludwig: Requiem for a Mad King;* three years later came *Confessions of Winifred Wagner,* and in 1977 *Hitler: A Film From Germany* (U.S. title: *Our Hitler*).[7] Richard Wagner functions as an absent focus in this grand narrative. In fact, Syberberg was planning a film on Wagner but this transformed itself into *Parsifal,* a film of Wagner's final musical work. The opera's very abstractness, as we have seen, lends itself to cinematic interpretation. With the imminent centennial of *Parsifal's* premiere at Bayreuth, Syberberg could pointedly take on Bayreuth and its meanings for German culture—a connection made more striking given that the opera was not allowed to be performed elsewhere for thirty years after its composition.[8]

Syberberg had difficulty obtaining financing for the project, especially since the German government blackballed him after *Hitler.* A consortium of French-German interests, led by Gaumont, provided support and a new musical recording was made. Syberberg implies that he could not use an existing recording because of the impact of Bayreuth's opposition to the project.[9] An "anti-*Parsifal*" sentiment colored the enterprise. The film was intended to run simultaneously with (or against) the centennial festival production at Bayreuth. Syberberg was offering a "rededicated" festival work: a reconceptualization of "Bühnenweihfestspiel," the label the composer assigned to the opera. It can be translated as a dedicatory stage festival work, with "dedicatory" connoting a sacralizing function.[10] As cinema, this rededicated work portends a broader public than that of a Bayreuth performance. But the difficulty of Syberberg's film and the video possibilities of a staged performance make the disparity less certain.

Although the two films discussed in this chapter differ in their appeal to audiences, they both emphasize theater and its conventions. In this respect they depart from film-operas treated elsewhere in this study, namely, Zeffirelli's *Otello*, Rosi's *Carmen*, and Losey's *Don Giovanni*, which involve spectacle. The stress on theatricalism reminds us that cinema has its roots in the stage. More pertinent to our purposes, it underscores the point that these cinematic treatments adapt works that were originally meant for the stage. The miracle is how the two films deploy fantasy to bridge the gap between theater and cinema and produce convincing works for the big screen.

TALES OF HOFFMANN

As in the opera, the film *Tales of Hoffmann* consists of three stories that are unified through a common protagonist, the poet E. T. A. Hoffmann, and surrounded by a prologue and epilogue that frame the narration of past episodes. The prologue gains length through the addition of a substantial ballet and a focus on the dancing talents of Stella, Hoffmann's current love whom he describes as a combination of the women evoked in the tales. Dance is also featured in an inserted transition from the third tale to the prologue. Besides adding weight to the outer frame of the narrative, these numbers illustrate the film's emphasis on performance. This thematic element functions as one of the main ways in which the film interacts with fantasy, and it occupies our attention in the next section.

Performance

Performance takes center stage in *Tales* and colors the film as a whole.[11] I use the term "center stage" intentionally, because

Tales makes a special point of emphasizing theater. This dramatic device serves many purposes, but one of its main goals is to question the so-called realism of cinema and suggest that it may be a sham—a theatricalism, set up and constructed as in the constructedness of theater sets. Theatricalism in cinema provides a means of highlighting cinema as a system of representation rather than a naturalistic rendering of the world. This helps create irony and a desirable distance between spectator and work. It also ensures that we not take the work too seriously. Still, *Tales* is clearly a cinematic work and, except for a section in the tale of Antonia, it does not allow the theater to take over mise en scène. The camerawork, magic effects, and extravagant color remind us that this is a conception for cinema.

The theater insinuates itself in several ways. Before each act a gloved female hand pages through a program book that gives time, location, and cast. A photo of each actor *en rôle* fills an entire page opposite a description of his or her character. As we peruse the program the introductory music to each act is heard. Labels that identify the title of each act emphasize theatrical divisions, and an "Intermission" sign appears before Act III. Although lengthy films may provide an intermission, for example *Gone With the Wind* and *The Ten Commandments*, *Tales* is only slightly longer than two hours and does not need one. Although the directors had concerns over length,[12] the insertion only strengthens the presence of the theater. One of the first images in the prologue, which now occurs in the theater as much as the tavern, is of the word "Theatre" emblazoned on a classical pediment. The angle is awry and we sense something odd about this theatrical space. Various accoutrements of the theater appear: a caped figure moving melodramatically over red carpet amid gilded chairs and sleeping ushers (all shot from above); a garderobe for hanging cloaks; a walking stick laid casually on a table with a theater program; and a shot from backstage of ballet being performed in the auditorium. Lindorf, a villain, directs his gaze and then ours to a poster announcing the ballet and its cast: a reflexive reference to performance itself.

Stella's Dragonfly Ballet, the first performance in the film, lasts some seven minutes. We encounter it in medias res, as eavesdroppers backstage. After various plot details are revealed, we become more formal viewers, observing the ballet from the front, and soon become immersed in multiple perspectives and distances. The combination of fantasy and abstractness in the sequence recalls the "Red Shoes" ballet. The sense of a theater returns with full force with the applause at the end, coupled with Lindorf peeking through the curtain at the emptying auditorium and at Hoffmann in particular. The second scene of the prologue, in the tavern, also hosts a performance. The through-composed section of Hoffmann's "Song of Kleinzach," where he waxes rhapsodic on the eternal feminine, becomes pretext for a drama in dance. Disneyesque fantasy turns sculpted beer mugs into real people who dance and mime around a come-to-life beautiful woman in white, portrayed by Shearer. Her cone-shaped headpiece recalls that of a fairy princess in cartoon animation.

The most memorable performance occurs in Act I, the Tale of Olympia, when Olympia the doll comes to life and performs her famous coloratura aria, "Les oiseaux dans la charmille" ("Birds in woodland ways are winging" in this rendition) (fig. 4.1). Followed by a spotlight, Olympia the star performer is also a virtuoso ballet dancer, in classic tutu costume. The theatricality is also underscored by camera angles, backdrop curtain, and gazes of real and half-real onlookers (more later), some of whom applaud at the end. The foregrounding of ballet dancer also characterizes the Tale of Giulietta, the second tale

Fig. 4.1 Pamela Brown (left), Frederick Ashton, Robert Rounseville (rear), Moira Shearer, and Léonide Massine in *Tales of Hoffmann* (1951). Directed by Michael Powell, in collaboration with Emeric Pressburger. (Courtesy British Film Institute)

of the film.[13] Played by dancer Ludmilla Tcherina, Giulietta the courtesan sports black leotard, tights, and ballet slippers. While seldom performing a set piece, Giulietta strikes stylized poses that keep alive the notion of the theater (see Frontispiece).

Although the camera exploits the freedoms made possible by cinema, the organization of space is theatrical. In Act I, gauze curtains replace traditional sets and define spaces as would a curtain, backdrop, or scrim in the theater. But while they confine space they also permit easy camera movement from one to another. The spectator feels unsure of location and depth, as if in a maze, but a maze that is nested in a theater space. Act II defines space through colors and images in the background that are created by lighting and painted sets. Occasionally the fantastic is crafted through visual effects that are amateurish in their simplicity, as in the cutout of a gondola that transports Giulietta and Dapertutto at the start of the act. The image would be laughable were it not for the ravishing display that appears with it: the bold colors, exotic makeup, and brilliant costumes; the shimmering water and facial reflection; and the sensual enticements of the music of the Barcarolle. Once again, montage and effects anchor the theatricalisms within cinema.

Moved to a Greek isle from the usual location in Munich, Act III has the most theatrical set and feels the most operatic. Some reviewers criticized its static quality and found it incompatible with the fantastic effects found elsewhere.[14] Justification for an operatic conception exists, of course. Antonia, the main character, is an opera singer, and when she sings there is an oscillation between diegetic and non-diegetic singing; some numbers represent her operatic talents as Antonia, while others reflect Ann Ayars the opera singer. This distinction becomes an urgent matter because Antonia will die if she exerts her singing voice (but whose singing voice?). Music, it is suggested, deceives and is not to be heeded. Her parents, as members of the musical community, become ambiguous figures: her mother, a dead opera singer whose beckoning voice she hears; and her father, a conductor. Both are replicated in marble statues.

Near the end these characters come together in a fantastic sequence that turns operatic performance on its head. In a quandary as to whether she should follow her own desires or be bound by a promise to her father not to sing, Antonia finds herself in the satanic grip of Dr. Miracle (fig. 4.2). He uses the most powerful weapon of all by saying that her mother speaks through him. Then the mother's voice, as operatic voice, is heard. Not believing him, Antonia turns to her parents' statues for guidance. Dr. Miracle is posed in meaningful ways in relation to one and the other, and we see the beginnings of a

Fig. 4.2 Ann Ayars and Robert Helpmann in *Tales of Hoffmann* (1951). Directed by Michael Powell, in collaboration with Emeric Pressburger. (Courtesy British Film Institute)

struggle for control over Antonia (Hoffmann is also a part of this, but he is not present in this sequence). Psychologically charged images follow one another. We see a glowing, halo-surrounded blow-up of the mother's statue. Later a back view of Antonia's theatrically outstretched arm replicates that of her mother's statue, both of which are in the frame: a portent of Antonia's fate? Theatricality turns macabre when the music picks up speed, at the Allegro section in B-flat.[15] The image of Dr. Miracle, bowing feverishly on the violin (the devil's instrument), is multiplied more than tenfold, filling the screen, and I am reminded of the musical-horror-fantasy film, *The 5,000 Fingers of Dr. T* (1953).[16] In the mounting frenzy Antonia finds herself on a stage made in hell and about to enact a nightmare of performance. We view the spectacle as if in a side box in an opera house. On a black stage ringed by golden footlights, both of which are suggested through artistic illusion, Antonia sings furiously, rushing toward her doom. A sketched-in outline of an audience watches her performance. In this virtual theater she is spurred on by her father, who is conducting her and a sketched-in orchestra; by Dr. Miracle, on the violin; and ephemerally by her mother, who briefly appears as a body, in white. The mother's body leaves the theater and journeys through an enchanted garden with white-flecked trees, Antonia in pursuit and looking up as if seeking a disembodied vocal presence.[17] Flames rise up and turn into outstretched arms of adoring fans. As the music builds toward a decisive dominant-seventh chord, the father's image rises out of the orchestra pit and he gives Antonia the conducting cue for her climactic high note—the musical cue for her to die. The zest that accompanies the gesture is horrifying. He is completely overtaken by the power conferred on him by music and the power he confers over it, and of course over his daughter as well. When the peak is reached the performance space returns to their house, with conductor-father in the same obsessive pose. At the resolution Antonia, on cue, dies in Dr. Miracle's arms. Completing the conducting ritual, the father takes a deep bow.[18]

This fantastic scene has rich implications for meaning. We witness an oedipal struggle between father and mother for the daughter—a struggle at the heart of another famous example of film-opera, Ingmar Bergman's version of *The Magic Flute*. While the theme is already present in Offenbach's opera, Powell and Pressburger's treatment sharpens the conflict and makes it more frightening from the standpoint of Antonia. The scene also levels a strong indictment against music as an organized system for power and deception. Selfishness, greed, and self-aggrandizement, we are led to believe, can be promoted by "pure" aesthetic activities. Another intriguing issue is the ambivalent role of the mother—also in Offenbach's opera but intensified here through fantasy. Is the mother an agent of deceit or salvation, a being who herself was doomed because she is a woman who sings? What does it mean that she is not a fully fleshed persona and mostly only a voice? And what does a mother's voice hold out for a daughter who follows in her footsteps? A satisfactory answer to these complex questions lies beyond the scope of the present discussion, but some have been taken up in relation to Offenbach's opera by Heather Hadlock, Carolyn Abbate, and Jeremy Tambling.[19] What seems clear in the film is that the virtual spaces at the end, which resemble the fantastic locations of MTV, convey more of a sense of reality than the naturalistic stage sets at the start of the act. Let us not be fooled by the latter's pretensions to reality.[20]

The film also contains more benign references to opera. Over opening credits we hear the random melodic fragments of an orchestra tuning before a performance, then the tapping of a baton that signals the expectant silence before the music begins. At the end of the movie the conductor returns as a seen presence for the final bars of the score. Sir Thomas Beecham, iconic British figure, conducts heartily, in tails. After the music ends he pointedly closes the score and lays down the baton. These representations of the conductor form a great contrast with the end of the third tale. An ironic counterpoint, they provide a wry means for the audience to withdraw from the heady world of fantasy. A surprising event occurs next: in a close shot a rubber stamp imprints "Made in England" on a leather-bound score of the opera. The act has several implications. One is the notion that film and opera are manufactured products.[21] Another is the idea that opera and England, long considered a nonviable combination, can fit together, and that includes the presentation of a foreign work in English. The stamp also satirizes English nationalism after World War II and affirms pride against the domination of Hollywood and other centers of film.[22] The absurd juxtaposition tells us that art and commerce are not far apart, and that the film just witnessed is really great fun after all.

Performance in the film has close connections with bodily movement, in dance, mime, and other kinds of physical stylization. This mannered aspect of image supplies an element of excess in the signifying system and works well with the excesses of fantasy. Let us examine the implications of bodily excess in dance. Stella, Hoffmann's framing beloved, is a prima ballerina instead of a prima donna—a suppression of opera, of the primacy of sound, in favor of the spectacle of image, which cinema can capture so successfully. While these issues will be discussed in the next section, it is clear that the jouissance embodied in coloratura in the opera is reconstituted in the film because of the additional element of bodily excess, at least for Olympia. This is not the case for Antonia, who signifies only with her voice, but this makes sense given that Antonia is a diegetic singer (and is portrayed by a real singer). In Stella's makeover as a dancer her connection to the three tales shifts to Olympia the dancer and away from Antonia the singer-colleague. This places greater narrative emphasis on Act I and makes it seem more continuous with the Prologue. That the same player, Moira Shearer, portrays Stella and Olympia only confirms (and of course has helped to create) the connection.

In any case Stella, a silent soprano in the opera, now has a vibrant vehicle for expression and subjectivity. In the Dragonfly Ballet in the Prologue she vanquishes her mate. At the moment of triumph, as rearranged love music from Act II resolves after a lengthy dominant build-up, Stella/Dragonfly exults physically through a strong pushing-down of her arms. Thus at the beginning of *Tales* woman triumphs over man: a counterbalance to the masculine search for mastery of woman that underlies the story as a whole. Of course, Hoffmann is unsuccessful in all three episodes and loses Stella, his idealized embodiment of femininity. The ballet, therefore, anticipates the end, or at least the idea that a woman will not be contained by a man. It also suggests male loss. Both could be reasons why Hoffmann looks so disconsolate after the performance. I find it interesting that the very gesture used by Stella for triumph is also used by Giulietta when Hoffmann succumbs to her sexual allure, to the same music. This provides an important connection between remote sections of the film and demonstrates the significance of stylized physical movement even when performance is not foregrounded as such, as in the place under discussion in Act II.

Dance also provides a vehicle for recapitulation. In the transition to the Epilogue, the four women, in their own costumes, reappear as dancers. Stella wears white. Shortly the images of the three women dissolve into Stella's and pictorialize Hoffmann's idealized view of Stella. Over the reprise of the Barcarolle she dances a pas de deux with a man, supposedly Hoffmann. The gesture splits into four and we see differing angles of the same dancing couple. Even though the three women have been sublimated into the fourth, the new arrangement implies that Stella is a multiply constituted woman. It also redefines the Barcarolle's relationship with desire. While the Barcarolle involved only Giulietta when it was first heard, its object of desire is now multiple and diffuse. As in the Dragonfly Ballet, these images signal that Stella cannot be contained and that Hoffmann will fail. The final image shows the couple proceeding to a utopian vanishing point on a theatrical set.

Stylized bodily movement also finds expression in mime. Puppets who move but do not speak appear in Act I. Even more fascinating are the human puppets — actual people who move in the herky-jerky manner of puppets manipulated by strings. The partygoers of Act I consist of such "half-human, half-puppet" figures. The film also offers fake imitations of the human imitations, as in the inanimate couples suspended from above during Hoffmann and Olympia's waltz. Cochenille, the puppet-master (portrayed by Ashton), typifies the ambiguity between reality and artifice in his movements, which range from the mechanical to the fully animate. In the end he reveals himself to be a puppet rather than a human.

Mime is not confined to make-believe figures or diegetic performance, however, and it surfaces in important places. In Act II, subtle movements memorialize the duel between Hoffmann and Schlemil. While spoken text occurred in the opera, the film converts the moment into a silent affair except for the instrumental accompaniment in the background. The absence of words, singing, and diegetic noise such as the clanking of swords marks a return to the world of silent film. Indeed, the scene is almost too quiet. It forces us to pay close attention to the hushed movements and to the power of bodily expression. Above all it shows how the film creates interesting relationships between sound and image.

Separation of Sound and Image

In *Tales* a separation of sound and image emerges as a prominent feature of the film. Of course, any film-opera or film musical that utilizes dubbing features a technical separation of the two elements. In *Tales* the separation assumes a major role and finds expression in unconventional ways. These imaginative arrangements help to structure fantasy, and generally expand the possibilities for the disposition of music and image in film-opera. They also challenge fundamental assumptions of classic cinema.

Classic cinema, according to many theorists, tries hard to

disguise the material heterogeneity that constitutes film.[23] Sound and image are meant to appear as a natural unity, and this helps the spectator to believe in the realism of what is actually a technical construction. Such strategies compensate for a feeling of loss that a viewing subject experiences because of a suspicion that cinema is not real and contains a missing referent or object. This absence can be symbolized as the loss at the heart of castration anxiety. Because a male's relationship to cinema thus has a great deal at stake, it is important that cinema conceal the loss and present itself as a unified basis of subjectivity. One of the main strategies in classical cinema to promote unified male subjectivity has been to keep the image and voice of a woman together. Although the idea seems paradoxical at first glance, film theorist Kaja Silverman argues that in this way woman remains farther from the heart of cinema, that is, from its technical apparatus, and the male can occupy a position at the center and ease his fears of loss more readily.[24] In other words, a divided representation of woman in sound film becomes a threat to male subjectivity. Adorno's famous statement on the inseparability of the recorded female voice and body is pertinent in this regard: "Male voices can be reproduced better than female voices. The female voice easily sounds shrill—but not because the gramophone is incapable of conveying high tones, as is demonstrated by its adequate reproduction of the flute. Rather, in order to become unfettered, the female voice requires the physical appearance of the body that carries it."[25] Although his remarks refer to a purely aural medium, they find resonance in the disposition of sound and image in the *Tales of Hoffmann* film.

Two major numbers in the movie offer intriguing challenges to the goal of a unity of woman's body and voice, the Doll Number and the Barcarolle. Each features an oscillation between embodied and disembodied sound, with fascinating consequences. The Doll Number, "Les oiseaux dans la charmille" in the Tale of Olympia, is particularly ingenious. In the opera the number serves as Olympia's official entrée into the animate world. The high-flying roulades of the demanding coloratura aria are supposed to prove her ability to function in this world. At the same time, the vocal excess reaffirms Olympia's real status as an automaton, as one who can be wound up and let loose on death-defying music. She represents a female on display who is controlled by her dual fathers, Spalanzani and Coppelius. Her bird-like chirps (and subject matter, at least in the French) suggest a caged persona who exists to absorb the male gaze and displace anxieties concerning loss.[26] Olympia cannot be wholly contained, however, for the jouissance generated by the song bolsters her subjectivity and deflects intrusive gestures from the others.

Will Olympia's singing bring her to life? Is it proof of a live human being, as Hoffmann believes? In the film, the disembodied status of her voice—or at the very least its confused status—suggests automaton: a role reinforced by her muteness elsewhere, except for a few perfunctory "yes" responses. She can never quite incorporate the voice and make it hers. Yet its independence acts to bolster Olympia. The Doll Number presents the complexities of the relationship between voice, image, and subjectivity for the character. As we know, in the Archers' movie Olympia is not merely a virtuoso singer but a virtuoso dancer. As the Doll Number proceeds, dance becomes the primary means of expression—a progression based on choreographer Ashton's recognition of the equivalence of vocal coloratura and intricate footwork.[27] Olympia begins the aria with moderated steps, a suitable visualization of the moderated vocal line. Lips mouth words and body shapes gestures. As the pace quickens and steps become more demanding, the lips stop moving. The sound, however, continues all the while. When the tempo slackens or an important structural event occurs in the music, the lips move again. Such synchronized passages tend to be shot in closer range than those that separate sound and image. Whether the pattern is cause or effect is unclear, but one consequence is that the spectator is less likely to notice the disparity because of the distance and because one's eye is drawn to the brilliant dancing of Shearer.[28] Worries over lip-sound synchronization fade in importance.

Nevertheless, this unusual construction has fascinating implications. Olympia experiences jouissance in multiple ways and this augments her power. The oscillation between synchronized and non-synchronized sound places the Olympia persona outside the diegesis, at least some of the time. It is almost as if that disembodied voice splits her subjectivity so that she is watching herself dance from the vantage point of that free-floating vocal signifier. Such reflexive looking displaces, or at least neutralizes, the controlling male gaze: of Hoffmann, of her "father" Spalanzani, and of the cinematic apparatus. The oscillation also suggests that the boundaries of her subjectivity are more elusive, flexible, and non-controllable. Through the free-floating voice she "spills over" beyond her visual representation, and according to Silverman such acts are transgressive. Hence Olympia's refusal to be contained in this way threatens to subvert that mechanism for displacement and associate her more closely with the cinematic apparatus itself than she would be in a unified representation.[29]

The disposition of voice and image in the number has several tantalizing meanings. Just as the free-floating voice watches Olympia, Olympia hears her song more attentively and dances to it when she stops mouthing the words. In these passages, Olympia/Moira Shearer pays greater heed to Olympia/Dorothy Bond, the actual singer, than in the embodied passages. As this implies, the notion of Olympia becomes more complicated:

there is Olympia/Shearer, Olympia/Bond, and Olympia/free-floating voice. Who are we attending and who is each of these personas attending? And what about the onstage audience that is watching, including Spalanzani, Hoffmann, Nicklaus, and a crowd of puppet-guests? No single answer can account for the many signifying systems at work here. Let us also consider the situation of Olympia/Shearer, a virtuoso dancer. She has to pay close attention to the music and use it as a guide to choreography and expression. Hearing the nontethered voice is of great benefit to her in the "coloratura" dance passages. But although she is listening to some outside presence, the act represents a reflexive interaction with herself.[30]

The famous Barcarolle, at the start of Act II, also reveals an oscillating relationship between sound and image. In the opera this number is a duet between Nicklaus and Giulietta. In the film it becomes a duet between Giulietta and herself, or rather Giulietta and her reflection in the water. It is not easy to determine the participants because some of the number is performed without moving lips in either part; we do see Giulietta most of the time, however. The situation becomes more complex when a chorus joins in but no chorus is seen. As in Olympia's Doll Number, the disjunction of body and voice tends to extricate Giulietta from the burden of assuming a masculine sense of loss. Yet the fetishizing of her face, sometimes duplicated in reflection, strongly reinforces the idea of woman as object of the gaze. She is also seen as narcissistic. While this quality mainly involves her body, it is also expressed in sound: the mirroring of the second vocal line, with reflective devices such as doubling of the line, singing in thirds, and imitation. But Giulietta is free to shed and recover one aspect of her subjectivity, her voice, at will—much as she trades in the reflections of men, collecting and dispensing their souls. When she does not move her lips, the effect does not seem as disembodied as in the case of Olympia because the camera foregrounds her body with closer shots. Furthermore, whereas Olympia oscillated in and out of sections in which she moves her lips, Giulietta abandons moving lips entirely after the opening. Embodied sound is apparently dispensable and the music is transformed into an accompanimental function, as in a non-diegetic film score. This allows attention to be fixed more exclusively on image — on Giulietta's body.

The emphasis on separation affects another famous number in Act II, Dapertutto's aria "Scintille, diamant" (here "Now gleam with desire"). The entire number is performed as an accompanied mime/dance. Robert Helpmann never acknowledges himself through moving lips as the source of the singing. The power of the voice and of the physical movements of mime enacts a complicated strategy of mastery. The plot provides the impetus. Dapertutto is mastering the alchemy of transforming an ordinary substance, wax, into valuable gems. This serves the ultimate aim of gaining control over Giulietta so that she will do his bidding and lure Hoffmann to his doom. We are confronted with two powerful discourses of persuasion. The pleading voice of singer Bruce Dargavel makes a strong case. Its status is ambiguous, however. Although it may belong to Dapertutto, it also takes on the quality of a disembodied voice-over, akin to an untethered voice of a narrator in a film or documentary. This phenomenon of a sourceless voice has characteristics of Michel Chion's *acousmêtre*, which he describes as a voice without a visible source.[31] That is not literally the case here, of course, for we see an apparent source, Dapertutto. Yet because the mimed dance operates as such a self-contained performance, the heard voice assumes its own independence instead of an accompanimental function. In this way the voice approaches an *acousmêtre*. According to Chion, who also theorizes a "partial" *acousmêtre*, the acousmatic voice forms an omniscient relationship with its environment.[32] Here the voice is affirming the attempt at mastery in the plot. But because the stylized body movements are also trying to dominate Giulietta, the relationship between voice and physical movement, or image, is not so clear-cut. The two entities express a split and flexible subjectivity in Dapertutto. The ambiguity of the number illustrates Chion's thesis that the acousmatic "creates a mystery of the nature of its source, its properties and its powers"[33] — an apt quality for the mystical magician of this film.

The Septet of Act II (No. 23) gathers several techniques in one number as it superimposes three different arrangements of the sound-image relationship. Hoffmann's embodied singing, the first and the most clear-cut relationship, continues for much of the ensemble. The music, incidentally, sounds like a variation of the Barcarolle, and so we meld our new impressions with remembered ones of the earlier piece. If this is Hoffmann's answer to Giulietta, it serves as a pale reflection of her vitality and reveals him to be a weak figure. The second relationship begins with the second musical entrance, that of Dapertutto, who does not mouth the words. As in his aria, he concentrates on mime and his music floats above. Physical action is foregrounded as he begins to circle around Hoffmann in a ritualistic invitation to a duel. Giulietta joins the circling maneuver and when her music is supposed to begin she also avoids moving her lips. In the ensuing trio, therefore, only Hoffmann is seen singing. Level three begins when a chorus enters. This chorus, however, is off-screen and invisible; we only hear the singing. At this point, Hoffmann has ceased mouthing and been taken over by mime; he too joins in the circling ritual that leads to a duel. We should note that three additional musical lines — those of Nicklaus, Schlemil, and Pitichinaccio — are eliminated, although Schlemil becomes a central figure in the mime. Nicklaus, as in much of the film, observes impassively (a weakness of the film), while Pitichinaccio is not even present (his role is greatly reduced). So in this finale-like number, various modes of separated sound and image interact with each other. They create a sense of suspended time largely because of the static quality of the music: its ostinato-like rhythm, its sectional repetitions, and its limited harmonic movement. It makes a perfect foil for the tense scenario.

Choral numbers also display a separation of sound and image. The first appearance of the human-puppets of Act I provides a good example. In no. 12, the reprise of the A-major Minuet, these hybrid beings gather for the party in honor of the special guest, Olympia. They remain to watch her virtuoso performance and partake of refreshments. In the opera these functions are sung by an onstage chorus, where sound and image emanate from a unified source. In the film, however, we encounter a separation of the two: we see the revelers, but the music does not seem to be coming from them because their lips are not moving. They are mute. And yet we assume that they represent the source of the music within the diegesis. Perhaps we no longer need proof of a sound source because we have internalized the film's irrationality. We accept the figures as fantastic beings and suspend our need for the appearance of a unified representation. If we thought about it, we could imagine off-screen ventriloquists as the source: puppet-masters who pass their voices into the mute receptacles that are seen.

The pretext of artificial beings, however, disappears in the choral environment in Act II, where the group consists of real people, revelers at Giulietta's bacchanal. As in the previous tale, we never see the congregated group move its lips in choral passages, and sometimes we do not see the group when the choral music is heard. Such instances of voice-off, or *acousmêtre*, tend to displace the dominance of the image and undercut our faith in the realism of what we are seeing. Identification becomes more diffuse and we gravitate toward a more objectified stance in relation to what is played out onscreen. This allows us to separate ourselves from the narrative and appreciate another thematic element of the film, its humor.

Parody

One might consider the most humorous aspect of the *Tales* film its resistance to the notion of the unified film. Just as it challenges the idea of a unity of sound and image, *Tales* explodes the myth of a unified approach to representation and narrative for a film. Perhaps this would be expected in a film of this opera because the plot consists of stories whose only common element is a character. Yet thematic similarities among the episodes and the existence of framing sections provide a unifying thread. Performance traditions have also narrowed the gap through single casting, as when the four evil men are portrayed by one bass. Although the film partakes of some of these devices, it still reveals an urge toward separation that pokes fun at the myth of the unified film. The fact that it does this in a film of an opera makes the parody all the more keen.

Many film critics were baffled by the centrifugal tendencies of *Tales* and found it bizarre, excessive, incomprehensible, and incoherent.[34] Raymond Durgnat, for example, speaks of "an all-stops-out expressionistic clutter." While finally admitting that it is "a minor classic," he pens the following fantastical description that itself has become a minor classic on the reception of the film:

> This gallimaufry of Gothicisms, this pantechni-
> con of palettical paroxysms, this meddle-muddle of

media, this olla podrida of oddsbodikins, this massive accumulation of immemorial Mighty Wurlitzerisms, follows Offenbach's operetta relatively faithfully and fills in filmically by ballet, decor and by-play, seeking, moreover, an operatic visual style with a splendid disdain of plausibility. It seeks nothing less than to recapture the full blown romantic urge. If that is weakened for us by time, then eclecticism will overwhelm us. . . . It's not courage this film lacks, it's taste, in the sense of economy and proportion.[35]

While Durgnat is baffled by the eclecticism, he recognizes and ultimately appreciates this quality in a filmic interpretation of Offenbach's opera. What is more surprising from a modern vantage point is how few of the reviews mention the film's humor. Unlike Durgnat most approached the narrative earnestly, guided by the fact that the film is based on an opera. Just as Hoffmann wears magic glasses in Act I and cannot see that the figures are not real, so critics sported magic blinders that blocked their view of the humor. Much of the humor comes from what we would identify as the film's deconstructive spirit: an exposé and reconceptualization of iconic assumptions such as the seriousness of art, film, music, this very undertaking, and even its attempt to get it right. Parody becomes a central aspect of this critique. Powell especially may have been motivated by a desire to reassert the advantages of silent film. As of midcentury, silent film was considered obsolete and people like Powell, who had begun their careers in the old medium, were forced to switch to the new format. The director's joy at being able to forget about dialogue and focus solely on pre-existent music created a freedom in shooting that resembled that of silent film. An improvisational spirit colored the project and fractured preconceived notions about a unified narrative. Mid-century modernism may have embraced a unifying vision in film, but *Tales* does not deliver one.

The Tale of Olympia contains many visual jokes, several inspired by the broad physical humor of silent film. We see such silly things as Cochenille sticking his tongue out at Spalanzani after Spalanzani corrects one of his mistakes. A puppet-spectator falls out of a viewing box when he applauds Olympia after her virtuosic aria-dance. Playing against type, Olympia herself throws a flower in Cochenille's face after she has been wound up. Other instances of slapstick grow out of her mechanical "turn-on" and tell us that the matter at hand is as lighthearted as a Disney animation. When the situation threatens to become serious, as when Olympia spins out of control and hurtles into potential danger, the film maintains a wry tone by offering a virtual staircase which the dancers descend (fig. 4.3). We know it is only an illusion because we are pointedly shown Cochenille unfurling a canvas that is painted like a staircase. The ruse implies that artifice is as good as realism and draws the audience into the technical side of cinema, breaking the illusionism of the medium. But the joke continues, for what we believe to be the staircase is actually a painted outline on the floor. We still perceive it as a staircase because of the position of the camera and the angle of the shot. Although the reason for using a painted staircase was lack of money,[36] the device has the effect of satirizing lavish production numbers that use architectural sets, as in Busby Berkeley films.

Opera also becomes the target of satire. Act I, for example, shows real people replaced by puppets or imitations of puppets—a suggestion that operagoers behave like automatons at the ritual that is an opera performance. During the final bars of Olympia's virtuosic aria, a female puppet in attendance extends her neck to outrageous heights when Olympia hits her

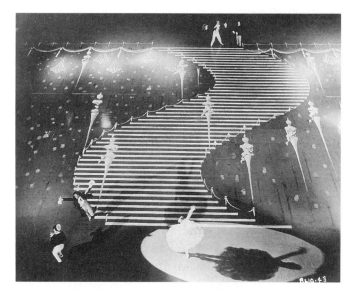

Fig. 4.3 The painted staircase in *Tales of Hoffmann* (1951). Directed by Michael Powell, in collaboration with Emeric Pressburger. (Courtesy British Film Institute)

climactic high E-flat before the resolution to the tonic. This is done by a "real" puppet, who sits amid human-puppets in the audience. Another comment on audience behavior is conveyed by the human-puppet who applauds too soon, in the middle of Olympia's aria, and is eyed disdainfully and hushed by his box-mates. The visual appearance of these human-puppets also satirizes opera. Their makeup is absurd and exaggerated and mocks the display that lies at the heart of the opera ritual. One goes to be seen as well as to see. And as discussed earlier, the film asserts that in opera the singers do not have to be singing, or at least not have to appear to be singing.

Some effects in the film promote a sense of irony. In Act III we see a loop shot of Antonia as she escapes from the right door of a theatrical set, reenters through a left door, runs across to the right and exits through the same door, reappears on the left, and so on. Pursued in her mind by a ghoulish Dr. Miracle, she resembles a heroine of silent film serials. The sequence is especially surprising because it forms a great contrast with the theatrical setting and seems an odd exaggeration of a small detail in the plot. As such it creates irony. Other places in the film ascribe undue importance to something insignificant or juxtapose it with something that is significant to underscore its triviality. I am reminded of an effect in the tavern, in the Prologue, when revelers clink their beer mugs on the table in time with the music. It occurs during a held note, and the added sounds subdivide the duration into small units, much as in a viola or second-violin part. It interrupts the narrative by calling attention to a momentary event, and we respond to its silliness. Today we would consider it a wonderful strategy of postmodernism. To these examples let me add the "Made in England" stamp cited earlier—an ironic and memorable parting shot.

PARSIFAL

Syberberg's *Parsifal* does not utilize parody, but it too pays a great deal of attention to meaning. A serious endeavor, the film engages weighty existential issues such as guilt, goodness, idealism, sin, nihilism, and depravity. Syberberg's film is more linear and unified than *Tales*. It presents a continuous story and anchors its images on a flowing stream of Leitmotifs that provide unity and shape meaning. At over four hours in length, *Parsifal* is much longer than *Tales* and moves much more slowly. Its visual tone is dark and gloomy. We enter a Wagnerian world of night—not one explicitly glorified as in *Tristan und Isolde,* where Night takes on metaphysical meaning, but one implicitly advanced as the appropriate setting for the issues under consideration. As in a long Northern night, Syberberg's palette favors icy-white light and grey-blues against a dark background. It creates an eerie but fitting context for the director's purpose of staging an ideological critique in cinema.[37]

Wagner's music is known for its power to overcome the listener's rational systems and engulf him or her in a regressive wash of sound. Syberberg does little to resist this quality. On the contrary, the director structures montage and mise en scène so as to reaffirm it. His effort to reflect what the music is doing—"to make music visible"[38]—is expressed in an extremely slow-moving camera. The film has a minimum of cuts and some takes are very long. For example Amfortas's monologue in Act I, some eight minutes in length, is shot in one take, an extraordinary effect in modern cinema. Because cutting is key to structuring narrative in film, Syberberg's technique places strain on the director to keep the film interesting and on the spectator as well. Syberberg also promotes music's seamlessness with other elements by stressing the actor's face, often in close-up, as he or she appears to be singing.

Contradictory tendencies abound in the film and they reflect Syberberg's relationship with the material at hand: a deep investment in the culture he is subjecting to critique. Showing many of the characteristics of Wagner and Wagnerism, Syberberg's protest has prompted Susan Sontag's remark that Syberberg is the greatest Wagnerian since Thomas Mann.[39] The director not only endorses the centrality of Wagner in Germanic consciousness through his intellectualized re-creation of Wagner but he affirms the idea of the uplifting powers of art— this as he simultaneously indicts Wagnerian art for its complicity in the moral decay of German culture.[40] The paradox marks Syberberg as rightist and leftist at the same time. Not surprisingly, this ambivalence permeates the film and contributes to its postmodernist spirit.[41] It also becomes a key feature in Syberberg's emphasis on ideology. As the next section demonstrates, ideology functions as one of the main vehicles for shaping fantasy in this extraordinary treatment of Wagner's music drama.

Ideology

Music makes audible that which is unspeakable, but it fades away. There are images that fix, that nail down, that preserve that which is not visible.[42]
—Hans-Jürgen Syberberg

In his incisive critique of the film Tambling puts it well when he states that "the composer is on trial."[43] Less sympathetically, Jean-Jacques Nattiez sees *Parsifal* more as a film about Wagner than as a rendition of the opera.[44] While I find his remarks extreme, it is true that Wagner's meanings for art, society, history, and morality form the core of Syberberg's reading of the opera. Wagner serves as sign and signifier of German consciousness. Through the composer's last work Wagner functions as a lead player in Syberberg's continuing saga of German cultural conspiracy. Here Wagner not only speaks through an authorial voice in the music but serves as the basis for mise en scène. He becomes the source for a prolific array of visual symbols that are much more than decorative; they function as defining elements in Syberberg's interpretation.

The most obvious symbol is the set. A blow-up of Wagner's death mask serves as the literal terrain on which the action is played (fig. 4.4). While its inertness seems to make it constricting, it becomes a flexible framework for shaping drama. In Act I, for example, Kundry arises out of a body of water in the eye cavity and visualizes the idea of sorrow through tears.

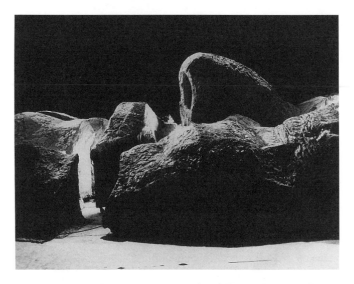

Fig. 4.4 Wagner's death mask in *Parsifal* (1982). Directed by Hans-Jürgen Syberberg. (Courtesy British Film Institute)

At the start of Act II, ingenious lighting converts part of the head into a glowing womb, lit with fire, and this may refer to Wagner's sexual ambivalence as an older man. At the end of the opera the head splits in two, below the nose, at a moment of reunion. It is significant that his death mask, rather than some other likeness, plays such a prominent role in the iconography. Wagner in death, we are given to believe, carries more weight than Wagner in life. Other allusions to his death appear, for example, a replication of the window in Venice where he died, and a skull at the very end. *Parsifal* was Wagner's last work before he died, and even while composing it he was not in good health. Thus *Parsifal* is a sign of artistic death. Wagner and his last work also become symbols of a culture in decay, a theme advanced by Nietzsche and Adorno among others.[45] Syberberg's film version finds visual analogies for the idea and sets them, for maximum effect, within that very work. Moreover, Syberberg's critique stresses this quality more successfully than most stage productions of Wagner's operas.

Wagner becomes part of an extensive parade of Teutonic icons. The background consists of front-screen projections of significant images, most drawn from German history and culture. Syberberg made more than 4,000 slides to serve his purpose and they indicate the intellectual spirit behind the project.[46] Images range from ancient civilization to German Romantic painting, to performances of Wagner opera. A projection of the Grail temple used in the first production of *Parsifal* occupies a prominent place. We also see a more updated reference to performance history in an image of the Valkyrie horse used in Patrice Chéreau's Marxist production of *The Ring* from the late 1970s. This ideological production of Wagner's magnum opus was probably influential in Syberberg's decision to make a film of *Parsifal*. Images of the Bayreuth theater also appear in the background. Considered as a whole, these changeable backgrounds form a flexible counter-rhythm to the musical drama and to the static camera and theatrical setting.

Props also play a part in Syberberg's ideological crusade. It is hard to forget the image of Bayreuth-in-a-crystal-ball held by a wild-eyed Kundry at the beginning and end: Bayreuth as key to a fearful future, to dashed dreams of a utopian order (fig. 4.5). At the beginning the image appears amid strewn postcard snapshots of bombed out cities and other evidence of mass destruction. We see the top of a broken Statue of Liberty, an image that is especially shocking to Americans. Puppets of famous figures of German civilization, including Marx, Nietzsche, and Ludwig II, appear before us, usually as inert figures who lie on the death-mask landscape. Sometimes nonhistorical puppets act out a scenario, as in the foretelling of some of the opera during the Prelude.

Wagner also receives special attention as a puppet. He ap-

Fig. 4.5 Edith Clever in *Parsifal* (1982). Directed
by Hans-Jürgen Syberberg. (Courtesy British
Film Institute)

pears in several poses, most modeled on famous images of
the composer: Wagner the conductor, Wagner the old man,
Wagner as caricatured with a big nose, Wagner assaulting the
ear.[47] Another attribute of Wagner assumes form in an unusual
theatrical gimmick. In his old age he had a fetish for sensuous
fabrics and scents—according to some authors a compensation
for declining sexual appetites.[48] He was apparently fond of a
particular blue silk dressing gown. Taking a cue from Chéreau,
who alluded to it in *The Ring*, Syberberg fetishizes the gown by
using it as the focus of several large projections and as a space
that characters inhabit for part of Act III. It becomes a way of
indicting Wagner the sensualist and pointing up the hypocrisy
between his own hedonism and the ethic of sacrifice and sexual

abnegation that is promoted in the opera. Use of the gown also suggests that Wagner's role as bourgeois materialist must be taken into account in a rendering of his art work.

Symbols of German oppression appear. As Parsifal and Gurnemanz proceed in Act I to the Temple (the so-called Transformation Scene) they have to pass through a maze-like space draped with flags. Among the historical flags of Germany is the Nazi flag, displayed prominently. In Act II a projection of a watchtower recalls concentration camps and East German outposts. More innocently, the stylized swan that is killed by Parsifal in Act I is modeled on that in Neuschwanstein, Ludwig II's pleasure palace.

Syberberg alludes to Wagner in another important way. Like Wagner, his prose writing extends the boundaries of the art work. The director wrote a dense metaphysical treatise on the making and meaning of *Parsifal* that becomes an important part of its ontology. The reference extends further because Syberberg imitates Wagner in tone and style. He is self-conscious, esoteric, verbose, cryptic, and often pretentious. In his third book on film, Syberberg presents himself as ideologue, social philosopher, and exponent of a new kind of synthesis between art and culture. The following excerpt is telling: "We see ourselves then on the search for the Grail under the maternal version of memories in the face of the death mask of knowledge, out of which spilled the blood of our sorrows, with a wound as tunnel to our hearts . . . , with longing for a phallic womblike paradise of a magical-mystical pre-existence, recouped as [if by] children in the artistic garden of the utopias and ideas and dreams and fantasies of the hopes and illusions of art."[49] This easily serves as an updated version of Wagner's writing and suggests that, short of composing music, Syberberg is establishing himself as a new Wagner. Of course, the writing style could be read as a rhetorical act of criticism that aims to expose

Wagner's foibles by adopting his swollen style. I find this less persuasive than the more straightforward interpretation, however, because the labored quality accords with the over-earnest tone of the film. Sontag's point is well-taken.

Separation

While Syberberg's film gathers elements and has the feeling of a collection, it also shows a remarkable propensity toward separation. On the most obvious level, all the parts in *Parsifal*, except for Gurnemanz and Klingsor (sung by Robert Lloyd and Aage Haugland), are portrayed by actors. As in *Tales*, this means a built-in disjunction between sound and image—actually a doubled disjunction, since the actors are mouthing the words of another's voice. Unlike *Tales*, however, the performers consistently move their lips when they are supposed to be singing, and we know this through the predominance of close-ups. Ironically, the use of actors instead of singers provides a way of realizing Wagner's goal of dramatically convincing works for the theater.

The film's impulses toward separation find their most sensational feature in the title role: Parsifal played by a man and a woman (fig. 4.6). We will call them Parsifal I and Parsifal II. In most of the film only one appears at a given time. The idea of multiple casting is not new to Syberberg. In *Hitler*, for example, all the actors, even a dog, take turns at playing the *Führer*. Here he uses two teen-age amateurs he met at a dinner party. They appear as androgynous beings on the screen: a feminine young man (Michael Kutter) and a masculine young woman (Karen Krick) who defy neat categorization. They seem like neutral beings whose essence lies beyond the framework of sex. Their gendered makeup is complicated by the fact that the

Fig. 4.6 Karen Krick and Michael Kutter in *Parsifal* (1982). Directed by Hans-Jürgen Syberberg. (Courtesy British Film Institute)

same male voice, that of singer Reiner Goldberg, issues from both of them. A case of kinky ventriloquism? I will return to the issue below. But however one analyzes the symbolic implications, the disjunction between a male voice and a female body is a formidable challenge for the spectator.[50] I found it odd at first but then adjusted so that it seemed a natural combination. One reason this can happen is the hypnotic power of the music, which can overcome challenges to logic. We also sense that if a character can change sexually in terms of body then a vocal alteration is not too surprising. Perhaps the most persuasive factor is the sound quality of Goldberg's voice—a light tenor that suggests androgyny. Its sexual mobility can speak through different kinds of bodies.[51] With Parsifal fragmented, the role of Kundry, especially in Edith Clever's riveting performance, can become the center of the work.

The creation of a specifically female Parsifal also contributes to the emphasis on Kundry. In The Kiss—that pivotal moment in Act II—the fateful change is enacted. Parsifal I has wandered around in a daze, lacking knowledge. Still a part of the imaginary stage, basking in the rich memories of the maternal plenitude, he finds himself being seduced. Tempting him in maternal-sexual terms, Kundry offers him the breast. At the moment of consummation, when their lips meet, Parsifal remembers the wound and spurns her. He gains knowledge and enters the symbolic stage—here perhaps to be interpreted as adulthood. At this point Parsifal II replaces Parsifal I. For the first time Parsifal's words focus on reason and ethical content; she becomes obsessed with "Erlösung" (redemption). A male Parsifal has struggled with oedipal conflict and paced out the journey toward the painful entry into language. Now past that hurdle, a female Parsifal can bring about healing for the social order. John Hoberman suggests that once Parsifal refuses Kundry's kiss he is symbolically castrated—a castrato—and hence a woman in the role is entirely appropriate.[52] In fact, the situation is that of an inverted castrato, namely, a woman's body with a man's voice.[53] The combination suggests an ideal of androgyny for the end.

The last appearance of Parsifal occurs at the end of the story. Parsifal I, who has just reappeared, and Parsifal II face each other and embrace. It is one of the few times in the film that characters interact in a human way.[54] Richard Mohr, a scholar of gay studies, sees the gesture as a promotion of heterosexual marriage and thereby inappropriate and offensive given the homosocial milieu of the Grail knights in opera and legend.[55] While I grant his inference, I inflect it differently. What I see is a coming together of close companions to share in the satisfaction of a successful venture. Given the ethical tone of the whole, the gesture seems more spiritual than sexual and the issue of marriage seems irrelevant. It is true that each Parsifal is marked sexually by the kind of vertical totem carried. Parsifal I sports a phallic lance and Parsifal II a demasculinized crozier, and when they reunite the two totems come together. This represents a kind of sexual reconciliation, but not in the sense of a marriage. I find the ethereal music at the end especially compelling as a sign of the spiritual emphasis. But I do agree with Mohr that the film in general dilutes the homosocial atmosphere of the brotherhood.

A female Parsifal also has an impact on the conception of Kundry. According to Syberberg, after the Kiss and the appearance of a female Parsifal, a part of Kundry forms a connection with the new figure. This is a better side of Kundry, as it were, and it "now admonishes her, as in an inner monologue. Old Biblical ideas of the evil in woman and the evil of the eternal Jew, as Wagner described it . . . , now no longer arise."[56] It is "no longer a matter of the rejection of the feminine through the man," but rather a self-induced caution, brought about through identification with the new Parsifal, that helps effect Kundry's turnaround. As such, the notion of what constitutes evil is deconstructed and tainted racial-sexual associations are defused. Parsifal II and her civilizing influence become a part of Kundry.[57] This feminine influence imparted through Parsifal II to Kundry has larger implications for the film. Kundry is placed in unexpected juxtaposition with Amfortas at the end and the film offers a new message on redemption. In Syberberg's version Amfortas dies. On the adjacent pallet lies the dead Kundry, a crown on her head. For the director this suggests a reconciliation of "lance and wound, male and female, Aryan and Jew in an impossible, lost, alternate universe."[58] Kundry has physically replaced the wound, which in the film has appeared as a separate object. It has female characteristics: it has vaginal lips and it bleeds periodically. Like a medieval relic it is on display, and it is dutifully carried around as symbol of Amfortas's misery. Kundry's location on the very place where the wound sat suggests that her spiritual purification brings about Amfortas's healing. Unlike the opera, in the film Parsifal's lance plays no part in the healing of Amfortas's wound. No prop or action ends Amfortas's suffering, other than his death. At this point the bleeding wound is seen no more, and Kundry takes its place. For the film as a whole, one can argue that female sexuality has been fetishized through Kundry and the pulsating wound. It has acted to displace male castration anxiety, and this includes Amfortas's genital wound of the original legend, Klingsor's actual castration, and a generalized fear of mutilation. As opposed to the traditional view of Kundry as the temptress who brings about the fall of man and who must be overcome, Syberberg proposes that woman brings about redemption and can be transfigured in death along with man. In this respect Kundry joins the pantheon of other Wagnerian heroines whose selflessness redeems the moral order.[59]

As Kundry, actress Edith Clever was keenly aware that she would be forming a special relationship with a voice, that of soprano Yvonne Minton, and thus be a divided persona. As a practical matter, how does an actor come to terms with appropriating and impersonating another's voice? This became a pressing concern for Clever. She met Minton and attended the recording session in order to acquire a physical sense of that voice and its real embodiment. She asked herself whether she has the right to take someone's voice and merge it into a single entity. "No," as Syberberg reports it. "She tried to play the role as if she *were hearing* this voice that she didn't want to make corporeal—as if they were remaining *two*."[60] Thomas Elsaesser describes this quality in his review of the film as "the listening hesitation in the actor's body [that] gives the gestures an intensity quite different from the usual operatic emphasis that comes from having to fill your lungs with a lot of air."[61] In Clever's case, therefore, a separation of sound and image becomes the basis for a dynamic physical rendition of Kundry, and it is no surprise that the character emerges as the center of Syberberg's conception.[62] At the same time Clever promotes a sense of pure voice, of its jouissance, even though she is not singing. She accomplishes this by physicalizing the almost violent implications of the voice. This comes through especially in the primal moans, laughs, and cries that Kundry is made to utter. As Michel Poizat notes, such a "systematic inscription of the trans-verbal," of the voice as pure object, is rare in opera.[63]

Clever's kind of ventriloquism requires that rare actor who can physicalize particular sounds without actually emitting them (although like many people who lip-synch, she probably uttered sounds while moving her mouth). For all its complexity, however, the role of Kundry uses one body for one voice. For the character of Parsifal, ventriloquism takes the form of one source and two dummies—Goldberg's voice and Kutter and Krick's bodies. Despite its androgynous sound, Goldberg's tenor voice provides an obvious disjunction with Karen Krick's female gender. Yet the male Parsifal (Parsifal I) brings the separation of sound and image more acutely to the surface because his lip-synching is so poor. Perhaps Kutter was encouraged not to perfect synchronization so that his character would seem even more an innocent, as one who has not yet entered the symbolic stage and its discursive mastery. This Parsifal is certainly no master of the music. Parsifal II, on the other hand, has the music-mouth relationship much more under control, although discrepancies still occur. Regardless of their skill at lip-synching, both actors approach dummy receptacles for sound by virtue of their wooden movements and blank looks. This feature may have been intended by Syberberg and explains why he chose amateurs for the roles. As novices ignorant of dramatic movement and gesture, they convey convincingly the idea of the pure-fool-who-lacks-knowledge that is the essence of Parsifal. Appropriately this quality is more apparent in Parsifal I, who depicts the Parsifal of the imaginary stage.

As these examples show, separation of sound and image through poor lip-synching can serve diverse ends. Nonetheless, its appearance is so pervasive in *Parsifal* that it prompts the question as to whether it was intentional. Dramatically the device foregrounds cinema as apparatus and inserts distance between spectator and narrative. Since other techniques in the film create the same effect, it seems plausible that the technique was intentional for sound and image. Syberberg's book implies that the director turned a negative into a positive when he realized that much of the footage had poor lip-synchronization. At that point he apparently recognized its usefulness for his interpretation and made no effort to correct it.[64]

Other elements in the film promote separation. Armin Jordan, the conductor of the music, portrays Amfortas and this means that the persona exists both inside and outside the diegesis. The juxtaposition suggests that Amfortas represents much more than himself, and allusions extend in several directions. The most obvious link is that the character now embodies control over the unfolding of a primal signifying system of the film, namely, the orchestral music. The character already has a link with the composer in that the balms and perfumes brought to ease Amfortas's agony, especially in Wolfram von Eschenbach's version, are echoed in Wagner's own fetishes when he was composing the opera.[65] In Syberberg's conception the connection becomes more apparent because of the idea that implicit in the figure of the conductor is the ruling presence of the composer, who in this case exerted much more control than merely composing the notes. I am reminded of the controlling conductor in *Tales*, discussed above, who directs his daughter to her death. But while the Crespel of *Tales* is a purely diegetic figure who symbolizes many of the ills of organized music, the dual or triple figure of Amfortas represents a benign critical presence in the story but a formidable entity beyond its borders.

Amfortas's alter ego, Armin Jordan, makes visible intrusions into the apparatus of cinema, creating distance. Twice in the film we become aware of the presence of the conductor and it breaks the spell of the disembodied wash of the music. This is ironic, of course, because Jordan is actually producing the music that his image works to demystify. In Act III, as Parsifal II and Kundry begin their journey to the Grail Temple, a sepia image of Jordan conducting the music looms large. A shock to the narrative, it also breaks the illusion of an immaculately conceived score. Such ethereal music should not require labor for its production. Jordan's sweat brings to mind Amfortas, who is bathed in the sweat of excruciating pain each time we see him. The conductor makes his presence known at another point in the film. At the very beginning, we hear Jordan conducting a rehearsal, in French (itself alienating in the context of Wagner). Sections are repeated and perfected, and we sense the labor that fuels the preparation of this mammoth project. Along with the images of destruction it accompanies, the device establishes a viewing distance from which the spectator can reflect. Art takes work and it can exact a human toll.

These devices produce Brechtian alienation in *Parsifal:* a distancing of the spectator from narrative and diegesis, toward greater reflection on what is presented.[66] On the whole, what the film offers is a fascinating amalgam of Brecht and Wagner, itself an act of alienation and separation. Wagner's aesthetic aims to abolish thinking in favor of a loss of self in the hypnotic music. This mainly affects the spectator, but the dazed expressions on characters' faces suggest that they too lose their ability to act as thinking subjects. Brecht advocates a pulling back and wants the spectator to objectify the action and reflect on it. Wagner abolishes distance, Brecht establishes distance. *Parsifal* does both at the same time.[67]

Memory and Time

We end with that voice of Kundry yet again, and let bells slowly end in the blackness of the last fade-out, like an echo of these memories of past cultures and of our life and human history and their adventure.[68]

When these eye-lids close at the end of the opera, the music of the inner vision . . . sets in motion the visions of our fate, as at the beginning, and so the circle closes.[69]
—Hans-Jürgen Syberberg

Like *The Ring*, Syberberg's *Parsifal* ends where it begins. It opens with an astonishing sequence that inscribes memory in varied forms and portends how memory will play out over the narrative. The three-part sequence is structured as a layering process that moves from fragmentation to coherence and knowledge, in effect the dramatic organization of the story. Sound is proffered as the first memory. Over a blackened screen, primal vocal fragments, in what we will later know as Kundry's voice, are heard. Tolling bells enter, and a wild woman holding a glass-encased totem is seen. The incoherence of pure voice continues, even sounding atonal at times. Are these the primal screams of birth, of the birth of memory? With the second section, organized around strewn photographs of destruction, we hear more fully formed fragments of sound. These are soundbytes, as it were, of the orchestra rehearsal. Many of the main themes are heard here, and we are to etch them in memory for later recall. They foretell much of the musical narrative of the whole.

The third section is the Prelude itself and thus fully formed music. In the opera house the Prelude is performed with closed curtain, allowing us to be totally engulfed by the music. In the film the Prelude is used for other reasons, although sound is given a brief chance to insinuate itself in our consciousness as it begins. During the course of this music the memory of the future is laid out before Parsifal. It becomes the memory of forgetfulness, however, for what he sees and learns will be forgotten by the time we encounter him in the story proper, in his role of pure fool. He enters as a young boy who is practicing with bow and arrow and attended by his mother (played by Clever). After glimpsing grown-up versions of himself, he comes upon a puppet show in which the prehistory is performed before his eyes: the pure Amfortas, the evil Klingsor, and how Kundry's seduction of Amfortas leads to the fatal wound. Next we see the wound-as-icon, as in the actual story, and an adolescent Parsifal puppet shoots a swan. After an array of Wagner puppets and the first glimpse of the Wagner-mask terrain, mother-Kundry lies with book open to the Grail story. As the music approaches the end of the Prelude, real figures take over, and we see the real Parsifal, in male and female guises. Parsifal I rises and begins the journey. The final image, over a sustained dominant-seventh chord, shows Parsifal II in repose, with sunken head on bent knees.

What this introductory tableau suggests is that just as these events will be forgotten by Parsifal—he has not learned from mistakes he knows about—so too will the mistakes of history repeat themselves. Memory is short. It also implies that the drama presented in this opera and in Syberberg's critique will probably not make a palpable difference. The past *will* be repeated. Thus, at the end, we are back at the beginning. This pessimistic message is conveyed not only in the look of despair on Kundry's face at the end but also in the large skull that forms a shocking contrast with the ethereal closing music. Poizat describes the image as the "death of desire."[70] It is an apt sign, he believes, because the opera's emphasis on the feasibility of a quest for the attainment of utopia is an impossible enterprise, and the only thing it can lead to is a death of desire itself. The skull also signifies the death of German culture as beacon to the world—in which case Syberberg is making a reflexive statement about his own enterprise. Nonetheless, for the director the film probably represented a necessary ritual of purification before German reunification could take place. As we view Germany after reunification, we see a new social order that has led to strained and dashed visions of utopia. Is this predicted in the purification ritual that is the film itself? If so, then Syberberg's cultural quest resembles that of Wagner even more closely.

A Tale of Two Movies: Epilogue

Fantasy works its magic well in these theatrical films, despite the fact that they are so different. *Parsifal* is deadly serious, *Tales* is entertainingly light. Each blurs boundaries between reality and artifice, rationality and irrationality, and the real world and the diegesis of the film; both, for example, contain real authors in the narrative—Wagner in one, Hoffmann in the other. Both tether fantasy to the mysterious workings of the psyche as they tap into aspects of memory and dream. Excess and exaggeration are fundamental to the representational apparatus: *Tales* with its surfeit of color, dance, mime, slapstick, and horror; and *Parsifal* with its overload of ideology, iconography, devoutness, and suffering. Fantasy helps structure the self-consciousness displayed by both films.

With its extravagant deployment of fantasy the Archers'

Tales can be considered an ideal, or possibly even the ideal, interpretation of the opera. Its novel effects seduce and bedazzle as it reperforms the fantastical quality of the original. Satirizing itself, the film infuses wit, parody, and irony into the narrative, and in the process shows how humor can serve fantasy and shape a personal vision of the opera. The film's success also rests on the quality of its cast and production team.

Powell and Pressburger's conception raises intriguing questions about the work. One concerns the meaning of the voice and its representation, including its relationship with the body. As *Tales* suggests, this now extends to dance and mime as well as more conventional movement. Another issue involves the opera's relationship with operetta and other lighter forms of opera. The lion's share of Offenbach's output consisted of such fare, and even though *Tales* was meant to be more serious it still retains the flavor of many of those works. One obvious vestige is that a few of its numbers are borrowed from them. In many respects the film underscores this aspect of its heritage. Aimed at a mass audience, it is in English translation, it cuts and rearranges music as needed, and indulges in gags and humor. It rewrites the opera as popular cinema and brings it into the fold of Mario Lanza-type operetta, film musical, and dance film. Indeed, when the film first appeared it was described as a ballet film, a sequel to *The Red Shoes*.[71]

The *Tales* film also sheds light on its relationship with the original. Powell and Pressburger's movie makes something wonderful, witty, and original of an opera that is regarded by some as frivolous and trivial. It does this by trading on frivolousness and triviality and reinterpreting them. Let us not ignore or belittle these qualities, the Archers might say, for they make for good cinema and great entertainment. As realized, the film reinscribes frivolousness and triviality, and extends them through satire and other creative modes of representation, especially dance and mime. This makes it very Hoffmannesque and thus extremely appropriate. The result is a landmark of film-opera.

Rich in social critique yet sparing in montage and mise en scène, *Parsifal* also constitutes a landmark of film-opera. It occupies an uneasy relationship to the spectator, however. The pessimism of the film is strong, and it prompts the question of whether the arduous experience of watching the film has been futile. Are we immersed in a new kind of Wagnerian nihilism, or a macabre world-without-end fantasy?[72] Perhaps. In addition, is the assault on the senses and the mind less problematic than the excesses the composer is charged with? That depends at least on one's relationship with Wagner and whether one is willing to sit through a movie more than four hours in length. In my view the film teeters on the edge of undercutting its effectiveness through an excess of meanings proposed on the screen. Nonetheless, Syberberg's journey through time, memory, and consciousness can be therapeutic as it attempts to salve troubling aspects of Teutonic culture. *Parsifal* joins *Tales of Hoffmann* in showing that fantasy can serve as the basis of successful cinematic versions of opera.

5

Opera *al fresco:* Rosi's *Bizet's Carmen*
and Losey's *Don Giovanni*

One of the main ways that cinema differs from theater is its
ability to draw on the real world for its images. It can deploy
exterior locations and place figures in relation to nature and architecture. As in still photography and realistic painting, such
images do not replicate the real thing but interpret it. Film accomplishes this in a variety of ways—through mise en scène,
through montage, and through other techniques that organize
space and time. Natural scenery is just as subject to manipulation as cinematic fantasy, the focus of the previous chapter,
because film is a medium of representation and not duplication.

Some filmmakers have taken opera outdoors in an effort to
construct a representation that involves the realism of the external world. Two films occupy us in this chapter: Francesco
Rosi's *Bizet's Carmen* (1983) and Joseph Losey's *Don Giovanni*
(1979). Each uses the external environment to shape narrative
and meaning, and the relationship between image and music.
Significantly, each deploys the real world to propose ideas on
class and other social structures, and in the process raises questions about notions of realism and naturalism. The movies reveal that a stress on the exterior still depends on certain theatrical qualities found in film and especially in opera. Each film
finds successful ways of reconciling the scenic unboundedness
of cinema and the theatrical confines of opera.

Why focus on these two films in particular? The Rosi offers
an incisive reading of the opera, brilliantly filmed and per-

formed. Many (including myself) consider it one of the best film-operas ever made.[1] It offers new interpretive insights on the opera, its reception, and the place of *Carmen* in society — what could be called the "discourse-*Carmen*"—and this is not easy to accomplish given the (over)familiarity of the story and music.[2] Musically it offers a complete rendering of Bizet's work, apparently the first such treatment, a surprising fact given the many *Carmen* films that have been made. From silent versions through glamour vehicles (Dolores del Rio, Rita Hayworth) through the Americanized *Carmen Jones*, the theme has attracted great interest. One reason for the late date of a complete version is that the score entered the public domain around 1980.[3] Within a two-year period no less than four major film versions of *Carmen* appeared. Peter Brook's *La tragédie de Carmen*, a film of his stage production, is a stripped-down, rearranged version of Bizet. Proceeding from the idea that the opera has become hackneyed and the only way to produce meaning is to reduce it to essentials, Brook gives us a drastically reduced orchestra (only fifteen players), an abridged and reordered score, and a story that foregrounds fate and "the tragedy of four people" (Brook).[4] Jean-Luc Godard's *Prénom Carmen* is so reduced that it barely deserves to be linked to the Bizet. The fourth treatment, Carlos Saura's *Carmen*, plays on multiple levels: a flamenco troupe performing a dance on the *Carmen* story, with the lead dancer named Carmen in a relationship with the male lead similar to that of the opera. In the end we are not sure which Carmen dies, the dance character or the dancer herself. These readings take us beyond Bizet, and as H. Marshall Leicester persuasively argues, they demonstrate the discursive power of the *Carmen* narrative in society and the ability of film to disclose it.[5]

Losey's *Don Giovanni*, dubbed the first modern film-opera

when it was released,[6] offers an important reading of Mozart's famous opera and deploys exterior settings in novel ways. Like *Carmen*, it was produced by a consortium headed by the French firm Gaumont and widely distributed. It is no coincidence that these big-budget films, shot on location and featuring major opera stars, are based on two of the most popular works of the repertoire. Losey's pessimistic reading generated much more controversy than *Carmen*. While his ideological treatment of the opera could be the reason, I suspect that the critical reaction also reflects the investment of the public in the two works. *Carmen* may earn greater latitude because of its status as a light work and because it is French. *Don Giovanni*, although in Italian, is considered an iconic work of the iconic Germanic composer Mozart. An assault on a key work of the Germanic tradition, which forms the basis of the Anglo-American canon, might be met with suspicion. I do not mean to imply that Losey mounts such an attack in his film. Nonetheless, the harshness of some of the reviews suggests that moral sensibilities were offended.[7] A more specific reason could be the film's return to a Romantic reading of the opera, one that stresses darkness and retribution. Although some of the excesses of Romanticism are reinscribed, Losey's film superimposes other concerns that reflect a late-twentieth-century ethos. *Don Giovanni* is a challenging work by an idiosyncratic filmmaker.

Bizet's Carmen and *Don Giovanni* represent important contributions to the history of film-opera. Despite major differences in tone and approach, the films share an interest in certain issues. The chapter focuses on these common concerns, and they include aspects of meaning, considerations of class and gender, and treatment of the music. Through these discussions we will see how each filmmaker draws on the outdoors to shape a personal interpretation of the opera, and how the very notion of realism is redefined through the interaction between the real world (or rather its representation) and the apparatus of cinema. We will also gain a better sense of the kinds of motivation that prompt such projects and which techniques work well in the transferring of opera to the large screen. Of course, *Carmen* and *Don Giovanni* are very different operas and suggest different kinds of treatments. The approach here is not so much a direct comparison as it is a discussion of common techniques and their success in each film. Rich in meaning and affect, Rosi's *Carmen* and Losey's *Don Giovanni* provide important insights into that vast creative area that we call screen opera.

MEANING

Francesco Rosi is not as well known as Italian colleagues Federico Fellini and Michelangelo Antonioni, but he shares their interest in social issues. His Neapolitan background informs his treatment of these themes and provides a natural link to the Andalusian culture of *Carmen*. As Rosi notes, this southern region of Spain shares many qualities with Naples: poverty, machismo, earthiness, climate, fondness for singing and dancing, and acceptance of superstition.[8] So while a film on the opera *Carmen* might seem an unlikely candidate for him, its culture is one he understands. Rosi's version reinterprets important issues of class, gender, and ethnicity in the opera. Unlike the traditional operatic interpretation, it presents a Carmen whose raison d'être is personal freedom. Her sexuality and jouissance allow her to control her life and make her own decisions rather than marking her as an evil temptress. She is an uninhibited, joyful woman as seen in the context of gypsy-peasant life and the social tensions of nineteenth-century Andalusia. Like the film overall, she has a frankness and matter-of-factness that re-

Fig. 5.1 Faith Esham in *Bizet's Carmen* (1983). Directed by Francesco Rosi. (Courtesy British Film Institute)

veal her acceptance of life as it is, without illusions and regrets. Julia Migenes-Johnson's extraordinary performance expresses these qualities well.

Many of Rosi's movies build on what film scholar Morando Morandini calls "documentary reconstruction,"[9] and the Andalusian settings in *Carmen* were chosen with an eye to authenticity. Rosi found Gustav Doré's illustrations of the region in the serialized book, Baron Davillier's *Spain* (1873), that he believes Bizet consulted when the opera was composed (it premiered 1 May 1875). For the third act, for example, Rosi uses the dramatic rocks and mountain paths near Ronda that were drawn by Doré (fig. 5.1). After consulting a historian on nineteenth-century bullfighting, Rosi set these scenes in the oldest Spanish bullring in Ronda.[10] But authenticity for Rosi is no sterile concept or an end in itself. He takes this realistic framework and uses it to heighten social concerns and provide his own reading of the opera. Although an emphasis on the "real place" could lead to an idealizing travelogue mentality, the film demystifies the surroundings even as it often makes them lyrical and wistful. As the director observes, "I want to show that there is at once the reality and the interpretation of reality, which leads at certain moments to a lyrical romanticism."[11] There is a healthy combination of respect, love, and objectivity. Importantly, the magnificent settings act to level and disperse major elements of discourse and narrative, including the operatic music itself. The result is frank, stark, and sometimes brutal: a gritty, almost cynical kind of realism.

Acts I and IV of the Rosi take place in daylight and feature austere, almost abstract, stone buildings.[12] The large expanses of wall could imply a feeling of monumentality, but the stark setting counterbalances any idealizing tendency. The lack of decoration suggests that the buildings are not only very old but the province of the lower classes, or at least not of the wealthy. Their off-white color blends with the dust that one can almost taste. The understated tone is replicated in the costumes in varied tones of beige—all earth colors, and suited for the hot, dry climate. This tendency toward spectral evenness creates a flattened-out visual discourse, which in turn affects other discourses and ultimately meaning. Acts II and III also display this sameness of color. In the interior of Lillas Pastia's tavern at the start of Act II, for example, the palette stresses sepia tones, and this tempers the glittering dance number. Or rather, it de-idealizes it and renders it more of a daily event than a special occurrence. Is this an effect of realism? The answer is yes and no. In the sense that it stresses the ordinary and the everyday it is. But the effect is achieved through non-realistic effects of lighting, by the application of filters and lighting that impart a yellow-beige tint. This is not realistic. There is an apparent split between technique and effect. But since cinema is a medium that creates illusions there is no operative contradiction. This serves as a good example of how cinema reconciles technique and effect.

Whether in town or countryside, the setting often disperses the narrative by absorbing some of the focus typically assigned to people and music. Figures frequently appear as insignificant details in a formal landscape reminiscent of Cézanne or Corot. They are overpowered by the setting, and their actions at that moment are inflected and diminished. Pauline Kael likens such movements to ritualized performance.[13] So, too, the music at that point often takes on different meaning. A good example of the shift in scale is the long shot of the protagonists, Carmen and Don José, in their fatal confrontation outside the facade of the bullring. Another instance occurs at the start of the melee in the factory, where a long shot of the street as formal architecture shows the people as tiny dots, scurrying around. The effect of showing miniature figures against a monumental element reminds me of Alfred Hitchcock's top shot in *North by Northwest* down the side of the United Nations building (or mock-up thereof) as the ant-size hero flees. Unlike the situation in the Rosi, Bernard Hermann's music stresses grandeur and irony instead of dispersed discourse.

Rosi's long shots of people also create distance from the spectator. We become less involved in them as individuals and see them as part of a class or community. Characters' subjectivity is also diminished by the intrusion of objects in our line of sight. For example, when Micaela and Don José approach the end of their Duet in Act I, they recede from view and blend into the point perspective. As the cadence is about to resolve, a donkey and peasant block them from us.[14] This serves as an insult to operatic convention, which would suggest a close-up to register the tender emotions expressed in their words. Rosi has the camera counter the sentimentality of their love relationship and the nostalgic memories of home. This becomes a wonderful example of the de-privileging of operatic musical discourse in the film. Moreover, the portrayal of this Duet challenges notions of realism. Does the music reflect their relationship, or does Rosi's insertion of a donkey inflect what we are to conclude about their feelings? That depends on one's vantage point, in several senses. The device underscores how the film articulates levels of realism and narrative, and how the distinctions among levels are blurred.[15]

Joseph Losey's *Don Giovanni* also uses the outdoors to shape meaning. His outdoors, however, consist of cultural icons as well as natural surroundings (fig. 5.2). Magnificent buildings of Palladio, including the Rotonda and the Teatro Olimpico in Vicenza, host the escapades of the mythic libertine and become the basis of a counter-reading that discloses cultural decay and incipient revolt. In this context, matters of realism and authenticity become less urgent than in the Rosi. Natural scenery assumes a more neutral role, although at times it seems to deceive.

Although *Bizet's Carmen* offers a matter-of-fact yet joyous reading—what could advisedly be termed optimistic—*Don Giovanni* proffers pessimism. An epigram by Antonio Gramsci at the beginning projects the tone of the whole: "Il vecchio muore e il nuovo non può nascere; e in questo interregno si verificano i fenomeni morbosi più svariati" (The old is dying and the new cannot be born; and in this interregnum a great variety of morbid symptoms occurs).[16] In its critique of class relations, this *Don Giovanni* affirms a death force rather than the life force that is often read into the opera.[17] Even *Carmen*, with its brutal ending and intimations of fate, is more life-affirming. Crudely put, Carmen enjoys life, Don Giovanni does not. The darkness of Losey's interpretation makes it more

Fig. 5.2 José van Dam and Kiri Te Kanawa in
Don Giovanni (1979). Directed by Joseph Losey.
(Courtesy British Film Institute)

Romantic than Rosi's, although it is a romanticism filtered
through modernist notions of existentialism and expressionism.
Don Giovanni's nihilism and anxiety have little to do with demonic forces and relate to the pressures of a corrupt order in
decay. Losey's approach is more labored than Rosi's, and in the
quest for meaning the seams may show.[18] For example, a jumpy
camera attracts undue attention and runs the risk of under-
mining the musical narrative. Like the scenery, the music is
read against the grain more than in the Rosi, and sometimes
good intentions are deflected through unfortunate cinematic

effects. I also see a very different approach to women in the two. While Rosi blasts through stereotype in offering flesh-and-blood portrayals of women in their complexity, Losey returns to some negative Romantic views of the women in the opera.

While the critical focus is centered largely in class relations (see next section), Losey's pessimism also extends to a critique of opera itself. One particular number presents his negative views of staged opera. The Sextet in Act II, a finale-like ensemble that resolves strands of plot midway in the act, becomes a vehicle for indicting the artifice of the medium.[19] In the film the number marks a return to the opera stage and a pointed denial of exterior locations and cinema's ability to roam freely. The first thing odd about the scene is that the preceding imbroglios take place outdoors and now we are in a theater (Palladio's Teatro Olimpico). Why do Leporello and Elvira, Ottavio and Anna, then Zerlina and Masetto enter the building? Perhaps it is because as opera singers they are drawn to the theater. A second striking feature is that the backstage area is a labyrinth and we (and they) are not sure where they are. An obvious reason for foregrounding the artifice of opera is that the dramatic situation at this point is a sham. Everyone thinks the man Elvira is with is Don Giovanni, whom they are pursuing, but it is actually Leporello. Moreover, Losey may believe that cinematic naturalism makes little sense in this number because of its theatrical qualities and *buffa* style. He had to return the Sextet to the stage, and once there could use it for ideological purposes.

After the characters have entered the stage, Losey places them in static operatic groupings before a gathering of aristocrats and church leaders. The camera remains fixed from the vantage point of an audience member in attendance. The players lose their three-dimensionality and perform in unidirectional perspective—a parody of relay broadcasts at the time, in which camera mobility was extremely limited. The scene also reminds us that singers themselves, even if portraying upper-class characters, represent a kind of servant class. They perform for audiences and have to please them. This was especially obvious when the nobility were the main patrons of opera, before 1800. Since the setting here is late eighteenth century, the connection is more apt. Of course, Losey's studied construction threatens to alienate the spectator—the movie spectator—and create Brechtian distancing.[20] The coolness of his approach in general, combined with his early experience in Brecht, make this a likely inference. The avoidance of close-up affirms separation.

The setting also marks a return to a location near the start of the film, when characters emerge from the backstage of the Teatro Olimpico to travel to Don Giovanni's factory. The connection not only suggests the centrality of theater to the dramatic action that is *Don Giovanni*, but that opera singers come from the stage and return to it if given the opportunity. But the singers appear constricted in the static environment they are forced to inhabit during the Sextet. Cinema, the film suggests, may be the only medium for their freedom as performers.

Opera is called into question through other symbols. The sound of waves provides our first aural experience in the film. It occurs over the opening and closing credits, and no music is present. At the beginning the sound accompanies various drawings, including the one of the Gramsci epigram written on a prison wall. The picture of a burning Palais Garnier, elaborate home of the Paris Opéra that was built in the nineteenth century, becomes a defiant symbol of opera's obsolescence. While Pierre Boulez's infamous remark to blow up opera houses was made in the name of musical modernism,[21] Losey's message appears to be that film now replaces staged opera. In light of the movie's reputation at the time of release as the first modern film-opera, the reading assumes great credibility. The image also recalls the destruction of Valhalla at the end of Wagner's *Ring,* a potent symbol for the death of the old so that a purified order can be established.[22]

Waves form a common aural motif in Losey's films in general,[23] and take on added meaning here by way of Søren Kierkegaard. In his essay on the opera Kierkegaard draws a connection between the Don and the hearing of waves: "Don Juan [*sic*] is a picture that is continually coming into view but does not attain form and consistency, an individual who is continually being formed but is never finished, about whose history one cannot learn except by listening to the noise of the waves."[24] By framing the film with these sounds, Losey affirms the elusive qualities suggested by Kierkegaard. In the opera, Giovanni is constructed as the absence of an inner core. He cannot be concretized as he is always in motion, never stopping to reflect. In this way, random noises which circle around on themselves without reaching a goal well represent him. I find it especially fitting that the film ends with these sounds, which form our final impression.

Water as a motif assumes further significance in the film. Characters often travel by boat, as in the nobles' journey to the glass factory or the masqueraders' arrival at Don Giovanni's villa. Don Ottavio croons his first aria, "Dalla sua pace," on a lagoon. These examples build on the idea that water's fluidity suggests class relations in transit, on their way to new patterns beyond the borders of the film. Water also implies the womb and a return to primal innocence. This trait pertains to the staging of the ending, where characters take to boats for their journey to a new life. Bright fugal music and cheerful facial expressions suggest optimism—characters almost seem ready to wave at the camera. Water can cleanse and purify, as in baptism, and this may represent Losey's hope for the individual and society at the end. The final image of the mysterious valet closing the doors of Giovanni's villa, however, makes that utopian vision less certain.

Water is also significant for its relationship with fire. In traditional cosmology, water serves as the antithesis of fire. Perhaps Losey wanted a balancing factor to the theme of hell and damnation that is built into the story. As noted, both fire and water are shown in a projection of a destroyed Opéra. But as for the literal appearance of fire, the director is not content with fire merely when Don Giovanni goes to hell. Hell is already present in Giovanni's life in the form of his profession. During the Overture we see Giovanni and his upper-class friends on a tour of his glass-blowing factory. They gaze into a powerful fire—an obvious portent of the industrialist's end. When he is dragged to the fiery abyss, hell becomes that same industrial site, transported to his house. It is a wonderful link in Losey's ideological conception of the story.[25]

CLASS AND GENDER

Ideology takes shape in Losey's interpretation mainly through a critique of class relations. Palladio's magnificent buildings, a fitting setting for Mozart's magnificent music, seduce us with their beauty.[26] Yet perfect architecture becomes an ironic counterpoint to the moral decay within. The upper classes own these buildings but wander through them aimlessly, like poseurs dropping in for a visit. Barely furnished, the interiors are dark and uninviting. This architectural negation of life bears out Losey's idea that "places are actors."[27] On the surface, however, these monuments showcase the power of the upper class, who inhabit the center of the story.

Set on the eve of the French Revolution rather than the sixteenth century as described in the libretto,[28] the film marks an end stage in Western society. Unchecked freedom for the upper classes is about to go up in flames. One could see that period of personal freedom as having been inaugurated in the Renaissance, which is symbolized by the Palladian buildings. Seen in this perspective they form an appropriate site for the drama and the destruction of its denizens and values. Furthermore, it is not only society that is about to change but music as well. The opera *Don Giovanni* displays a musical violence seldom heard before and mounts a challenge to number opera that will bring greater continuity in opera. Losey is marking the end of a unified musical style, that of late-eighteenth-century musical style, through his visual fragmentation of the music (see next section). This historical moment in music becomes part of the film's location at that "interregnum" between the dying-out and the newly born.

Scenery becomes a site of confrontation between classes. "Là ci darem la mano," for example, shows Don Giovanni and Zerlina moving to various places in the palace. At several points the seduction plays against a grand opening to the exterior. It discloses masses of peasants lined up on the steps, watching, looking. The two principals may be oblivious to the watchful eyes but we are not (they face us). One senses that the observing group circled around the palace to arrive at the new doorway and watch the principals in each location. Their look has little to do with sexual voyeurism but implies a studied watchfulness that threatens bodily harm. While other seductions in the film do not show these groups, Losey probably staged "Là ci darem la mano" in this manner because Don Giovanni is preying on a member of the lower class, namely, Zerlina.

The feeling of imminent explosion of the lower classes is even more apparent in the finale to Act I. This composite number already contains a dramatic confrontation between the principals (except Leporello) and Don Giovanni, who barely escapes. Losey layers this with two striking massed confrontations. At "Viva la libertà," Don Giovanni's toast to libertine values, the peasants gather en masse and stare at the others. At the start of the final section, "Trema, trema," where the tonality wavers between major and minor, the peasants follow Don Giovanni's flight across the piazza after his attempted rape of Zerlina. Gathered in numbers, they resemble a mini-army but stop short of storming the building. The intensity is great, thunder roars over Don Giovanni's head, and we sense that revolution cannot be far away. This massed uprising is also interesting because in pursuing Don Giovanni the lower classes are joining the ranks of the upper-class characters who are pursuing him — Donna Anna, Don Ottavio, and Donna Elvira (so are the lower-class Zerlina and Masetto). Because the story shows Don Giovanni as a predator of his own class as well, Losey may have difficulty indicting the Don as a predator of the lower classes. Moreover, as discussed below, Don Giovanni preys on women as much as on the lower classes.

While these examples describe the more dramatic places, the lower classes appear elsewhere in the film. We see them in the background in many numbers, as they attend to busy-work or stand still. For example, near the start of the film servants appear after the duel between Don Giovanni and the Commendatore. After rushing out to the loggia, they stop suddenly and refrain from going to the wounded man. Their inaction is striking. Is it fear of Don Giovanni, who is still present, or fear of the dead? A feeling of social impotence or a hostility toward the powerful? The next morning, we see Don Giovanni and Leporello on horseback in the countryside, with workers and peasants at their tasks. Shortly thereafter, the "Champagne" Aria is performed al fresco against servants' chores and preparations for the party. The device becomes mannered in the film, however, and detracts from the main focus. For example, indoor numbers, such as Donna Anna's aria "Non mi dir," become muddled when servants putter in the background. Their activity dilutes the self-importance of the aria's music and text and of Anna herself, an upper-class character. In the film as a whole the device clarifies a pecking order in the lower classes. Leporello becomes a master-servant who is almost equal to his boss, a status that is stressed in many stage productions.[29] As we will discuss shortly, the presence of an added figure—the valet in black—complicates Leporello's position in the narrative.

Don Giovanni is particularized in Losey's conception. A capitalist predator, he is owner of a glass-blowing factory. This industrialist represents the modernism to come and fills Losey's general Marxist agenda rather than a specific historical picture of a class that will be routed with the Revolution. This view accords with the film's ending, which suggests that little changes with the demise of the Don. His identity is also shaped by his appearance. He looks ghoulish much of the time: whitened face, blackened eyes, wide-eyed looks, reddish lips (fig. 5.3). Ruggero Raimondi, who plays the Don, calls it "makeup as a sign of the end of a certain world." [30] It also recalls the silent-film era. This is an apt connection given that Raimondi/the Don resembles a silent-film star as he gestures mutely to his own recorded singing (not in the secco recitatives, which were recorded live).[31] Like the stars of that era, the Don looks effeminate. Excessive bows and flounces, floppy wide-brimmed hats, fluffy ostrich plumes, and trailing fabrics accentuate the feminization and suggest an ambiguous sexuality. Is Don Giovanni gay? The query continues the speculation whether his lust for women masks homosexual desires.[32] While it remains an open question, the feminized looks and androgynous valet in the film make it more of a possibility than usual. If Losey is proposing a link between homosexuality/bisexuality and decay then the ruse is disturbing. I also see the connection as a repre-

Fig. 5.3 Ruggero Raimondi (left) and Eric Adjani in *Don Giovanni* (1979). Directed by Joseph Losey. (Courtesy British Film Institute)

sentation of such through the lens of conventional (read bourgeois) morality, and it is consciously foregrounded in order to be criticized.[33] If so, then decay is being represented positively and negatively at the same time.

Many of Losey's later films display a menace that is similar to that conveyed by the Don.[34] Like the misanthropic antihero in many Losey films,[35] this Don Giovanni is joyless, cold, desperate, and cruel; some critics liken him to Casanova.[36] While a Romantic figure, Losey's Don Giovanni symbolizes a death force rather than the Kierkegaardian life force. The "Champagne" Aria ("Fin ch'an dal vino") shows these features. A paean to wine, women, and song, the aria praises the hedonistic life and in many productions ends with a champagne glass thrown across the stage.[37] In Losey the joy gives way to a Don who strides purposefully in the outdoors and sneers at the world and his underlings. He is driven and a bit crazed. As in most productions strength born of desperation carries him at the end, however, as he refuses to repent. Like Carmen he accepts death rather than betray his principles. This act of courage resonates with Losey's own background. Called before the House Committee on Un-American Activities in 1951, Losey refused to provide names. He was blackballed from Hollywood and began a career in exile, mainly in England. Many themes in his work, especially hypocrisy and the abuse of power, stem from this life-defining experience and find a place in *Don Giovanni*.

The valet in black adds to the feeling of decay. His very ambiguity makes him shadowy. He is mute, everpresent, and robotic. I agree with Philippe Carcassonne's wry comment that the figure exudes a disdainful superiority that hints at a hip (post)modernist attitude toward classic works.[38] The valet looks down on this classic opera and removes himself from it as he simultaneously acts as a deus ex machina to help the Don out of difficult situations. In this way he not only relates to Baroque *opera seria*, symbol of an outmoded cultural form, but complicates Leporello's relation to Don Giovanni. Played superbly by Eric Adjani, the valet has other notable attributes. Made up with white face and dark eyes, he suggests a young and androgynous Don Giovanni. Is he an illegitimate son of the Don? He becomes proprietor of the villa at the end, and his succession is implied when he usurps the Don's chair at the final feast. But the sickly demeanor also signifies death, and hence his triumph when the Don dies. Moreover, the doting on the Don hints at homosexual desire—an impression strengthened by his jealous reaction to the Don's attentions to another androgynous youth in the film. The valet in black holds up a mirror to Don Giovanni: not as conscience but as reflection. He is a kind of Don Giovanni "in potentia," to use Kierkegaard's term. In his essay "The Immediate Erotic Stages or the Musical-Erotic," Kierkegaard sketches three progressive stages of sensual desire and Don Giovanni occupies the third and fully realized stage. Papageno represents the second stage (Cherubino the first), and I can imagine the valet as Papageno's replacement. The major problem with placing the valet in this framework, however, is that he is totally unidealized. In Kierkegaard even Papageno embodies ideal qualities. The valet could become the second member in a new progression that is based on the unidealized tone of the film. Losey's Don is cynical and cold, and his heir apparent has similar qualities.[39]

Rosi's *Bizet's Carmen* offers a different slant on class relations. Here the lower classes occupy the center of attention, and their environment is life-affirming and optimistic rather than one caught in the grip of upper-class decay. Rosi links class with nature and the workings of nature. The lower classes, consisting of workers, peasants, and gypsies, identify strongly with the outdoors. They are defined by the natural world and conversely help to define it. Their garb, sun-baked faces, and dark skin extend the natural world. The director used local inhabitants for crowd scenes, something he has done in other movies, and this strengthens the bond with the environment. Comfortable with themselves and their bodies, the lower classes move around freely. Noises of the everyday world accompany their actions, and this continues when music is heard, even during formal numbers. The continual presence of noise becomes a major marker of realism and, to almost the same extent, of class. Losey's film, concerned with ideology rather than realism, keeps noise to a minimum.

The effect of these elements in the Rosi is illustrated in several places in Act I. After the tensions of the bullfight and religious procession near the start, Rosi cuts to the dusty streets of the town. For a few moments there is no music, only crowd noises and close shots of earthy people on the way to work, approaching the camera like a secular army. The sense of an emerging workday is taken up by Bizet's music too. A sotto voce dominant pedal point in the bass sets things in motion and gradually builds toward a stable musical phrase, sung by a chorus. In the film we do not see moving lips; it is rather like a disembodied description of the scene. The music-image partnership in creating expectation is striking. The text speaks of people coming and going on the street. We see a wealth of lived-in faces—faces at home in the sun-drenched setting. The noises continue throughout. Another memorable shot of the local people occurs a bit later, as the camera lingers sensually on the faces of the *cigarières,* who are enveloped in lazy smoke. (I have often wondered why cigarette companies do not use the scene in their advertising, it is so persuasive.) This is a world that takes pleasure in the everyday, although we could accuse the director of slipping in some idealization. The images complement Bizet's sensuous music, a languorous waltz in the chromatic key of E major, with muted strings.

The everyday is also captured at the end of the act. After Carmen escapes from her ropes, confusion erupts on the street, people scatter in all directions—a suggestion that her release leads to anarchy (fig. 5.4). The odd occurrence of the everyday comes when we see baskets of fruit held by peasants spilled onto the street. The moment is held in freeze-frame and leaves us with a curious kind of genre scene to end the act. In fact, tableaux vivants that recall a genre painting are enacted often in the film. In the Don José-Micaela duet, for example, a family of artisans at work on their wares appears prominently in the frame. The scene suggests that overheated operatic discourse and its purported seriousness are out of place and possibly irrelevant. The everyday blunts the operatic.

The upper class, essentially absent from the Bizet, assumes an interesting role in the Rosi. In its dissociation from the natu-

Fig. 5.4 Plácido Domingo and Julia Migenes-Johnson in *Bizet's Carmen* (1983). Directed by Francesco Rosi. (Courtesy British Film Institute)

ral world it becomes an Other to the narrative. The aristocrats we see are indoor people who appear to be sealed off from the outside. With alabaster faces that have not registered the sun, they bear the trappings of a constricted interior world. They never move their bodies, show emotion, or sing and dance. No noise intrudes on their environment and they remain removed from the music of the opera. This is quite a different picture from that of the lower classes, for whom the out-of-doors and the natural function as a foil against the aristocracy.

Escamillo serves as the fulcrum between the two groups.[40] He interacts with both camps and is present in the three scenes where we see the aristocracy. In his mobile role of matador he offers a pretext for their appearance. Looking is stressed in two of the scenes. At the start of Act II, over the instrumental music of the entr'acte, the aristocrats perform the ritual of observing a gentle flamenco dance (by Antonio Gades, choreographer for the film and star and choreographer in Saura's

Fig. 5.5 Confrontation between factory workers
and soldiers in *Bizet's Carmen* (1983). Directed by
Francesco Rosi. (Courtesy British Film Institute)

Carmen). Their contained decorum forms a striking contrast to
the bodily abandon expressed at the end of Act I and forthcoming in the Gypsy Dance at the start of Act II. Later in Act II
the second ritual of observing takes place. In an elegant carriage
the aristocrats accompany Escamillo into the countryside and
impassively observe his "Toreador Song" and sexually charged
introduction to Carmen. We see no reaction from them; blank
and wooden, they signify absence. While Losey's upper classes
represent active agents of social decay, Rosi's upper classes convey a more passive presence. They appear to be of little threat to
the social order and are criticized for their self-exclusion from
the joys of life.

Although Escamillo is the most mobile figure between the

upper and lower classes, the bourgeoisie also fills in the middle. The soldiers and Micaela inhabit this broad area, and their relationship to the external world is more ambiguous than those at either end. The soldiers do not show any special attachment to the outdoors; they merely exist in it or use it for their duties. Literally or not, they amount to colonizers of the environment.

Gender

The soldiers are also colonizers of women. Even though Micaela is basically equivalent in class, in her first appearance the soldiers form a tight circle around her that threatens gang rape.[41] Before that she was objectified by the leering male gaze of passersby and soldiers on balconies in the tall fortress (women today might liken it to going through a construction site). The height differential underscores the power hierarchy between male and female. It also depicts the relationship between the military and the women. Soon after the melee erupts in the cigarette factory ("Au secours"), a top shot from the viewpoint of the military authority miniaturizes the female workers below into ants. In another example, Zuniga turns voyeur as he peers from up high through binoculars at the factory women on a break. This pastime of the soldiers marks power differential in several respects, including class, gender, and ethnicity. It also sharpens the difference between the hard work of the lower classes and the easy lot of the military (fig. 5.5).

Objectification inevitably leads us to Carmen. As mentioned, the film is notable for its presentation of a Carmen whose raison d'être is personal freedom and the ability to control her life. Yet as in the opera she dies in the end—like Don Giovanni, holding firm to principles at the risk of death—and can be viewed as a sacrificial victim. Rosi likens her to a bull in the bullring:

a forceful symbol of nature in Andalusian culture.[42] In the extended opening sequence, we form sympathy with the agonizing death struggle of the bull. The angle of the shots, level with the bull's head, and the slow-motion photography are gripping. We are meant to identify with the victim-bull, rather than the victor-human, and this inversion extends to the representation of Carmen. Instead of indicting Carmen for supposed sexual excess, we are persuaded to see her sympathetically as a victim or at the very least as a site of contradictory impulses. Her link with the bull continues. In the entr'acte before Act III we see bulls roaming the mountainside. Carmen herself wanders the same terrain, the realization of her rallying cries for freedom and liberty at the end of Act II.

Carmen's death takes place next to the bullring just as a bull is being vanquished in a real bullfight. Her red dress, a dramatic departure from the film's muted look, symbolizes the blood of her death but also refers to the red cape the matador uses on the bull. The dress is a false temptress, a kind of Trojan horse. She was apparently given the dress by Escamillo, who has invited her as his guest. We had seen a red dress worn by the flamenco dancer performing for the aristocrats at the start of Act II. For Carmen, however, this special clothing suggests that when she takes on the trappings of established society—when she engages in artificial display—she is doomed. She cannot exist in such an environment, just as she cannot take Don José back under false pretenses. She will not live a lie. She will also not be trapped, and the physical constraints alone of such a dress mean that she is not free. Bodily movement is like the lifeblood to Carmen, and restrictions would separate her from nature. Even in this scene, however, Rosi does not give us a real red. It, too, is muted, and infected with the dust and earthiness of Andalusia. This tells us that Carmen can never be tamed by conventional society.

While Carmen and others are affirmed as women in Rosi's film, women receive short shrift in the Losey. If lower-class women in *Don Giovanni* evoke sympathy, it is because of their class and not their gender. Women do not interest Losey a great deal in this film, and they are mostly excluded from its critical concerns. Don Giovanni is not interrogated as a predator of women, nor is he guilty because of his conduct toward women. In fact, psychological neurosis is (dis)placed onto the women, especially the noblewomen (Elvira and Anna). They are the furies, the madwomen; they are irrational hysterics, and he has to hide from them.[43] They engender little sympathy from us. Furthermore, the film implies that they have strong sexual desires toward Don Giovanni and hence are guilty. In making Anna a sexually voracious woman who turns into a hysteric, and Elvira a hysterical fury who withdraws into asceticism, the film reinscribes Romantic notions of the women in the opera.

According to Losey, Anna is in love with Giovanni at the start. "She is an aristocrat who demeaned herself, cannot admit it and provokes the death of her father and ultimately Don Giovanni."[44] She is guilty on several counts: her class, her sexual desire, her father's death, and even Giovanni's death. An astonishing indictment, the view demonstrates the myopia (or misogyny) that can result from a heavy investment in a particular ideology. And what about Giovanni's responsibility and guilt as a rapist? He is not placed in that category and effectively gets off scott free.[45] Losey also absolves Giovanni of guilt in the killing of the father and disposes of the oedipal undercurrent in the story.[46]

In the nineteenth century Anna attracted the most interest of the female characters. She embodied the whore-madonna dichotomy so dear to the era. Pure and chaste on one level, she fiercely desired Don Giovanni on another. In E. T. A. Hoffmann's famous story "Don Juan" (1813), she is "a divine woman" who becomes engulfed with "the fire of a superhuman sensuality." Character and singer merge in this male fantasy, and she can only expire in the end.[47] To preserve the ideal of the eternal feminine, Anna's moral demise is attributed to the demonic seduction of Giovanni. In the film the theme is updated in that Anna is sexually attracted to Giovanni of her own free will. They even exchange glances on the factory tour.[48] The main problem with this interpretation, however, is the violence of the music and the appearance of the two during the struggle. Anna is extremely upset, a reaction that does not make sense if she desires the Don. Furthermore, why is Giovanni trying to conceal his face? These elements point to rape rather than consensual sex.

Except for the rape scene in the loggia, Anna's numbers take place indoors and suggest psychic confinement as a character. Even Don Ottavio, her boring counterpart, gains a degree of freedom through his outdoor arias. Anna is also static most of the time, making only slight movements and gestures. In this way she is doubly confined. In "Non mi dir" Losey depicts the confinement through the use of a mirror, a favored device of the director.[49] The camera remains still for quite a while. Don Ottavio is also caught in the reflection, in a static (operatic) embrace with Anna. As aristocracy both cannot escape their class. As the enunciating figure, however, Anna's words are trapped in themselves and ultimately impotent.

As for Donna Elvira, Losey describes her "as a kind of hysterical witch, an upper-class witch, a woman gone mad from desertion—a fiend really."[50] The director thus agrees with Don Giovanni's characterization of her as "pazza" (mad), uttered when he discredits her to Anna and Ottavio (in "Non ti fidar"). Elvira's clothing undercuts her credibility from the start. In the aria-like Trio, "Ah! chi mi dice mai," she looks like a clown with excessive bows and a headpiece that resembles a windsock or a beehive. Furthermore, why is she striding through field and wood, and in that outfit? Her gestures are jerky and unpredictable. Losey reads Elvira's jagged musical lines here and elsewhere as signs of hysteria. But they can just as easily be markers of courage.[51] In many numbers she wears a grey wig, a sign of obsolescence and artifice. Only when she goes off with Giovanni/Leporello in Act II—that is, only when touched by the romantic attentions of a man—is her hair color natural. In another major aria, "Mi tradì," the clownish look returns, mixed with a quasi-religious demeanor. The dark purple garb (still with too many bows), the bent knee and confessional, and the sacred book affirm her purpose. Overall, Elvira's depiction takes her from one stilted role to another and prevents us from seeing her as an individual and as a woman with the sensitivity to express conflicting emotions. She is, after all, the only character to stand up to Don Giovanni, a feature that is stressed in Peter Sellars's version.

Women come to the fore elsewhere and sometimes difficulties arise. Near the end of Leporello's "Catalogue" Aria, we see a nude woman bathing. Young and idealized, she is shown when the text describes how Giovanni's favorite conquest is the virgin. In an odd moment, the camera locks in on an extreme close-up of Giovanni's eyes as he gazes intently at hers. Perhaps we are to infer lust or eroticism, but I read it as a predatory maneuver that instills fear in the young woman. After a series of shot-reverse shots, she looks away and covers herself. There is no joy, only fear and shame. This Don is cold and cruel. What disturbs me is that the surface titillation and the focus on Giovanni's reaction conceal the gravity of the woman's fear. She is object of sensual display rather than subject, and there is scant criticism of her victimization.

This takes us to a truly gratuitous example of female nudity. After the Duet between Giovanni and Leporello near the start of Act II, the two engage in casual chatter. A naked woman lies sleeping amidst their conversation as they sit on the bed. The men are fully clothed, and Giovanni rests a casual hand on her buttock as if she were a table. She is completely dehumanized. If the act is meant to show Giovanni's coldness, it is successful. But in the total scheme it functions as another means of deflecting serious attention from women. In addition, because Giovanni is hardly seen in a joyous, lusty way with women in the film, the place offends all the more. Losey may hope that our disgust alienates us, in a Brechtian manner, from the narrative, but the image runs the risk of alienating us from the enterprise as a whole.

MUSIC

Losey's film likes to juxtapose distant or unrelated locales, creating an unusual narrative rhythm. These juxtapositions occur within numbers as well as between them. In many places they become a way of reading against the music and challenging traditions of musical coherence in Mozart's opera. As mentioned above, one purpose is to show that the musical style of the late eighteenth century is fragmenting. Other ideological aims prompt these effects, and Losey's larger goal in the film is to reveal the social ruptures that lie below a calm surface. Some of the camera cuts map class dialectics through the contrast of dark interiors and bright exteriors. We also see purposeless motion of characters, especially upper-class figures, who wander hither and yon in their arias: a sign of their aimlessness. An excessive number of locales occur. Is this cinematic surfeit, a mannered way to counter the theatricalisms of opera, or an ideological ploy to represent social excess that leads to ruin?

Before exploring specific places, we should keep in mind that much of the opera is episodic and challenging to stage. The score itself is a pastiche. As performed, it typically consists of the original Prague version and most of the Vienna additions. Act II is especially problematic and this partly has to do with Da Ponte's rushed appropriation of an existing libretto, from early 1787, by Bertati. Its loose construction opens the window to scenic juxtaposition. But does the device work in Losey's film? The following examples offer some of the more unusual relationships between music and setting and suggest the mixed results in the film as a whole.

One of the great moments of the opera is the Quartet, "Non ti fidar," midway through Act I. It draws together various antagonists of Don Giovanni for the first time, namely, Donna Elvira and the pair Donna Anna/Don Ottavio, who from this point will act in concert. Their animus will culminate in the collective confrontation of Don Giovanni in the Act I finale. The Quartet actually begins in the preceding recitative. Anna and Ottavio waylay Giovanni to converse. Elvira arrives, and true to her habit of ruining Giovanni's plans she turns to the others and tells them not to trust him. At these words the Quartet begins. Not only is the story continuous from the recitative to the number, but the music overlaps. The cadence ending the recitative resolves on the first chord of the Quartet proper and not in the more usual way within its own boundaries. The first harmony under the vocal line underscores the connection because it is a continuation of the B-flat chord. In other words, Mozart has elided the recitative and number to achieve continuity. Elvira's words are to be a direct continuation—a more measured, elongated version—of the declamatory discourse just uttered.

In the film, however, this continuity is interrupted with a mannered effect, the insertion of a major scene change. The dialogue has taken place in a courtyard, around a carriage in which Anna and Ottavio are sitting; Giovanni joins them.

Elvira tries to rush in but is confined behind a wrought-iron gate, like a prisoner, as she begins to plead. The carriage drives off as the recitative ends and resolves tonally. Then comes a noticeable pause as the scene changes to an elegant interior. A female voice is heard, at the start of the Quartet, as Anna and Ottavio make a grand entrance. One assumes that Anna is singing—she is the only female we see—but her face is covered by a veil. Those who know the opera know that Elvira is singing. Soon she too appears, and we see her lips moving. From that point nothing unusual happens. But the sequence is problematic, for there is little sense in fragmenting a unit that is coherent musically, temporally, and scenically. Furthermore, why create confusion as to who is singing at the start of the Quartet; why have the spectator believe that Anna rather than Elvira is saying "Don't trust him"? The only reason I can see is that Losey wants to rob Elvira of some of her power against Don Giovanni. We do see her behind bars, unable to reach him, and now somebody else seems to be the main gadfly, at least at first. Her credibility as a dramatic force is weakened as a result. In addition, if Losey's purpose is to create psychic disturbance, he succeeds. The spectator feels unsettled and confused as to what is happening. At this important junction, however, the disjunction is gratuitous and does not work.[52]

Don Ottavio's arias also display an unusual relationship with their setting. The two numbers become memorable visual experiences for the spectator, indeed more than their dramatic function merits. Both place him in nature, in the great outdoors. Both show him on the move, restless, which I interpret as a sign of the aimlessness of the upper class rather than of his dramatic force as a character. He is not sufficiently interesting for such emphasis.[53] The first aria, "Dalla sua pace," in Act I, is an odd fit anyway in the narrative, for it was a later addition in the opera (originally a replacement for "Il mio tesoro"). In the film the preceding number, Donna Anna's "Or sai chi l' onore," is performed indoors. Then there occurs a quick cut to lagoon and sky, which fill the frame. We hear Ottavio's recitative as voice-over. As the aria begins a tiny boat can be seen in the distance, and presumably he is the standing figure in it. Why is he cruising a lagoon, and why is he so far away? Ultimately the idiosyncrasies of this scene remain a mystery, but maybe there is some rationale behind Losey's choices. As for site, Losey may have feared the static quality of the music and believed a way had to be found to sustain interest. Placing him on water would provide visual focus and distract the viewer. At the start of the B section the strains are eased as the camera cuts to a medium close-up, and for the rest of the aria we are never far away. Nonetheless it is too late to rescue the abrupt dislocation and mannered composition.

The other aria, the virtuosic "Il mio tesoro" of Act II, shows Don Ottavio roaming the grounds of the estate. In this refined version of a vengeance aria Ottavio strides purposefully across lawns and fields. Servants doze in siesta along the way. At one point Ottavio kicks a sleeping peasant and steps over him. While intended to show upper-class cruelty, the action, as one reviewer describes it, is a bêtise, a shallow, gratuitous, and sensational act.[54] Metaphorically it might represent Ottavio/Kenneth Riegel's frustration over the challenging coloratura he had to negotiate at the end of the B section. In any event, one wonders why the character is wandering al fresco during the aria. Is this another ruse for Losey to find a cinematic solution for a number whose focus is more musical than dramatic? As in "Dalla sua pace," perhaps the staging was intended to strengthen the character by making him seem independent and determined. Yet Don Ottavio seems more irresolute because of the inappropriate action, and that may be Losey's way of further indicting the upper classes.

Although Losey's treatment of the music in many places serves his aim of exposing corruptions of class and power, it reflects a cynical attitude toward music and opera that leads to a weakened narrative role for music. I see this as an aspect of Losey's general dislike of opera and its cultural power, as symbolized in the image of the Paris Opéra in flames at the start of the film. We also saw how staged opera was subjected to criticism through a mannered setting of the Sextet. On the surface Rosi also appears to diminish the power of musical discourse in *Carmen*. But unlike Losey, Rosi actually has a healthy respect for music. He removes the glittery excesses from this overfamiliar score—he disperses and de-privileges the operatic music as a discourse—and by so doing increases the power of the music. As is the case with the understated visual tone of the film, less becomes more in terms of dramatic impact.

In Rosi's film the music of *Carmen* seems less operatic, and by operatic I mean a heightened discourse of emotional extremes that are compressed into relatively brief periods of time. The musical tone in the Rosi seems more ordinary, more natural, and more a part of the everyday world. Music is asked to yield some of its functions to other elements, especially noise, spoken dialogue, scenery, and movement. Noise, for example, is present in most of the film and in most of the musical numbers, especially those associated with the lower classes. Noise not music forms the first aural impression in the film, as the arresting visual sequence with the bull is accompanied by a steady stream of noise and cheers from the crowd. Since the image unfolds in slow motion, noise serves as the main marker of realism in the scene. Although the extent of spoken dialogue in Rosi's film is far from that in a regular film, it does occur occasionally. Considered together, these elements conspire to further a sense of realism. The music, stripped of some of its operatic artifice, does the same.

This environment in which music has a reduced role means that other discourses for representation and narrative can share these functions with music. As a result change from one discourse to another can occur easily, for example, from spoken dialogue to full-fledged music or from noise to scenery. Such virtuosity in the treatment of discourse is a trait we see in Carmen as well, and the parallelism is one way in which the film shapes the character of its lead figure.[55] Another aspect of the leveling effect upon music is that Bizet's music may resemble background music in some places. As explored in chapter 3,[56] the spectator usually pays little attention to a film score. In the Rosi, the very familiarity of the music of *Carmen* may mean that it is similarly ignored. The situation suggests that Rosi, like Saura and Brook, is practicing a kind of deconstruction of the cultural discourse-*Carmen*. Unlike their film treatments of *Carmen*, however, Rosi's treatment reinflects the music rather than cuts it out to make his point.

Rosi's use of music for background purposes is aided by the structure of Bizet's opera, which includes entr'actes and substantial instrumental sections in vocal numbers. Tailor-made for film, they allow the director to show us Andalusia and its social climate. For example, the entr'acte to Act II accompanies a display of authority. First it provides a background to a formal shot of a soldier on watch and then becomes dance music for the flamenco performed for the aristocracy. Before Act III the lyrical entr'acte introduces us to the mountains and its denizens, and we see bulls roaming free and Escamillo and Micaela on horseback. As prelude to the final catastrophe, the entr'acte to Act IV registers the anticipation of the bullfight. In line with the dispassionate tone of the whole, the scene is decidedly understated. What would Zeffirelli have done with this opportunity for spectacle? I would expect banners filling air space and crowds gesturing wildly. Rosi's restraint shores up the discursive organization of the film.

Although the instrumental music resembles the behavior of a film score, the disposition of much of the other music in the film shows similarities with the film musical.[57] In asserting this I am saying that Bizet's score of *Carmen* shares these similarities, for the Rosi essentially uses Bizet's score intact. In a popular style, Bizet's score sports individual numbers, tuneful melodies, clear-cut phrases, repetitive structures, folk-like idioms, dance, spectacle, and production numbers. It has spoken dialogue, although to a much lesser degree than most musicals.[58] In fact, a musical has been made from the opera: Oscar Hammerstein's *Carmen Jones,* produced on Broadway in 1943 and made into a film a decade later (see chapter 2).[59] The connections become closer because the musical as a genre grew out of the operetta. Although officially labeled an opéra comique, Bizet's *Carmen* is often considered an operetta. Its dark undertones and sexual explicitness fit neither category, however. Another similarity between Bizet's opera and the film musical is that many numbers are performances or concern performance. The show musical in particular features those kinds of numbers, as in *Cabaret, A Star Is Born,* or *The Band Wagon.*[60] But there are major differences between *Carmen* and this genre. A typically American affair, the film musical tends to affirm optimism through a happy ending, carefree outlook, emphasis on individual ingenuity (at least for the man), sentimentality, nostalgia, faith in the future, and the idealism of heterosexual love. Social problems may lurk in the shadows but they are not brought to the surface.[61] Bizet's *Carmen,* on the other hand, amounts to a social text that eschews idealization in favor of a realism rife with cynicism and brutality.

Enter Rosi's movie project of the opera, and who does he

cast in the title role but a performer who has done as much musical comedy as opera. While many reviewers pointed out the lightness of Migenes-Johnson's voice in comparison to the husky mezzo or contralto timbre usually heard in the role,[62] her significance for the role entails other qualities. A performer in musicals is typically more of an all-around performer than an opera singer, especially in terms of dance and bodily movement. Because Carmen's "discourse" is her body, it is a distinct advantage, especially in a visual medium such as film, to have a bodily virtuoso such as Migenes-Johnson in the role. Another telling aspect of Migenes-Johnson is that her voice sounds much less trained than that of the typical opera singer. Its quality is much more typical of the musical, where a natural vocal style is valued over the cultivated style of the opera singer. As Rick Altman observes, the folk musical sub-genre (and *Carmen* could be considered a folk tale) aims for naturalness and a nostalgic simplicity. Voices that sound effortless and natural, such as those of Frank Sinatra, Judy Garland, and Gene Kelly, have been valued in such films.[63] Carmen represents a "natural" figure, and a more natural vocal style in the role is highly appropriate.

Perhaps the most significant resemblance to the film musical is the way in which the film effects transitions from one musical discourse to another. The opera *Carmen* already contains these transitions, be they from spoken dialogue (in some versions) to full-fledged music or to some hybrid format such as melodrama. The interesting point in the present context is how such transitions in Bizet's score assume additional meaning because of the presence of the camera and a stress on realism through natural scenery. A stage production, no matter how "real," is still theatrical in its setting and means of presentation. For these reasons, even though the Rosi uses Bizet's music intact, comparison of the Rosi with the film musical is apt. In the following discussions I am not proposing a lockstep relationship between Rosi's film and the more popular genre. What I am suggesting is that the film musical, as a kindred cinematic genre, offers useful models for understanding some of the ways in which Bizet's music works when it is transferred to the screen, especially in Rosi's successful treatment.

The film musical, as well as the musical in general, faces the challenge of reconciling the idealism and abstractness of music with the realism and concreteness of spoken dialogue. How can musical numbers seem credible as a medium for communication when it is not natural to sing one's thoughts? How can the spectator move beyond skepticism when a character breaks into song in an environment in which communication occurs through real speech? According to Altman, the solution in film occurs through the audio dissolve.[64] The audio dissolve, like the image dissolve, involves the superimposition of elements. For sound it means a controlled dovetailing of certain elements of the noise and music tracks, which are typically separate. In order to create a smooth transition from the diegesis of the noise/dialogue track to the abstractness of the musical track, a pivotal diegetic element is often inserted. This can be a song, such as a selection heard on a radio, a rhythm, or an abstracted tune as in a character humming or whistling. At some point the diegetic music is converted to a non-diegetic musical number; sourceless elements such as an orchestra or chorus join in. Typically the process is reversed in the return to the diegesis.

The model applies to some of the musical behavior in Rosi's *Carmen,* which as we have noted uses the music of the opera. Diegesis is obviously not the same concept in opera as in the musical, whether on stage or on film, because in the musical spoken dialogue functions as the normal means of communication and not music. In Rosi's film, however, music yields some of its control of discourse to other elements, including spoken dialogue. Moreover, several numbers in the film are conscious performances and show similarities with diegetic numbers in ordinary film or the film musical.

As in the opera, many places in Rosi's *Carmen* deploy discursive transitions that involve speech, music melodrama, full-blown music, and their rhythmicized abstractions. In the film, noise is pervasive, even in many musical numbers, and this aspect of realism creates an environment that is hospitable to such transitions. Noise de-idealizes the music and renders it closer to speech. It is interesting that even the film musical tends to have little or no noise in full-blown musical numbers,[65] as noise would subvert the idealism of the genre. In the Rosi, noise acts as a foundational cement that one finds in regular films but rarely in one with so much music.[66] Noise is also much less pervasive in staged opera than in Rosi's film (see chapter 3 regarding noise in the relay broadcast). I want to emphasize again that even though the surface musical events of discursive transitions occur in the staged *Carmen* as well, the point is that they interact with filmic elements in the Rosi and together contribute to a realism that approaches that of regular film.

An example of discursive transition early in Act I of the film typifies the process. The players are Don José, Zuniga, and a boys' chorus. The passage begins in the soldiers' parade ground and brings us the first speaking in the film. Actually it is speech with a musical accompaniment, or a melodrama. The two soldiers converse about Micaela, and a cello-violin canon underneath provides a bridge with the preceding number—not only because it continues the musical thread but because it is based on it thematically. Then comes a reprise of the boys' chorus (number 2). As that is taking place, with disembodied choral sounds, we get additional dialogue between Don José and Zuniga, who appear on the parapet. The choral music fades away under their speaking voices and soon is gone, leaving pure speech as they descend the path. While we obviously cannot stipulate a "normal" discourse such as is found in the film musical, we nonetheless have transitions between various levels. The distinctions among them become blurred and we hardly notice the move from one to the other—another component in the leveling process in the film.

Act II offers interesting passages of overlap. After the Gypsy Song, an extended dialogue takes place among Zuniga, Pastia, Carmen, and her friends. When Carmen says "Alors, tout va bien," we hear the outdoor chorus singing "Vivat," the start of number 13. The compression returns at the end of that chorus. Immediately upon its termination, Zuniga (a completely spoken role in the film) toasts the arrival of the matador. Yet he is not given a chance to finish for number 14, the Couplets (better known as the Toreador Song), breaks in. The two overlaps create a cumulative excitement. A third example involves the instrumental reprise of the Toreador Song (number 14c), which closes the scene. After Escamillo rides away in the first half of the number, spoken dialogue is superimposed against the fading refrain, much of it consisting of nostalgic-sounding chord progressions over a tonic pedal point. Dramatically it creates an effective transition from the heroic to the everyday, and the insertion of speech, creating melodrama, furthers a sense of realism. We should keep in mind that in these examples it is difficult to say whether the arrangements are the same as in Bizet because there is no definitive score of the opera or general agreement on the use of spoken dialogue or sung recitative. Viewed in this light, the transitions between different discourses in the Rosi take on a more meaningful role than they would otherwise.

Perhaps the most intriguing examples of discursive transition involve Carmen and diegetic performance: Carmen as the performer par excellence. She knows many discursive languages

Fig. 5.6 Plácido Domingo and Julia Migenes-Johnson in *Bizet's Carmen* (1983). Directed by Francesco Rosi. (Courtesy British Film Institute)

and how to make transitions between them. In these numbers especially, Carmen's talents affirm the discursive dispersing that is central to Rosi's conception. The numbers have much in common with the workings of audio dissolve as laid out by Altman.

The first example begins in the middle of Act I. Don José has gone into the factory to fetch Carmen, who reportedly started the fight (fig. 5.6). He has brought her out into the street. The camera is fixed and we see Zuniga, Carmen, and Don José in the dusty square. Zuniga speaks to Carmen, asking her if she has anything to say in her defense. Receiving no response, he tries again: "Parlez! . . . J' attends." After another tense silence she responds. But instead of capitulating to his discourse, which is speech, she invents one of her own. As in Bizet's opera she utters meaningless musical syllables, "Tra la la la," and in song dares him to slash or burn her, but she will say nothing. Her friends laugh approvingly. Carmen has made a transition to music through a rhythmicized abstraction of music, namely its syllables, as per Altman's theory of audio dissolve. For Carmen it is a natural-sounding activity and thus cannot be considered a completely subversive response. This becomes a clever ruse to make a transition into a musical discourse of her own, which she does after those initial syllables. This can provide her with mastery. We sense that these natural rhythmic sounds are a calculated performance, and as such they take on a diegetic character. This feeling is intensified by the reiterations as the number progresses. As the bare instrumental accompaniment continues, Zuniga speaks again, over it, creating melodrama — melodrama an operatic counterpart to cinema's non-diegetic film music. In any event, throughout the scene Zuniga's speech is always accompanied and in this sense Carmen's discourse has won the day. The remainder of the scene consists of alternations of her "Tra, la, la" sections, on varying pitch (and dramatic) levels, with Zuniga's melodrama sections. The final section presents purely instrumental elaborations of the "tra la la" motif, which act as a non-diegetic accompaniment to Carmen being taken to jail.

In summary, an abstracted form of music, strongly rhythmic, has acted as a transition between speech and song. It has provided Carmen with mastery and kept the diegesis in a relatively narrow range even though it is composed of several elements. The multiple functions of Carmen's musical motive create a fascinating sense of ambiguity for the scene and for her character.

The seduction scene of Act II, also built on Bizet's music, similarly utilizes rhythmic abstraction for discursive mobility. It represents even more of a diegetic performance, as Carmen performs a seduction in private for Don José. The scene begins with spoken dialogue. Then comes a surprisingly formal recitative for Carmen, in which she announces her intentions of dancing for him. The performance proper depends on three forms of rhythm: the physical rhythm of her dancing, the "La, la" rhythm of her song, and a rhythm in the castanets (in the film we never actually see them). In Altman's formulation these three devices are often transitional, yet here they form the number itself. It is also interesting that the heightened rhetorical level of the recitative leads into this kind of ambivalent discourse. One would expect a formal aria, such as Don José's upcoming "La fleur que tu m' avais jetée," to follow immediately. Perhaps the detour is signaled by the mannered progression toward B-flat at the end of the recitative. In any case, Carmen's discursive ambivalence is heightened by the nature of her melody, which swirls ambiguously around the fifth of the key rather than affirming the tonic. What we seem to have in this scene is a flattening of the distinctions among discursive levels. When the military bugle call contributes a counterpoint, we get yet another diegetic rhythmic strand. Then comes a musical conversation between Don José and Carmen. This is a move away from performative discourse, except that the diegetic bugle calls continue underneath—another instance of overlap (or dissolve in Altman's terms). The climax comes when Carmen makes up a dramatic musical counterpoint to the bugle calls as she exultantly sings that those bugle calls falling out of the sky make a wonderful orchestra for her own purposes.

Eventually the structure collapses. She finally heeds his protests, stops the performance, and the bugle calls end. Carmen launches into a declamatory musical style as she mocks him. This culminates in the only response available to Don José, full-blown lyricism. Overall, the scene has gone from spoken dialogue to heightened operatic discourse, but with a discursive flexibility that minimizes gaps between levels: a leveling-out typical of the film as a whole. Furthermore, even though the scene is based on Bizet's music from the opera, it shows how discursive flexibility finds a welcome home in cinema.

As these illustrations demonstrate, Altman's model for the film musical is suggestive. The mobility created by these transitions obviously does not pertain as neatly to film-opera as to the film musical, but many of the ideas apply to Rosi's dispersed environment. Cinema's propensity for naturalism, which implies a flexibility in discourse, and Rosi's frank depiction of the physical environment make the connection apt. They help us to understand why Bizet's opera works so well in this version for the big screen.

Conclusions

In the final analysis Losey's *Don Giovanni* is a mixed success. Regaling us with gorgeous architecture and scenery, the film uses these images as the basis of a critique that stresses cultural decay in that pivotal moment between the ancien régime and the new order to come. A labored quality colors the Marxist enterprise. Unlike the Rosi, the outdoors does not concern itself with realism, local color, or authenticity, but acts as a constructed frame for a self-conscious political interpretation. In its ideological mission the film often reads against the music, with varied results. We have discussed some questionable scenic constructions and their effect on music. Incidentally, the music displays more fundamental problems, as sound quality and synchronization are often poor. Recitatives, shot live, sound vital and convincing, but full-blown music is sometimes unfocused. The break between the two is noticeable. Synchronization often suffers in the post-dubbed numbers (Masetto's aria in Act I is a particularly bad example). While problems in synchronization can serve dramatic ends in some films, as in Syberberg's *Parsifal,* this does not seem to be the case here. *Don Giovanni* also reveals serious gaps in alignment between the singing and the orchestra, and this appears to be a less understandable weakness from a technical point of view.

Losey's film offers a dark and pessimistic reading of the opera. In the end we do not have the sense that anything has changed for the better. Unlike many productions, the remaining characters do not seem lacking now that Don Giovanni is gone. The result is a draw. This indifference typifies the coolness of the film toward the characters, the narrative, and the music. In a Brechtian way the characters stay remote from us. This approach does not work easily with this extraordinary music and probably prompted Julian Rushton's assessment of the film as an "elegant imbecility."[67] While I disagree with his extreme position, I do see problems in the representation of the music, especially the odd scenic juxtapositions. For me the disdain of the valet, Losey's alter ego in the story,[68] serves as the most fitting sign for what is at work in the film—and this in spite of, or in Losey's eyes because of, magnificent splendors of art and nature.

Rosi's film uses natural settings more positively in connection with meaning. They form an essential element in his evocation of an unassuming earthiness that attends the lower-class figures and their behavior. They take on the qualities of their environment. As a consequence, discourses for the communication of narrative, including music, shed some of their heightened qualities and approach each other in function. This ease extends to the film as a whole. Unlike the Losey, the Rosi is decidedly not labored or self-conscious. Ideology also propels Rosi's project, but the touch is light and we sense that less is definitely better. The film is neutral toward opera itself, a decided contrast with the critical view that comes across in *Don Giovanni*. Rosi is comfortable with the work-*Carmen,* or at least is choosing to trade on its populist qualities and use it for an affirming view of Andalusian culture. Little is affirmed in Losey's project except the destructive tendencies of the upper classes. In a larger way, of course, Mozart's opera is affirmed as a text that can accommodate diverse interpretations.

The success of the Rosi prompts a general question. When a film-opera tends so strongly toward realism, does it run the risk of self-destructing? In other words, do we become so accustomed to realism that the music of opera becomes a rude intrusion? This anomaly lay at the heart of Altman's discussion on the need for diegetic transition in the film musical, and it remains a thorny issue in discussions of film-opera, especially by its detractors.[69] With the opera *Carmen*'s realist tendencies it is a potential problem. Rosi, however, resolves it beautifully—in fact, defuses it before it becomes a problem. Rosi's film *Bizet's Carmen* gives us a realism that is both constructed and natural, and utterly convincing as a cinematic treatment of opera.[70] Moreover, it is that rare film of opera that manages to capture the musical spirit of the original and offer a personal interpretation with something significant to say about society and culture. Bizet's opera has rarely looked this good or seemed more important.

6

A Matter of Time and Place:
Peter Sellars and Media Culture

American director Peter Sellars has become a "bad boy" of the operatic world, a pop-culture rebel who has infiltrated the sacred grove of opera. His controversial productions have elicited strong reactions from critics and audiences. Many consider him a charlatan—a director who subjects classical works to sophomoric tricks and ruins them in the process. To admirers Sellars represents an innovator who brings welcome freshness in his updated treatments.[1] Regardless of one's opinion, most agree that Sellars's interpretations leave an indelible mark on the viewer and encourage new thinking about the work. A traditional production may never seem the same as a result.

To date, four of his updated productions have appeared on video: the three Mozart-Da Ponte operas and Handel's *Giulio Cesare*. These are not relay broadcasts but videotaped versions made in a studio, tailored for television screening and video distribution. Released in the early 1990s, the four are based on actual stage productions. The Mozart group became famous at the Pepsico Summerfare Festival, in Purchase, New York, over several years in the late 1980s. The Handel was introduced at Pepsico in 1985 and staged elsewhere before it was taped. All four take place in the present and substitute an American plot for the European original. These video texts are saturated by popular and youth culture and show an America that is hip and dangerous. Life is played close to the edge, with little thought of consequences. The narrative in these videos displays features of media culture, especially a sense of a continuous present that is characteristic of television and video.

In short, updating and media culture join forces to create the resituated opera texts that are Sellars's four video operas. Temporal manipulation not only results in a contemporary setting but permeates many levels of narrative and discourse. Popular genres such as soap opera, MTV, and American daytime talk shows exert a strong influence on image and music, and represent one means by which the meanings of high art and popular culture are questioned. Another means of interrogation occurs through the new setting. The American venue brings important aspects of cultural ownership to our attention, particularly America versus Europe and youth versus establishment.

These themes raise important questions and they form the basis of our inquiry. What does updating mean in these four videos in terms of time, place, and cultural ownership, and how is it accomplished? How is the relationship between high art and popular culture expressed? How does television affect these meanings and relationships, especially in terms of narrative, representation, spectatorship, and genre? How does the camera produce meaning? How do performance and presentation affect the video versions? And finally, what is the relationship between these video productions and other operatic texts, and who is Sellars trying to reach with them? As we will see, these issues bring to the surface thorny aspects of postmodernism and the challenge of discussing media culture against the rapid pace of technological change.

Background

Born in 1957, Sellars came to opera from theater, specifically American theater. This makes him different from the other directors treated in the study. Rosi, Losey, Powell, and Syberberg are filmmakers and European (Anglo in the case of Powell).[2] As Europeans (this includes Zeffirelli), they consider opera natural products of their culture instead of imports. These figures belong to a generation that paid more attention to opera. Like Sellars's, their operatic work has a political or ideological message. But each director shows a basic respect for time, place, and language that Sellars does not necessarily share. He is ready to manipulate these elements to reveal meaning that he believes is lost on contemporary audiences in traditional interpretations. In this regard he shows the influence of innovative European figures such as the Russian theater director Vsevolod Meyerhold, the Italian opera director Giorgio Strehler, and Brecht.[3] Aspects of Asian theater also leave traces in his productions, especially in terms of stylized movement.

Sellars is prepared to give up other aspects of traditional opera for theatrical ends. Large houses, big voices, and big stars do not interest him much for they prevent the long rehearsal period and painstaking choreography that characterize his productions. He relies on a repertory ensemble of actor-singers drawn mostly from Emmanuel Church in Boston, headed by conductor Craig Smith. This group, especially Susan Larson, James Maddalena, and Sanford Sylvan, has worked with Sellars since the early 1980s. They lack star-image as opera singers and their names play almost no role in the marketing of the videos. Most have small operatic voices, sufficient for television or video and similar to the type used in Hollywood musical or operetta. Larson's voice, for example, recalls that of Jeanette MacDonald or the young Shirley Jones. Amenable to Sellars's idea that a production is always evolving, the ensemble is ready to improvise and exert themselves when they sing. Their appearance in more than one opera creates interesting connections among the works. Larson, for example, links together the characters of Cherubino, Fiordiligi, and Cleopatra, and Sylvan joins Figaro and Don Alfonso. If watched in close succession, the videos begin to resemble a continuous saga akin to a mini-series or soap opera. Although unusual in professional opera, at least in the United States, the repertory-ensemble concept is common in American theater, especially experimental theater. So are the smaller house (500 to 600 seats) and populist in-terpretations. What Sellars is attempting is the creation of an American opera-theater experience.[4]

Sellars claims that he wants to create "a 20th-century per-forming tradition of opera, in whose image we can re-create the past," and this means new works as well as old ones.[5] In 1987 he directed the premiere of John Adams's *Nixon in China*, at Houston Grand Opera. Four years later, in Brussels, he staged another new work of Adams, *The Death of Klinghoffer*. It is no accident that both are not only political themes but recent his-torical events, centered on America. Other new works include Nigel Osborne's *The Electrification of the Soviet Union* (1987), Adams's *I Was Looking at the Ceiling and Then I Saw the Sky* (1995), and György Ligeti's *Le Grand Macabre* (1997).

While the 1980s were occupied largely with the Mozart trio, other productions took place. In 1988 Sellars staged an un-usual *Tannhäuser* at Chicago Lyric Opera. Alongside its TV-evangelist protagonist, it featured three simultaneous streams of surtitles, each in a different color: one with a typical surtitle text (although sometimes colloquial), one with subconscious thoughts of characters, and one with quotations from classic German writers. This created a tapestry of cultural references that were woven into Wagner's rich imagery. Practically it is hard to imagine how the audience could digest so many ref-erences at once. Perhaps one is supposed to create one's own web of meanings, drawing on one and then another stream—

Fig. 6.1 Herbert Perry (left) and Eugene Perry in *Don Giovanni* (1990). Directed by Peter Sellars. (Photo by ORF. Courtesy Forum Media, Dr. Eberhard Scheele.)

a practice that hinders the creation of any single coherent narrative. The layering of cultural meanings in a Wagnerian work reminds me of Syberberg's project in his film *Parsifal,* although the techniques differ considerably.

Giulio Cesare marked Sellars's operatic debut at the Pepsico Festival, in 1985. The production was later given in Boston, Brussels, and Nanterre. *Don Giovanni* bowed at a festival in Manchester, Vermont, and appeared at Pepsico in 1987. By 1989 some members of the cast had changed. The most striking difference were two African-American singers who are twins, Eugene and Herbert Perry, as Don Giovanni and Leporello (fig. 6.1). This casting, captured in the video version, stresses the similarities between the two characters and contributes to a multiracial cast (Masetto also African-American, Zerlina Asian-American, and the other singers white). *Così fan tutte* was the first of the Mozart to appear at Pepsico, in 1986, and was repeated the next year. Sellars had first produced the opera for the Castle Hill Festival at Ipswich, Massachusetts, in 1984. He took it to a festival in Stuttgart in 1987. *Figaro* debuted at Pepsico, in 1988, and joined the other two the next summer. Later, the productions were performed at various venues in Europe and taped in Vienna that fall. They were televised in America, on PBS, to usher in the Mozart bicentennial: *Figaro* in December 1990, *Don Giovanni* and *Così* in January 1991. They aired shortly thereafter on European television.

The four works typify Sellars's American-centered productions. They depict contemporary American culture and stress its dark underside, especially excesses of sex, violence, addiction, and psychosis. While *Giulio Cesare* exports an American presidential entourage to a political hotspot in the Middle East, the Mozart group plays in and around New York City. *Don Giovanni* is set in gang-ravaged south Bronx, *Figaro* the tony world of an apartment high in the Trump Tower, and *Così* a diner amid a summer vacation spot in Westchester. Surely it is no coincidence that these locations are very close to the site of the festival. As a group, the four are imbued with an urban, east coast outlook; one could not imagine them set in a small town, especially in the south or midwest.

Don Giovanni stands out from the others because, with one exception (Lorraine Hunt as Donna Elvira; as Sesto in *Giulio Cesare*), its cast does not come from the repertory pool. This Giovanni functions as the "boss" not because of his class but because of his macho authority and power in a violent neighborhood. He does drugs, as does Donna Anna, who is caught unawares after attending an opera (!) and is forthwith raped by Don Giovanni. Both shoot up before technically demanding arias: a suggestion that an extra hit is needed in order to get through them. Elvira, although dressed as a punk, proves to be the courageous antagonist of Giovanni. Zerlina's "Batti, batti" finally comes across as a meaningful number for today's audiences, for it occurs directly after we hear Masetto slapping her around for being a slut. Her request in the aria for him to hit her emerges as an all-too-typical response of women to assume guilt for the assault.[6] Another memorable moment occurs when Giovanni strips down to his briefs to sing "Viva la libertà!" — a libertarian visualization of the ringing sentiment. Near the end, a little blond girl rather than the Statue clasps Giovanni's hand and leads him away: a hint of pedophilia, one of the most reviled of sins. Finally, the other characters (except Leporello) end up in purgatory, popping out of glowing manhole covers. We are all implicated in the sins of Don Giovanni, Sellars is saying.[7]

Giulio Cesare resembles *Giovanni* in its cruelty and despair. Ostensibly the "bad guys" are vanquished in the end, yet only Caesar and Cleopatra, shown as vain and shallow, put on a happy face. Caesar, an American president whose characterization was probably conceived when Sellars was working on *Nixon in China,* is conducting poolside diplomacy at a bomb-damaged hotel in the Middle East. The setting repeats a poolside location from a production of Shakespeare's *Antony and Cleopatra* that Sellars mounted in college. In *Giulio Cesare* Ptolemy is a punk sadist with kinky sexual practices, which include physical and psychological torture. Cleopatra is vain and hedonistic yet courageous in crisis, especially when raped by her brother. Sesto is driven and suicidal in his struggle to live up to his father's name. Caesar, in fact, is one of the least interesting characters, with few visible neuroses: a comment on the actual President at the time, actor Ronald Reagan. Yet the character of Caesar is ambiguous. Is Caesar portraying an American President or is an American President portraying Caesar? As I watch I am inclined to believe that a person named Caesar is the American President and thus sense an added persona attached to the figure. The dualism results from the fact that both are recognizable and strong historical figures. It adds another layer to Sellars's dual construction, to be discussed below.

In *Le nozze di Figaro* the Count and Countess Almaviva occupy a glass-lined apartment in a skyscraper in Manhattan. Figaro and Susanna are live-in servants, and Cherubino, Marcellina, Basilio, and Bartolo are satellite figures who revolve around the household. The upper class is bored but the age-old double standard applies to male-female relations. The Count, in a jealous rage at the start of the Act II finale, beats his wife and threatens her with a gun. By the end and the revealing arias of Act IV, all the characters, except perhaps Susanna and Cherubino, are psychologically spent and have passed through a suicidal crisis. This is a much darker production of *Figaro* than most (see chapter 2 for a discussion of Ponnelle's film). Like *Don Giovanni,* the setting is winter, and specifically Christmas season.

Così, in contrast, takes place in the summer, at Despina's Diner. The owner, who is the main waitress, is the longstanding girlfriend of Don Alfonso, a cynical Vietnam veteran. Class virtually disappears as a significant factor. The two pairs that are involved in the wager are naive and shallow. Deep and passionate feelings are awakened in one pair, Ferrando and Fiordiligi, after the switch but not in the other. Those left as observers, including Alfonso and Despina, are stunned by the emotional depth displayed. With funky references to Shirley MacLaine as a seer and the genital-charging properties of a Die-Hard Battery, *Così* becomes the most erotic production of the four. The pairing at the end is ambiguous and fluid, but it is clear that the principals have been jolted by the experience (fig. 6.2).

Fig. 6.2 Sanford Sylvan, Sue Ellen Kuzma, Janice Felty, and Susan Larson in *Così fan tutte* (1990). Directed by Peter Sellars. (Photo by ORF. Courtesy Forum Media, Dr. Eberhard Scheele)

DUALITIES

The updated setting is one of the most obvious characteristics of the productions. Yet Sellars rejects the notion of updating as a description of what he is doing. "I *hate* updatings as a gambit. I resent it actively—it's cheap and vulgar and obnoxious and not to the point. My productions are never updated."[8] He seems to resist the notion because he takes it to mean that the present and its values replace fundamental aspects of the original. And this is not what he does. Instead, his productions work two tracks at the same time. Past and present are juxtaposed alongside each other. This dual focus is not intended to obliterate the past but underscore the existence of history in the present. As Sellars notes, "Opera has a role to play in giving people a space for historical reflection in their own time, which is otherwise not happening in this absurd rush-to-judgment journalism."[9]

This respect for the past is one reason why Sellars insists on re-taining the original language in the sung music, even in the face of serious inconsistencies with the new settings, and presenting the score in a complete version.

Past and present do not merge but remain distinct entities. The director wants the audience to be involved in two centuries at the same time, in this case the eighteenth and the late twentieth centuries.[10] Yet the dualism runs the risk of collapsing and leaving a sense of a timeless interpretation in its wake. Furthermore, the more time that passes since the videos were made, the more likely that the viewer will be seeing two *historical* streams juxtaposed—the late eighteenth century and the late 1980s—with a third, the actual present, superimposed on the two.

The temporal juxtaposition accords with Sellars's belief in Brechtian alienation. Sellars offers viewers outrageous acts in the production because he wants to shake up audiences. He wants them to reflect on what they see and hear, and to think twice. Del Ray Cross plausibly suggests that Sellars likes to do opera because its audiences expect traditional productions and are themselves traditional, and hence greater distance will be created between the productions and their expectations.[11] The danger is that distance may turn into hostility and his productions are avoided. Like his resituated characters, Sellars enjoys living on the edge.

Sellars contends that alienation also involves the music of opera. He implies that technical aspects of singing, including glancing at the conductor and coordinating with the orchestra, interrupt the flow of pure narrative. This can alienate the singer-actor for it distracts from the main business at hand and creates distance through an added level of discourse. The singer has to deal with the duality of being inside and outside the narrative at the same time. The important point for Sellars may be that the audience in the opera house becomes aware of the interruptions. At the same time, the audience is affected by the intensely emotional quality of music. From these two properties, one of alienation and the other of pulling-in, a higher-level alienation results, one that qualifies as Brechtian in its theatrical impact.[12]

Sellars has explained the rationale for his modernized productions numerous times. The basic idea is that because we cannot recoup the reactions of eighteenth-century audiences to the shock value and avant-garde aspects of these works, we have to recast them in the "image language" of today.[13] That means the contemporary United States, which provides the means to access the core of the work. Furthermore, he believes that the modern setting does not exist for its own sake or to critique American culture but to serve dramatic ends. Yet Sellars is myopic when he posits American culture as the absolute reference point for his productions. For American audiences, and more narrowly for young Americans and those who watch television regularly, Sellars is right. But these productions, especially on television and video, have reached Europe as well as the United States. Is contemporary American culture the most meaningful point of reference for these audiences? It certainly is *a* meaningful reference point, but not in the same way that it would be for American audiences, even for those Americans who are older and not media saturated.[14] For many Europeans, I suspect, the image language means another layer of alienation. On the other hand, this becomes an object lesson for Europeans in operatic Otherness: on how many Americans feel when confronted with European opera.

Sellars sees his hip settings as backdrops to the real issues of the productions, which are people and the social structures they inhabit. He uses such locations "because they are movie locations, the locations of all this pop culture that is already in people's heads."[15] It is tempting to speculate whether Sellars's dependence on contemporary culture amounts to a masquerade: a strategy of concealment for social or political ends. The contradiction between an eighteenth-century work and a contemporary setting could imply satire or a criticism of the operas. Critics accuse him of destroying masterpieces through an irreverent tone toward the original.[16] Yet Sellars's form of alternative garb for the operas is meant to highlight their ability to be meaningful to audiences that are removed from them in time. The masquerade of updated versions allows him to display the power of the works for contemporary audiences.

Another aspect of the duality in the videos concerns the relationship between image and music. The director speaks of setting up a "visual counterpoint" to the music, in order to maximize the range and intensity of emotional reaction.[17] This has been interpreted by Jeremy Tambling, a Marxist critic, as opposition between image and music.[18] But counterpoint does not necessarily indicate opposition, and merely describes contrast or two (or more) entities operating in tandem with or against each other. For example, a red and a beige wall adjacent to each other can be in counterpoint but not in opposition, and the same is true of two musical lines or visual and musical entities that accompany each other. In Sellars's updated treatments, music and image do not oppose each other, although they may contrast with each other. Sellars understands the kinetic and narrative qualities of the music very well, and deploys images that underscore those qualities. The surface images, which show the contemporary setting, may seem to contrast with the eighteenth-century music. But the underlying properties do not, and certainly do not amount to an opposition. Despite my disagreement with Tambling, however, I agree that the surface duality foregrounds difference. Difference represents another way of characterizing Sellars's notion of "dual vision" as the sensibilities of two different historical eras that are in juxtaposition with each other.

Duality also extends to the text. Sellars retains the original words, in Italian, along with the original music. For the stage productions he was opposed to surtitles and in its place distributed a lengthy prose description that he wrote. This is included in the video box but is obviously missing from the telecasts, which do, however, offer a "talking head" introduction by Sellars himself (for the Mozart operas). As is customary, the videos include subtitles in English. In conjunction with the original text this translation creates a dual-vision text that corresponds in several respects with the historical dual vision. The translation is hip, street-wise, and irreverent. Often it departs from the original to such an extent that it resembles the glossing that accompanied his updated staging of *Tannhäuser*. Examples include slang contemporary phrases, as in "classy guy," for the class-based "cavaliere" (cavalier) in *Don Giovanni;* and explicit phrases, as in "My God, what balls!" uttered by Fiordiligi in *Così* for "Stelle che ardir!" (Heavens, what impudence!).

The updating leads to some odd inconsistencies. In *Don Giovanni* the subtitles retain the "masqueraders" idea of the original while we see no one in masks. More typical is the elimination of nonsensical concepts in the translation. In *Figaro*, Bartolo's line "Tutto Siviglia conosce Bartolo" (All of Seville knows Bartolo) is rendered simply as "Everyone here knows Bartolo." Marcellina's "l'argent fait tout" (in French, money does everything) loses its elitist veneer because the subtitles make no reference to a separate language. Later, Susanna and the Countess's "Sotto i pini del boschetto" (Under the pines in the grove), a poetic phrase in their assignation letter to the Count, is not translated as there is no thicket of pines on their high-rise balcony. Antonio refers to Cherubino in New Jersey (instead of in London). Yet in a misguided retention of the learned discourse of the original, Don Giovanni's line "Amor,

consiglio" (Cupid, help me) is rendered as "Now what, Cupid."
Can we imagine this street hustler invoking Cupid?

From a realistic perspective, therefore, the updated translation is highly problematic. It has been suggested that Sellars
(and his subtitlist, Brooks Riley) rely on the fact that television
and video audiences do not know the original Italian. This
allows them to create a text that has little to do with the original but attempts to support (not completely, as we have seen)
the updated time and place.[19] But why not begin anew and use
a new sung text, in slang and the vernacular? For one, Sellars
cherishes textual duality. Second, as opposed to his fondness
for such a dualism, he believes that the original music and language form an inseparable unit. While this shows respect for
the music and its integrity, it amounts to a purist view that dis-
regards music as lived practice in a larger context. Sellars's third
reason for keeping the original text is that he does not know of
any suitable English translation.

The problems in the subtitles raise the issue of the purpose of
subtitles in general. Even in traditional productions, subtitles
do not convey a full or exact translation, for that would insert
an intrusive element that distracts from the drama. Arguably
Sellars extends the practice a bit farther, to the extent of a gloss,
and adds support to the updated track in his dual-vision conception. But if the viewer does not know this, then he or she
may assume that it is the literal translation. Perhaps the inclusion of Sellars's lengthy description in the video box is meant to
add weight to the independence and pertinence of the English
text on the screen.

Duality is also present at the level of medium. The video version, our main concern, suggests interesting relationships with
other forms of the production. Dual structures apply to the
recorded work for video and television alongside the staged ver-

sion, and to the video as separate from the television broadcast. In addition, the excesses of pop/youth culture that are emphasized in the video create a second track alongside the original. Although such excesses can subvert the original,[20] they can also deconstruct the very culture they are based on as they show how the original is broad enough to accommodate a range of interpretations. We should remember that these videos are not so much a recorded version of a stage production as the stage production is already a video-influenced phenomenon, especially in terms of youth and pop culture, staging, and imagery. Nonetheless, the video versions constitute an independent entity because of the camera and its control over what we see. They are strongly influenced by popular genres such as MTV and soap opera and how they structure meaning.

Given the experimentation of Sellars's stage versions, it is surprising how conservative these video works are as video art. The only innovation lies in the film openings of the three Mozart works and the superimposed images at the end of *Don Giovanni*. Sellars affirms that he is a man of the theater and not a video artist or filmmaker. Nonetheless, as the next section demonstrates, the camera constructs narratives that reflect innovative aspects of media culture.

The Camera: Time and Space

Video's only about energy, it has no pictorial weight. Theatre is always playing against the edges, and in TV there are no edges, there's only a center. So you have to treat the video camera as an emotional thermometer, and point it at where things are hottest.[21]
—Peter Sellars

I feel your pain.
—attributed to Bill Clinton

Sellars's video productions elude a specific historical position. This shows the influence of MTV, the 24-hour network in the United States that presents music-videos. MTV, according to E. Ann Kaplan, "blurs previous distinctions between past, present, and future, along with its blurring of separations such as those between popular and avant-garde art, between different aesthetic genres and artistic modes." Time becomes a continuum from which one can draw at will, and meaningful spatial distinctions are similarly leveled.[22] Soap opera, another influence on the videos, also denies defined space,[23] and a feeling of virtual space permeates Sellars's videos. Even in *Così* and *Figaro*, where we know we are in Despina's Diner and an apartment in the Trump Tower, the emphasis on detail makes us forget the larger context most of the time. This effect helps to contribute to a sense of an absence of time, or rather an absence of a specific time.

The concept of a timeless continuum ties in with theories of televisual flow, which were proposed by television theorist Raymond Williams in the 1970s. Drawing on his experience with British television, which was devoid of commercials, Williams advanced the notion of television as a continuous flow. Constantly available, television presents few divisions and is like a stream that is ever-available and ever-flowing. Television tends to deny closure and this makes it open-ended. The viewer knows that more is always available and can never get enough. Desire is continually unsatisfied, and thus emerges the lure of the medium.

Later theorists, especially Kaplan and John Fiske, have amended Williams's work to include American televisual experience. In their formulations television is still a flow but has divisions, and they result in a segmented flow. This means that the relationship between successive units is more complex. As

Fiske expresses it, "The television text . . . is composed of a rapid succession of compressed, vivid segments where the principle of logic and cause and effect is subordinated to that of association, and consequence to sequence. Flow [now means that] the movement of the television text is discontinuous, interrupted, and segmented. Its attempts at closure, at a unitary meaning, or a unified viewing subject, are constantly subjected to fracturing forces."[24]

This aesthetic describes the rhythm in the four videos, where extremes in pacing create a mannered sense of time and space. Many techniques in the videos—quick editing, fragmented angles, and mannered juxtapositions of shots—show the impact of MTV. Soap opera exerts influence in the incessant use of close-up and probing of inner emotion. Yet despite their contradictory pulls—MTV toward speed and incoherence, and soap opera toward depth and emotional excess—the two genres promote an open-endedness that keeps viewers eager for more. For *Giulio Cesare,* with its static Baroque dramaturgy, this is no mean feat. The endings of the four are ambiguous, resisting closure, and stir up unfulfilled desires that are characteristic of MTV and soap opera.

The visual pacing in Sellars's videos approaches schizophrenia. On the one hand, lengthy pauses occur in recitatives or at the borders of musical numbers. On the other, the camera assumes a frantic pace, cutting quickly from one image to another. This occurs partly because characters move a great deal and Sellars prefers tight shots. In order to capture the successive images, the camera has to make big jumps. Either it moves quickly with the character or cuts to another shot. In both cases the result is a succession of quick, disconnected fragments. The discrepancy is often transferred to the music. In *Don Giovanni,* for example, "Là ci darem la mano," the famous duet of seduction, is built on extremes of musical pacing.

The first section, usually leisurely, is much too fast; dramatically it exposes Giovanni's insincerity and his discomfort with such sentimental wooing. The second part, "Andiam, andiam, mio bene," typically faster and more dance-like than the first, is excruciatingly slow. The discrepancies suggest that Giovanni is on a drug-induced trip and his musical reflexes are impaired. The camerawork thus far has prepared us for such imbalance and implies that other numbers may be under the influence of this drug-addled force as well. The literally drug-induced "Finch'han dal vino" ("Champagne" Aria), at a furious pace, is such an example.

Soap Opera

The insertion of pauses, some very long, becomes a mannered feature of the four video productions. Those familiar with opera buffa may find them a rude shock in a genre that relies on fleetness and speed.[25] Their appearance on the television screen brings to mind the dramaturgy of soap opera. (I can't help but be struck by the term, a pop derivative of a high-art genre, which here is used as a point of departure for a discussion of opera.) An American daytime genre geared mostly toward women, soap opera inserts pauses so that a character's words register for maximum emotional impact. The device is particularly useful to close off a segment, before a commercial break. In the Sellars, lengthy pauses invite the viewer to insert and rewrite meaning. They illustrate the director's aim of exploring "secret worlds": filling in meaning in the textual and dramatic gaps of the libretto and the larger narrative.[26] While Sellars is referring mainly to his updated settings and his own insertions, the technique covers other elements in the videos and creates a larger role for the viewer—what Fiske calls a "producerly text" in the context of soap opera.[27] Sellars's use of the device creates a kind of nineteenth-century dramaturgy—one in which mannered looks by the camera replace the symphonic connections between numbers that appear in operas by Puccini and others. This helps to explain why eighteenth-century opera works well for Sellars: it offers a framework that he can fill with his media-intensive devices.

Many examples of inserted pauses take place. In *Figaro* they begin early. In the second section of the second duet, which already contains halting stops, the lines hinting at trouble with the Count ("You know the rest") assume metaphysical import through extended pauses. In the following recitative, when Marcellina shows Bartolo the contract and asks if he will support it, his tortured reaction is underscored by a lengthy silence; angst replaces comedy. In *Don Giovanni*, Act II takes on added weight through the insertion of pauses. After Giovanni and Leporello supposedly exchange clothes, lengthy silences interrupt the conversation. When Leporello, as Giovanni, speaks with Elvira, their recitative is also greatly extended through meaningful pauses. Sellars emphasizes the psychological investment in identity that is, in the end, illusive. Later in the act, a two-minute silence, the longest in the opera, marks the spiritual disintegration of Ottavio as he shuffles away after seeing Anna shoot up with drugs. After this dramatic high point—an insignificant moment in most productions—the story plays out to the end. Similarly, Sellars underlines the dramatic high point of *Così* with a lengthy pause. After the climactic "Fra gli amplessi," the magnificent duet in which Fiordiligi's passion is revealed, a substantial silent space is inserted for the emotional afterglow to take hold and the characters to show their feelings physically.

While pauses slow the dramatic rhythm, fast cutting adds vitality and excitement. Sometimes, as in *Giulio Cesare*, the device becomes so excessive as to be tiresome. Again we can look to camera techniques in soap opera for a model. In that genre, according to Sandy Flitterman-Lewis, "a visual rhythm which depends on fragmentation is built. Within a single sequence there is never any *sustained* camera work (the camera hops about from place to place), nor any sustained focus of the representation. . . . The soap opera form confirms that TV viewing means the eye is constantly in movement; it never rests, and always has something new to see."[28] Sellars too keeps the viewer's visual receptors busy as the camera flits from image to image, most of which are close-ups of faces, body parts, or objects. Like visual "sound-bytes," these fragments of image form little connection with each other and typify a digital aesthetic, the very foundation of media culture. They also resemble the practice of "zapping" or "surfing" from one channel to another. Zapping, however, invests the viewer rather than the director with the ability to create a collage of images. Fiske describes it as "a form of scratch video that produces an individualized television text out of its mass-produced works."[29] Of course, when Sellars's videos are played back on the television screen, the viewer also has the power to control images: they can be lengthened or shortened in time, repeated or skipped altogether. These modes are clearly open-ended.

Soap opera fosters an intimate relationship with the viewer. Sellars's videos capitalize on this feature in their visual construction. With the typical shot from mid-chest through forehead, the videos court intimacy and draw the viewer into the innermost emotions of the characters. This occurs in the tight close-ups of the face, so that expressive features, especially eyes and mouth, fill much of the screen. These partial shots exclude background and further the sense of a timeless, placeless drama: another similarity with soap opera.[30] Our attention is to be riveted exclusively on psychology of the characters. This includes

Fig. 6.3 Sue Ellen Kuzma (left), David Evitts, Jeanne Ommerle, Sanford Sylvan, and Susan Larson in *Le nozze di Figaro* (1990). Directed by Peter Sellars. (Photo by ORF. Courtesy Forum Media, Dr. Eberhard Scheele)

their fixation on objects of violence, especially guns, knives, blood, and hands, which appear in tight shots in each video. In *Giulio Cesare* the device is so insistent that it becomes its own fixation: an obsessive *Leitmotif* that wears out its welcome through the strain it places on the viewer.[31]

Soap opera is notorious for postponing closure indefinitely and stressing neurosis. Sellars's videos similarly replace closure with ambiguity, self-doubt, or parody.[32] *Figaro* has characters who pass through death urges and come out the other side (fig. 6.3), *Don Giovanni* a new protagonist who himself is doomed (Leporello), *Così* a group scarred by a brush with real passion, and *Giulio Cesare* characters who cannot face themselves any longer. The narrative of each borrows from the aesthetic of confession and victimhood that underlies soap operas and daytime talk shows. Eager to bare their souls and elicit compassion, Sellars's characters express their identity in their dysfunction; this is created by the music, the spaces inserted in the music, and the stress on inner feeling. The dramaturgy emphasizes the individual as a single unit. He or she may interact with others but, as in American culture in general, the individual's concerns form the primary social unit. Isolation takes precedence over community. I find it ironic that as Sellars criticizes capitalism and consumer-culture in these productions, he endorses their social base, the individual. The hyper-intensity of the camera captures a self-absorption that was characteristic of the 1980s and early 1990s in the United States. Bill Clinton's "I feel your pain," a parodied slogan of the 1992 campaign, supplies an apt description of Sellars's intended effect in this intimate medium.

The camera's obsession with the individual has important consequences for drama. One is that many ensembles are broken up into isolated shots of individuals. "Cosa sento," no. 7 in *Figaro,* provides a good example. Labeled a trio, it begins in media res and actually involves four people. Cherubino, who hides, is the silent focus of attention in the number. In Sellars's version, most of the shots are claustrophobic close-ups of one or two characters. The sense of a whole and of an interaction among the four is greatly diminished. The effect is especially noticeable when the second musical group of the number's sonata form (modified) returns to the tonic key, B-flat major (m. 168). In Mozart's operas this generally signals dramatic resolution or a coming together of individuals and situations. The characters need not be in agreement with each other— they might have different texts—but the point is that they are relating to each other more directly and the musical lines are closer temporally. A sense of expansiveness often results and musical textures tend to be thicker, louder, and more homophonic. Here, although the characters sing together (with differing texts), the camera works against expansiveness and fragments a sense of community, as fleeting as it might be at the time. In the Mozart, the music soars as the individuated lines heard earlier in the ensemble coalesce in rich sonorities. Yet Sellers keeps the drama in separate fragments through a camera style that is similar to that at the beginning. This conveys the idea that equilibrium is illusory and each character still has his or her own agenda. Sellars's way of showing the divisions is to jump from one character to another, in tight shot, instead of shooting them together and highlighting their differences.

The close camera can change comedy into neurosis. Bartolo (mentioned above) sings his revenge aria "La vendetta" in a state of anger and frustration. Close-ups and pauses probe his feelings of failure, and he lays blame squarely on others. From a Classical point of view, however, this is a comic aria of revenge. Elements of Baroque style serve to mock him as being socially obsolete, and patter lines show him to be a buffoon. He is not to be taken seriously. In the Sellars, however, the camera presents a different character. He is pained that Marcellina is about to betray him by executing the contract to marry Figaro, and bitter about his general lot in life. "La vendetta" becomes personal and deadly serious.

The registering of emotion by another character is a device that Sellars uses on several occasions, often in close-up. It operates as a kind of mirroring process: a character's emotions are reflected on the face of another, although a cracked mirror may produce divergent reactions. A prominent feature of soap opera, the device is also used in television programs that promote closeness between narrative and viewer. One example is *Designing Women*, an American situation comedy from the late 1980s. In this series the camera likes to shift momentarily from the speaker to register another character's emotional response while the person is still talking. While its excessive use is unfortunate, it draws the viewer into the emotional climate of the group and makes one feel part of it. A major difference from the Sellars, however, is that the camera includes much more than faces in the frame. This helps to keep the tone light.

Many examples of this visual intensification occur in *Giulio Cesare*. Cornelia's arioso in Act I, "Nel tuo seno" ("On your breast"), accompanies her visit to the tomb of her husband, Pompey. During the opening ritornello we get extreme close-ups of Cornelia and these draw us into her despair. As the number proceeds we have quick glimpses of the reactions of others to her plight. Her son Sesto, expectedly, is moved and distraught, but we also see tight reactions of sympathy from the soldiers in the background. Similarly, in Cornelia's "Deh piangete" in Act II, when she contemplates suicide with a sharp garden tool, meaningful reactions on the faces of the guards intensify our involvement. Yet as this emotional hook pulls us into the narrative, the alienating tendencies of Sellars's dual vision provide a healthy counterbalance. We are not in over our heads.

The intimate reaction shot is also used to good effect in a famous ensemble, the Sextet in *Figaro*.[33] Like Bartolo's aria "La vendetta," this buffa number becomes deadly serious. The camera transforms it into a set of deep emotional reactions that betray the influence of soap opera. These reactions come from characters who are part of the group of six but may not be singing at the moment, and who are reacting to what they are hearing. Sellars utilizes fast cutting from face to face and a fair amount of shot/counter-shot technique. In this way he relates individuals or groups with each other, as if they are answering each other emotionally. In addition to the shared intimacy with the viewer, the number seems serious because of lengthy pauses and sustained looks in the prior recitative.

Although the deep looks of the camera seem mannered by Act III in *Figaro*, the device is critical to Sellars's psychological conception. In *Don Giovanni* it reveals the gripping relationship between Giovanni and Elvira. Sellars's interpretation foregrounds the courage of Elvira as the only character to stand up to Giovanni as an equal. This antagonist pursues Giovanni relentlessly and succeeds several times in thwarting his designs on other women. An important turning point occurs in the Quartet, "Non ti fidar," in which Elvira warns Anna against Giovanni and he attempts to discredit her by calling her "pazza" (crazy).[34] Sellars ends the number with a very tight shot of their faces cheek-to-cheek as they continue to fend off the other. This literal face-off encapsulates their relationship and forms an indelible image for the remainder of the opera.

Space and Narrative

As noted earlier, space is ambiguous in the video productions. *Don Giovanni* is the most abstract spatially, and one hardly knows where the action is taking place. Even when markers appear, such as the cracked-glass door of Elvira's building or the grocery store plundered by Giovanni's thugs, we have no idea of how they relate to a larger context. In *Giulio Cesare* the spatial environment is also ambiguous. Close-ups mark off a limited space in a given aria, and it is hard to figure out how that space relates to slices of space in other numbers. But that is precisely Sellars's purpose: we are not supposed to form a notion of a coherent space. Our attention is to be focused on the emotional "hot spots" captured by the camera, and we are to become intimate with the foregrounded elements. The ambiguous space is also intended to illuminate ambiguous relationships in the narrative—between people, people and their emotions, and people and their environment.

As if to puncture the mystical quality of the ambiguous

space, Sellars occasionally wrenches the narrative out of its fiction through the intrusion of the performing space and its technical apparatus. In *Così* this first occurs in Guglielmo's aria in Act I, "Non siate ritrosi." We are given a glimpse of the orchestra pit and made aware that the story is unfolding on a stage. That it happens in this number suggests that Guglielmo may be an independent fellow, someone who, like Don Alfonso, refuses to be contained by the diegesis. This trait comes boldly to the fore later, in his other aria, in Act II. Both arias display the simple vocabulary of a buffo character, in key, melody, texture, and motif. Guglielmo is more superficial than his male counterpart, Ferrando, whose depths of feeling leave lasting scars. Sellars's satire of Guglielmo's feigned seriousness through narrative interruptions is highly appropriate.

In his second aria, "Donne mie la fate," Guglielmo surpasses the earlier intrusion and literally jumps the gap by running into the studio audience. The camera is forced into a high-speed pan typical of the amateur videoist. Meanwhile we see two or three other television cameras at their positions in the front row. Imitating David Letterman, Guglielmo shakes hands with the cameramen, totes a hand mike in the aisles, and acts as if he is asking questions about the fair sex to individual audience members. As a modern man on the go he receives a phone call. The Viennese audience, meanwhile, is bewildered by the ruse. When Guglielmo returns to the stage, he looks directly at the camera and moves closer to it (another Letterman trick). A sudden high-speed zoom to a medium close-up of Ferrando onstage takes us back to the main story.

A relay telecast will also show house and audience, and it is interesting to compare the two situations. In the relay the audience in the opera house is kept separate from the work. This places the television viewer in a subject position that causes us to identify with that audience and feel as if we are in the opera house as well. In the Sellars the studio audience, an unusual presence in any studio taping, is integrated into the presentation of the narrative. This maneuver instills a more mobile subject position in the television viewer and allows us to identify with performers as well as spectators.[35]

Giulio Cesare, the other abstract work, also ruptures the narrative. Before Act II, we are met with a display of technical apparatus, and this ushers in a string of numbers that have extra-diegetic features. The preliminary action exposes the labor and confusion behind-the-scenes. We see cameras moving into position, Larson primping for her entrance, stagehands walking dogs on stage, and a stage manager calling out "Quiet, are we ready." During Larson's recitative, the first number in the act, we catch a glimpse of a large prop suspended from high above the stage. This previews the full appearance of the crescent a few numbers later, when it descends as the seat of Cleopatra's spectacular entrance from above.

These events in *Così* and *Giulio Cesare* bring to mind Ingmar Bergman's film *The Magic Flute.* Bergman shoots the audience during the overture and returns to it (and one little girl in particular) at certain points in the story. He takes us backstage a few times, including during intermission. But Bergman's purposes are different. He naturalizes the audience from the beginning so that they are an integral part of the narrative and his universalist conception of the opera.[36] The excursions backstage similarly extend the narrative. Furthermore, Bergman keeps audience and singers as separate entities and refrains from showing the technical process of filming. Sellars collapses boundaries to ensure that *Così* and *Giulio Cesare,* two abstract works, do not become overly idealized.

When the operas were taped, Sellars told the camera crew to improvise and "live dangerously" in their shots. He did not want establishing shots and full-body shots; he did not want

Fig. 6.4 Lorraine Hunt (right) and Drew Minter in *Giulio Cesare* (1990).
Directed by Peter Sellars. (Photo by ORF. Courtesy Forum Media,
Dr. Eberhard Scheele)

to see anyone's feet. He counseled the crew to stay with the
characters and try to get inside their head and reveal inner
emotions.[37] As a result the camera furthers the cognitive split
between mind and body. Sellars has us see the face, a part of the
body, but it lacks the context of an integral body and thus seems
disembodied. The disembodiedness also comes from close-ups
of other body parts or objects, and they can signify psychosis
or addiction on the part of a character. While they can alienate
us from the characters, they provide a healthy counterbalance
to the tendencies toward shared intimacy that are created by
close-ups and pauses. We might pull back in a Brechtian way
to reflect on the social conditions that produce such misery.

The strong image of blood leaves a lasting impression in two
of the videos (fig. 6.4). Blood becomes a fetish early in *Don
Giovanni*. In "Fuggi, crudele" Anna forces Ottavio to swear revenge against her father's murderer and the man who raped her.

The text of the oath is a pledge sworn on her eyes, and blood ("sangue") is mentioned nearby. Sellars gives us a literal blood-oath, however. Anna and Ottavio cut into their hands, and the camera lingers, in very tight shots, on the generous and sensual spreading of the life fluid. The image, which also suggests sexual union, is shocking and alienating. It reveals a masochism in Anna (and Ottavio) that will be borne out later and establishes the idea that she will resort to excessive behavior to get what she wants.

In *Giulio Cesare* we encounter blood in the suicidal Sesto, who harbors Oedipal insecurity about his ability to fill the shoes of his father, Pompey. Like the *Giovanni* example, the aria "Cara speme" concerns vengeance for the murder of a father. Unlike the Anna-Ottavio situation, it has stronger hints of masochism. The brief text, only two lines in length, makes no mention of blood. Sellars has Sesto cut deeply into his skin at the elbow and let it bleed. As the aria begins, a very tight shot shows blood pouring down his arm. The obsessive flow continues through the da capo, where close-ups depict the blood being rubbed on the shaft of his automatic weapon: a phallic image of his attempt to shore up masculine power for revenge. In the number as a whole, the progression of the blood imagery in relation to the music illustrates how Sellars reshapes the stylized dramaturgy of the da capo aria to create a more modern flow. At the same time the fragmented images resist linearity and create a motivic organization: an appropriate scheme for the motivic character of Baroque music.

Knives and guns in close-up become thematic. Cornelia's "Priva son" in *Giulio Cesare* presents disembodied shots of a revolver, which fills the screen. These alternate with recurring close-ups of hands and Sesto's face. Although Cornelia never fires the gun, the image creates suspense about her intentions, and suicidal urges resurface in "Deh piangete." In *Giovanni* weapons in close-up figure persistently. A vivid moment occurs when Zerlina threatens Leporello with a butcher knife as he tries to escape after the Sextet, in "Per queste due manine," a duet that is usually omitted. Zerlina brandishing a weapon makes her a member of the corrupt order, and she is sent to purgatory with the other characters.

Although weapons do not play a significant role in the imagery of *Così*, objects that fill the screen become a critical Leitmotif. Reflecting the slow pace of the drama and the focus on inner feeling, the camera likes to isolate suggestive body parts and linger, a prime example of the video camera as emotional thermometer. Entwining hands, sensual touching, slow petting—these are frequent images that fill the screen as "disembodied" entities as they assume an existence that departs from the singing bodies that contain them. The mesmerizing display reflects the sensuality of Mozart's music and typifies the stylization of the production as a whole. It visualizes the obsessive theme at the heart of *Così:* the confusing workings of erotic love (fig. 6.5).

Sellars also relates space to narrative through direct address, a manner of communication that is characteristic of television. Direct address strengthens the sense of a continuous present in television for it makes events seem live. Intimacy comes from the feeling that someone is speaking directly to you, in your own living room, under normal living conditions, outside a constructed narrative. While news programs furnish the best example of direct address, its influence can be felt in many areas of televisual discourse. In the Sellars's videos, direct address occurs mainly in the more abstract works, *Giulio Cesare* and *Così.* In the former, Sellars latches on to the reportage function of television and uses it as a framing device. Reportage takes literal form as a press conference in the story. Caesar, the American President, holds a press conference at poolside as the

Fig. 6.5 Janice Felty and James Maddalena in
Così fan tutte (1990). Directed by Peter Sellars.
(Photo by ORF. Courtesy Forum Media,
Dr. Eberhard Scheele)

opera opens. This sets the stage for multiple levels of discourse
in the production. It also places the medium of television at the
forefront of our attention—a pun given that we are watching
it at that very moment on television. The press conference returns at the end to close the production. Besides shattering the
fiction of the story, the gimmick emphasizes the similarities of
politics and performance.

In *Così* we meet a different kind of direct address. Assuming a thematic role, direct address is used several times to break
through the fiction of the story and create a familiarity that

is characteristic of television. In a recitative midway through Act I (before "Smanie implacabile"), Despina speaks directly to the camera over her hot chocolate as if she were doing a commercial. In no. 13, "Alla bella Despinetta," Ferrando and Guglielmo address the audience directly as they introduce their new personas. They mock themselves through a stylized pop routine, itself a kind of direct address (see also "Movement and Gesture" below).[38]

Even more striking is the direct address adopted by Don Alfonso in Act II. As the drama progresses into the depths of human feeling, Sellars reasserts a dual vision through an additional discourse and keeps the narrative from becoming maudlin. Shortly after the ethereal "Secondate, aurette amiche," a wind serenade with vocal accompaniment, the men make awkward attempts to woo the women. Alfonso points directly at the camera and says to the audience, in English, "Wipe that old-fashioned look off your face"—a crude remark in the prevailing sensual climate. This kind of address emphasizes a present. Alfonso returns to a direct mode later, in no. 30 ("Tutti accusan le donne"), which ends with the "Così fan tutte" words and music. An obvious place for a discourse removed from the fiction, Alfonso offers his wisdom on women. Repeating the earlier gesture, Alfonso points and looks directly at the camera during his disquisition. For the first "Così fan tutte" statement the camera zooms in close. Typical of Sellars's contrarian urges, for the second statement, which is sung tutti with Ferrando and Guglielmo, the group fragments and the players look down.

Direct address can affect the way we view singer and character. Andrew Goodwin's ideas on personas in MTV are suggestive. He notes that in MTV, where a sense of direct communication is strong, the star-image of the performer threatens to overwhelm the character in the narrative. Usually the situation projects a kind of doubled address that engages both character and singer simultaneously.[39] When the narrative in the Sellars's videos is interrupted with another mode of discourse, and especially one that speaks directly to the viewer, the integrity of the character is similarly challenged. Unlike the situation in MTV, however, the singers in the Sellars do not emit much star-image and thus their personas do not pose a major challenge to the characters. Nonetheless, the use of direct address hints at a real present and in this way the singer as an actual person is more likely to emerge here than anywhere else in the opera. The link accords with the emphasis on the present that is promoted by the updated setting.

MOVEMENT AND GESTURE

Movement and gesture form a major element in Sellars's narrative structures and are central to *Così* and *Giulio Cesare*. They function as a way of visualizing the music and offer counterpoint and contradiction as well as reinforcement. They provide a visual emphasis that serves several purposes. Movement and gesture fill in static moments in music and action, and hence their suitability to the slower pace of *Così* and *Giulio Cesare*. The added points of interest enrich the rhythmic aspects of time and expand the possibilities for the camera. Sometimes movement and gesture are used in the service of meaning, especially for creating parody or describing social groupings.

Eclectic and stylized, movement and gesture in the Sellars show the influence of many traditions, including Asian theater, American sign language, Greek tragedy, and contemporary popular music. They have been described as choreography,[40] a term that captures the expressiveness of the movements as well as their orderly nature. *Così fan tutte* offers interesting examples. Stylized movements act as a structural device that unifies the artifice at the beginning and end of the opera when the characters exist in their original guise. The gestures of the principals correlate nicely with their music: the sisters stuck in the convention of parallel thirds, each woman a slavish reflection of the other; and the men, especially near the end of the opera, similarly tied to each other. At the beginning of the opera, Ferrando and Guglielmo share similar musical gestures but are not stigmatized by the monotonous thirds they will have later.

The camera pinpoints subtle gestures throughout the production, and they become mesmerizing patterns of abstraction in their own right. Two examples occur in successive numbers of Act I, the farewell Quintet (no. 9) and the Trio "Soave sia il vento" (no. 10). Both numbers are static and leave ample room for visual insertions. The Quintet is an astonishing number. The first six measures present "robotic" music: music with a simple one-bar pattern that repeats over and over. The vocal line is not much different, with its halting notes on the beat that accompany the promise of the sisters to write every day. The lovers are automatons who are guided by the social script. Only when Fiordiligi manages an arching melody in bar 7 do harmony and pattern start to progress. Don Alfonso, meanwhile, punctures the artifice with a rhythmically active bass line in which he says he is dying of laughter.

Sellars visualizes the number with sensitive motions. Just as this F-major music circles back on itself, so the lovers engage in a slow circling motion. Like a do-si-do pattern in square dancing, the four form brief hand connections with different people as they wander around each other. This signals the fluidity of their relationships and the possibility for realignments among them. The dramatic significance of the choreography is underscored by the fact that Sellars returns to it in the last number of the opera. Here the glancing touches as the characters intermingle are more forceful. Unlike the trance-like farewell before the switch in identity, by the end the lovers have been taken to the depths of emotional involvement. They have made themselves vulnerable, and the abrupt turn-about after the ruse is revealed leaves them shell shocked. At the end they regress to the state of automaton; they are wind-up dolls that have lost their power, spinning and flailing out of control.

The Trio "Soave sia il vento" represents one of the most sublime moments in Mozart. Written in a reverential style reminiscent of the late motet "Ave verum corpus," the Trio has a lyrical text that prays for gentle winds and waves for the departed lovers. It is a dramatic "time out" that reveals the potential depths of their feelings. Several elements contribute to the musical delicacy: the affective key of E major, the use of muted strings, and the imitation of waves in the continual stream of thirds in first and second violins. Against this surface motion of sixteenth-notes occur the sustained lines of the voices, along with the slow-moving harmony. In the video Fiordiligi, Dorabella, and Don Alfonso stand in a line and look slightly away from the camera. With gentle hand motions that resemble sign language for the deaf, they physically describe the waves of the text and the music. The lighting becomes darker to imply that they have moved from the world of appearances to a reality at a deeper level. We also see hand gestures that tend toward masturbation, as the women rub their hands sensually along their bodies, in close-up. This hints at the latent passion that will be awakened later.[41]

Much of *Così* invokes parody in conjunction with straight drama, and Sellars deploys movement to stress the multiplicity of discourse at a given time. A good example occurs at the beginning of the finale to Act I. Having been introduced to the new men, the sisters lament their fate in poetic language. Musically the artifice of their sentiments is conveyed by the nearly parallel lines of the two; as at the start of the opera, they have no will of their own and are being manipulated by society's expectations. In the videos Fiordiligi and Dorabella accompany these sentiments with stylized hand and arm gestures that mock their characters. Soon the two men run in with knives and perform a mock suicide drinking ketchup and mustard (the text calls it poison), and all four enter into stylized movements that mock themselves and the contrived seriousness of the situation. At this point the persona of each is split, as it were, into the diegetic character and his/her observer. This creates distance, on several levels: between the story and its parody, the character and its observer, and the narratives and the viewer. Genuine feeling soon overtakes parody. As in "Soave" the lights dim, and sensuality rises to the fore as the lovers engage in serious petting.

Giulio Cesare also makes frequent use of movement and gesture. A moving example is "Son nata a lagrimar," a duet for Cornelia and Sesto that ends Act I. As in nos. 9 and 10 of *Così*, the music is slow moving and ripe for elaboration. Mother and son have been captured by Ptolemy's forces and the lament expresses their despair. Dotted rhythms underlie suspended dissonances and intertwining vocal lines that bring out the pair's hopelessness. As we saw in *Così*, the characters use very slow, stylized motions, which beautifully visualize the undulations of the music. Cornelia and Sesto bend over, and turn hand and arm gently to the musical flow. At the da capo their enemy Achilla joins in the slow movements and intertwining hand gestures, and Cornelia's words and gestures take on a pleading tone: another example of how Sellars resists self-reflexiveness in the da capo aria and creates a linear dramatic flow. A close-up intensifies the physical movement.

Stylized movement is also used to describe power relations. A striking example occurs at a famous place in *Don Giovanni*, the section of the finale to Act I where three orchestras with different tunes play simultaneously. Musically these contrast three class levels: upper class with the minuet, middle class with the contredanse, and lower class with the teitsch. Characters of the given class dance to their own music, with Giovanni a mobile element among the groups. This organization in the Mozart poses a problem for Sellars because traditional class structure is replaced by a hierarchy based on power in the ghetto. How will he choreograph these dances, which are tied closely to eighteenth-century social structures? His solution is to treat the music as a barometer of individual rage and frustration. Giovanni, relaxed and confident, moves erotically to the moderate pace of the contredanse and engages Zerlina in a sexual seduction that will lead to an attempted rape. His comfort level is signaled by his state of half nakedness (he wears only jockey shorts). The three visitors to the party—Anna, Ottavio, and Elvira—move at a slower pace that corresponds to the slower-moving Minuet. Their gestures, which consist mainly of violent finger-snapping and head thrown back, convey controlled anger and frustration. These are well-bred people who behave in public and hold emotion in check. Masetto, the most rhythmically active, moves to the livelier teitsch. His body seems out-of-control as arms flail wildly, body spins, and torso buckles over. The movements reflect deep frustration over Giovanni's appropriation of Zerlina and his inability to do anything about it. Without the constraints of an upbringing from the better part of town, Masetto feels free to physicalize his emotions and run amok. Even though each group of dancers has ties to a particular dance, the situation is fluid as a whole. Giovanni and Zerlina, for example, also dance to the slower pace of the minuet, just as the trio of antagonists moves to the contredanse too. This can happen because the three musical strains fit together rhythmically, and a dance step that fits one is likely to fit all three. In other words, Sellars choreographs the scene according to physical contrast more than social standing. The connections to the musical strains are flexible.

Movement and gesture often take on the trappings of popular culture to make larger statements about opera and its status as high art. Each production includes one or more segment in which movements of a pop singer occur and confuse boundaries between opera and mass culture. The postmodernist strategy mocks or at least questions the seriousness of opera, and interrupts the fiction of the narrative to cause the spectator to reflect on cultural meanings of the medium (actually media). *Don Giovanni* presents such a rupture in its first vocal number. Leporello's "Notte e giorno" shows Don Giovanni's henchman play-acting in his aria. Sporting black leather jacket, this denizen of the ghetto holds mike in hand and mimics the movements of a rock star as the accompaniment supposedly issues from the boom box nearby. He moves and gestures in time with the "beat" of the aria. The performative mode, in which he adopts another persona, suggests that his complaints in the aria against Don Giovanni are not to be taken seriously, and that he would like to become as famous as his boss through the celebrity that is conferred on rock stars. This spectacle drawn from popular culture provides an apt way for Sellars to update Leporello from an eighteenth-century servant to a hip modern figure.

In *Giulio Cesare* Nireno presents a pointed parody of opera in her aria "Chi perde un momento," near the start of Act II. She steps in front of the curtain and uses exaggerated rhetorical gestures to mock opera, especially Baroque stylization. In this campy arrangement, several layers are superimposed: operatic music rendered by a light voice in a popular context, conveyed through a parody of serious opera that mixes popular and traditional modes of presentation. As in the example from *Don Giovanni*, Nireno's aria implies that opera stars and pop stars use similar theatrical techniques when they perform. Nireno makes the more obvious point than Leporello, for she performs in front of a closed curtain and that places her further from the narrative. *Giulio Cesare* is a more stylized work than *Don Giovanni* and lends itself to a more mannered break.

Sellars also has groups of people assume the exaggerated movements and gestures of popular culture. In *Così*, "Una bella serenata" offers the gestures of consumer culture as it turns the trio among Ferrando, Guglielmo, and Don Alfonso into a commercial for beer. The three man vamp for the camera as they show off the product with exaggerated gestures—an act that satirizes popular culture and opera at the same time. The characters appear to be automatons caught in the clutches of consumer culture. Near the end of Act I, a stylized pop-group routine of the principals suggests that operatic conventions for ending an act—the tutti finale—take themselves too seriously. The physical movements adopted from popular culture in these examples help to prevent *Così* from becoming overly idealized. They demonstrate yet again that the opera can accommodate a wide range of meanings from a broad spectrum of society.

CULTURAL RESONANCE

Sellars's video productions are controversial, and as we noted at the start they have drawn strong reactions from critics and audiences. As interpretations that depend on popular culture, the videos have suggestive implications for the role and meaning of opera. In the final pages of the chapter I would like to consider some of the important cultural consequences of the videos. They shed light on Sellars's treatments but also open a window on the future of screen opera.

One issue concerns the notion of distraction, a term that has been applied to video culture and other media discourses that involve technology and popular culture.[42] Sellars's treatments of Mozart and Handel obviously belong to video culture, and the question is whether distraction is a meaningful concept to describe them. Distraction has several connotations. It implies a deflection from serious pursuits by something frivolous and fleeting. Distraction suggests entertainment that leads to short-time gratification rather than serious and lengthy reflection. Something that distracts stimulates briefly and causes interest to shift to another attractive stimulus. In Brechtian terms, distraction promotes a bourgeois mentality in its appreciation for the superficial. For Brecht the antidote is to highlight the superficial and create a distance that encourages reflection on the object. Only through a self-conscious separation from the stimulus can the proper perspective be gained.

How do these characteristics apply to the Sellars videos? Video watching, as compared to attending a live opera, fosters an aesthetic of the sound-byte. One can watch in small units and interrupt the experience with other kinds of activities. This accords with the short attention span that is encouraged by postmodernist culture. In the Sellars is the viewer distracted, in the sense of being entertained, by the quick pacing of the camera? Do the updated settings distract from serious contemplation? Do the light voices qualify as entertaining? In short, do Sellars's videos provide distraction from the notion and experience of traditional opera? And if they do, is this the main point of the videos?

I do not believe that this is the main point of Sellars's enterprise. Elements of distraction are directed mostly toward encouraging reflection on the meanings of the operas. Sellars may be clumsy or extreme at times in his narrative and representational choices, such as excesses in camera movement or violent imagery, but the fundamental purpose is apt and beneficial for the vitality of the works. I agree with Andrew Porter that I would not want these productions to be my only experience of the operas. Yet as new interpretations they offer valuable insights that affect the way we approach every other production we see.[43] In this light it is surprising to read Tambling's assessment of Sellars's videos. As a committed postmodernist Tambling favors new readings that encourage reflection on high art. Yet as in his harsh assessment of Syberberg's *Parsifal,* he views Sellars's project as a failure largely because the director respects opera.[44] He is correct, however, in identifying Sellars's respect for classic works; Sellars believes that opera has a great deal to teach us about ourselves. The surface details of the video versions may distract us momentarily but their underlying seriousness elicits as much sustained thought as a traditional production, if not more.

While Tambling faults Sellars for respecting opera too much, most of the criticism against Sellars comes from those who believe that he does not respect opera sufficiently. Some of the harshest attacks betray a moral outrage that goes beyond ordinary criticism—a reaction that bespeaks offense at a deep level. This may reflect a strong sense of ownership in the traditional canon and the values behind it.[45] Within these criticisms ownership is cast in terms of competing interests: America versus Europe, outsider versus insider, young versus old, high versus low culture, and present versus past. In the historical pair, the past becomes an entity that "owns" itself and cannot (and should not) be manipulated. This represents a false premise, of course, as the past cannot remain pure in a later representation. The issue becomes a matter of degree, and for some critics Sellars goes too far.[46] Even many proponents of screen opera in general feel that Sellars's video productions exceed the boundaries of its canon.

Sellars's videos represent Americanizations of European classics. These operas were composed in a certain cultural context, and their plots reflect European structures of class and deportment. I realize that to speak of Europe so generally is a distortion, but the point is that the works are not American. In a manner that recalls the imperialism that he satirizes in *Giulio Cesare*, Sellars has appropriated American culture and used it to take over masterpiece (European) culture. Considered in this light, his videos are subversive as well as decadent. The combination of original language and hip-American subtitles, at least in the English-language version of the videos, may be especially galling; I can only imagine the reaction of a historian of Italian literature to the arrangement.[47] Resistance to Sellars's project also rests on the fact that he is an outsider to the operatic establishment and that the counter-culture values he purveys threaten idealistic values that are promoted in traditional productions, especially love, heroism, and sacrifice. Sellars's values shift the object of identification from a European period in the past to an American era in the present. This can be disturbing.

Another perspective on ownership concerns the composers of these video operas. Unlike such figures as Wagner and Verdi, neither Mozart nor Handel is exclusive to any country. Their cultural malleability makes them more likely candidates for Sellars's transformation, even if such transformations are not well received. Mozart was Austrian but not well loved in Austria during his lifetime; he garnered success elsewhere. *Don Giovanni*, we may recall, was commissioned for Prague after the great success of *Figaro* there a year earlier. Mozart belonged to the pan-European culture of the late eighteenth century rather than any individual nation. In our time Mozart has become an international commodity whose "wares" belong to everyone. Nonetheless, it is not coincidental that Austrian television and a German production company decided to produce new versions of the Da Ponte operas for the Mozart bicentennial. Perhaps this is a fitting reappropriation of the operas. Yet the video versions retain a strong American identity and must have been an odd import for the Viennese studio audience at the taping and Austrian viewers in general. They become strangers to their favorite son as pride of place yields to American popular culture.[48] Handel has always been available for adoption given his split career in Germany, England, and elsewhere as a young man.

One of the inescapable paradoxes of the videos is their permanence as a document in the face of Sellars's belief that opera is a production-in-progress. The aesthetic resists the notion of a finished product, of a perfected art work. In Sellars's kind of updating it also means a contemporary setting that has to be up-to-the-minute. This is impossible in any production captured in a repeatable format, such as video. As of the present writing, almost a decade after their taping, the productions are beginning to look dated—they look like a late 1980s updating of an eighteenth-century work.[49] This is not a problem in and of itself but, as suggested earlier, it means an added layer of temporal meaning. Instead of the past and the present we have the distant past, the recent past, and our present from which to read the four. The conundrum underscores the postmodernist dilemma of having to reconcile its emphasis on the present, an evanescent point of time, with the fact that the present immediately becomes the past: a process made glaringly apparent by the speed of digital communication. Cyberspace, with its false sense of reality, is the perfect sign of the contradictory impulses at work in the desires for currency and tangibility.

Sellars's videos exude media culture as a hip, up-to-date phenomenon. But just as their content may become history, so may their format. Opera-as-video may become obsolete as it yields to opera-on-Internet and opera-on-CD-ROM (on DVD). Images will flash on the screen but it will probably be a computer-television screen that can gather opera from a wide variety of sources. Thus we end on a quizzical note regarding the paradoxes of writing about current phenomena, especially where technology is involved. Media culture is a moving target that is difficult to hit. Whatever the specific format, however, it seems unlikely that screen opera will fade from the cultural scene, predictions of the demise of classical music notwithstanding. As suggested by this book, opera on screen offers a wealth of possibilities for representation and interpretation. With any luck, socioeconomic conditions will continue to support projects and promote experimentation. This will probably lead to treatments we cannot imagine given the current state of technology. We should be encouraged by the prospect.

Notes

CHAPTER I

Introduction

1. Citron, in *The Musical Quarterly* 78/4 (Winter 1994): 700–41.
2. Jeremy Tambling wrote the first major study of opera on film, *Opera, Ideology and Film* (New York: St. Martin's Press, 1987), which unfortunately ignores music. His edited collection, *A Night in at the Opera: Media Representations of Opera* (London: John Libbey and Co., 1994), is more eclectic and includes a few studies that consider music. Two dissertations are devoted to the genre: Alexander Simpson, "Opera on Film: A Study of the History and Aesthetic Principles of a Hybrid Genre" (Ph.D. diss., University of Kentucky, 1990); and Jeongwon Joe, "Opera on Film, Film in Opera: Postmodern Implications of the Cinematic Influence on Opera" (Ph.D. diss., Northwestern University, 1998). Joe is co-editor with Rose Theresa of a forthcoming collection from Garland Press, *Between Opera and Cinema,* which includes contributions from a variety of disciplines. David Levin addresses opera on film in *Richard Wagner, Fritz Lang, and the Nibelungen: The Dramaturgy of Disavowal* (Princeton: Princeton University Press, 1998); a few pieces in his edited volume concern the genre: *Opera Through Other Eyes* (Stanford: Stanford University Press, 1993).

Major independent essays are Citron, "A Night at the Cinema"; H. Marshall Leicester, Jr., "Discourse and the Film Text: Four Readings of *Carmen,*" *Cambridge Opera Journal* 6/3 (November 1994): 245–82; and Joe, "Don Boyd's *Aria:* A Narrative Polyphony Between Music and Image," *Journal of Musicological Research* 18/4 (1999), forthcoming. Opera on screen is enjoying keen interest in several fields, as witnessed by presentations from a variety of disciplines at the "Dramaturgy" Conference of the Lyrica Society, at Northern Arizona University, Flagstaff, October 1–3, 1998, and the Society's session on film-opera at the annual meeting of the Modern Language Association, San Francisco, December 1998. In musicology, growing interest in the genre reflects a trend toward interdisciplinary topics and acceptance of research that incorporates aspects of popular culture.

3. Availability on video can be elusive, however. While major films and relays will probably remain in print on a steady basis, others may slip in and out and be difficult to track. Moreover, a given version may be available in one country and not another. Market conditions and licensing agreements play a role, but the different video formats of various countries complicate distribution. For example, a video sold in the United States in NTSC format will not play on a machine in England, which has its own format.

While I advocate video for viewing these works, I am aware of its drawbacks. Motion pictures especially suffer on video because the proportions of the television screen differ from those of cinema. Not only is part of the image excluded, but the focus and scale may be quite different from the original. Nonetheless, except for the "envelope" format that is increasingly being used for art films, this is probably the best we have at present.

4. For an intelligent description of the adaptation process see various discussions in Joseph Kerman, *Opera as Drama* (New York: Knopf, 1956).

5. In Abel's chapter "Opera Through the Media," in *Opera in the Flesh: Sexuality in Operatic Performance* (Boulder: Westview Press, 1996), 163–78.

6. In *Illuminations,* ed. Hannah Arendt, trans. Harry Zohn (New York: Schocken Books, 1969), 217–51.

7. In this set of critical essays, whenever a film director is reputed to pay attention to the source opera or opera in general, Tambling finds the project a failure. The most serious example is Syberberg's *Parsifal.* The volume suggests that opera cannot be redeemed, except possibly by film, for it is a regressive art form that is socially harmful. This theme also permeates Tambling's later books on opera: his contributions in his edited collection *A Night in at the Opera* and his monograph *Opera and the Culture of Fascism* (Oxford: Clarendon Press, 1996).

8. *Imre Fabian im Gespräch mit Jean-Pierre Ponnelle* (Zurich: Orell Füssli, 1983), 52.

9. See, for example, Dominique Jameux, "Le Film Opéra: Histoire d'une Illusion," *Diapason-Harmonie* No. 327 (May 1987): 60, and Gerhard Persché, "Lauter Mesalliancen: Welche Oper für welchen Film?" *Opernwelt* 25/12 (1984): 64–65.

CHAPTER 2

A Stroll Through History

1. Although entirely instrumental, Korngold's score has been described as being "perched right on the edge of operetta style," in George Burt, *The Art of Film Music* (Boston: Northeastern University Press, 1994), 206. For a detailed discussion see Martin Marks, "The Sound of Music," *The Oxford History of World Cinema*, ed. Geoffrey Nowell-Smith (Oxford: Oxford University Press, 1996), 251–55.

2. Juxtapositions of various kinds occur in avant-garde stage productions. For an account of the leading experimentalists of the 1980s and 1990s, especially in England and the Continent, see Tom Sutcliffe, *Believing in Opera* (Princeton: Princeton University Press, 1996).

3. Benjamin, "The Work of Art in the Age of Mechanical Reproduction," *Illuminations*, ed. Hannah Arendt, trans. Harry Zohn (New York: Schocken Books, 1969), 217–51.

4. For an exploration of the meanings of kitsch in relation to high and mass culture see Paul Coates, "Introduction: Kitsch, Art and the Audience," *Film at the Intersection of High and Mass Culture* (Cambridge: Cambridge University Press, 1994), 1–8. Theodor Adorno wrote about the dangers of "the culture industry." In an excellent summary essay, Miriam Hansen charts the changes in Adorno's views over his career and their relationship to conditions in cinema and society. See her "Introduction to Adorno, 'Transparencies on Film'" (1966), *New German Critique* No. 24–25 (1981–82): 186–98.

5. Naomi Greene, "Coppola, Cimino: The Operatics of History," *Film Quarterly* (Winter 1984–85): 28–29.

6. Mark LeFanu, "Pageants of Violence: Problems on the Staging of History," *Monogram* No. 6 (October 1975): 6–7.

7. Peter Franklin, "Movies as Opera (Behind the Great Divide)," *A Night in at the Opera: Media Representations of Opera*, ed. Jeremy Tambling (London: John Libbey, 1994), 77–112.

8. Franklin, "Movies as Opera," 88–89.

9. For a contemporary view of the role of opera in legitimating the new medium see E. H. Bierstadt, "Opera in Moving Pictures," *Opera Magazine*, October 1915, 30–32.

10. Schoenberg's views appear in "The Future of Opera" (1927) and "Art and the Moving Pictures" (1940), in *Style and Idea: Selected Writings of Arnold Schoenberg*, ed. Leonard Stein, trans. Leo Black (Berkeley: University of California Press, 1975), 336–37, 153–57.

11. For the view that cinema caused a demise in opera see Alex Ross, "An Unequal Partner Raises Its Lovely Voice," *The New York Times,* 12 March 1995, H15, H26, and H27.

12. As quoted in Edward Rothstein, "A Night at the Opera (Sans Song)," *The New York Times,* 13 March 1994, H29.

13. Kemp R. Niver, *The First Twenty Years: A Segment of Film History* (Los Angeles: Artisan Press, 1968), 74.

14. For more on Méliès see Alain Garel and Marc Salmon, "Cinéma et Opéra (II)," *La Revue du Cinéma* No. 429 (1987): 58; and "Trente Classiques du Film-Opéra," *L'Avant-Scène Opéra* No. 98 (May 1987): 54-55.

15. Richard Evidon, "Film," *The New Grove Dictionary of Opera* (London: Macmillan, 1992), vol. 2: 195. See also Walther Freisburger, *Theater im Film* (Emsdetten: Heinrich & J. Lechte, 1936), 42; and Gerhard R. Koch, "Vom Nutzen des Grenzgängerischen: Wie sich Oper und Film befruchten," *Oper-Film-Rockmusik: Veränderungen in der Alltagskultur,* ed. Hans-Klaus Jungenheinrich (Kassel: Bärenreiter, 1986), 18.

16. Bierstadt, "Opera in Moving Pictures," 30.

17. Evidon, "Film," 195.

18. Garel and Salmon, "Cinéma et Opéra," 59.

19. "Film Timed to Strauss Opera Hailed as New Era in Music," *The New York Times,* 12 January 1926, 1.

20. Koch, "Vom Nutzen," 23-24.

21. For a fuller discussion of this period see Evidon, "Film," 195-96. For an excellent list of early titles, as well as those over the entire history of filmed opera, see the Filmography at the end of Garel and Salmon, "Cinéma et Opéra," 68-79. Probably the most complete list, continually updated as a database, appears in IMZ, *Opera on Screen: Ein Projekt im Auftrag des Oesterreichischen Bundesministeriums für Wissenschaft und Forschung,* 2 vols. (Vienna: IMZ, 1995).

22. This project and research are discussed in Rothstein, "A Night at the Opera."

23. The description in terms of a shadow was apparently coined in the silent era. It is used, for example, by Bierstadt, in 1915, in his "Opera in Moving Pictures," 15.

24. For a summary see Martin Marks, "Music and the Silent Film," *The Oxford History of World Cinema,* 183-92.

25. Harrison Lawler, "Opera on the Screen," *The Etude* 34/5 (May 1936), 283-84. On the movie theaters see also Rothstein, "A Night at the Opera."

26. Antheil, "On the Hollywood Front," *Modern Music* 14/2 (1936), 48.

27. "Trente Classiques du Film-Opéra," *L'Avant-Scène Opéra* No. 98 (May

1987), 63–64 (by "C. B.," probably Claude Beylie). See also the discussion of the film in Alexander Simpson, "Opera on Film: A Study of the History and the Aesthetic Principles and Conflicts of a Hybrid Genre" (Ph.D. diss. University of Kentucky, 1990), 21–22.

28. Evidon, "Film," 196–97, and Herbert Graf, *Opera for the People* (Minneapolis: University of Minnesota Press, 1951), 212–13.

29. Garel and Salmon, "Cinéma et Opéra," 62.

30. See Peter Conrad, *A Song of Love and Death: The Meaning of Opera* (New York: Poseidon Press, 1987), 266–67; Koch, "Vom Nutzen," 25; Evidon, "Film," 196; and for a contemporary account Trude Weiss, "The First Opera-Film," *Close-Up* (December 1932), 242–43.

31. Koch, "Vom Nutzen," 25.

32. Koch, "Vom Nutzen," 25–26. For a postmodernist interpretation see Lawrence Kramer, "The Singing Salami: Unsystematic Reflections on the Marx Brothers' *A Night at the Opera*," *A Night in at the Opera*, ed. Tambling, 253–65.

33. "Trente Classiques," 66.

34. "Trente Classiques," 64–65.

35. Comuzio, "Opéra et Cinéma: Des Origines aux Années Soixante," *L'Avant-Scène Opéra* No. 98 (May 1987), 9. Originally written for an Italian exhibit, the essay is an excellent portrayal of Gallone and the Italian tradition in general. Gallone's own ideas appear in his essay, "Il valore della musica nel film e l'evoluzione dello spettacolo lirico sullo schermo," *Musica e Film*, ed. S. G. Biamonte (Rome: Edizioni Dell' Ateneo, 1959), 203–06.

36. Visconti was intimately familiar with opera, having directed it regularly on the stage. For more on the operatic dimension of his films see Koch, "Vom Nutzen," 27–29.

37. Altman, *The American Film Musical* (Bloomington: Indiana University Press, 1987), 139.

38. See Otto Preminger, *Preminger: An Autobiography* (New York: Doubleday, 1977), 133–37; and for a summary of Hammerstein's views, see Susan McClary, *Georges Bizet: Carmen* (Cambridge: Cambridge University Press, 1992), 131–32.

39. James Baldwin, "Life Straight in De Eye; Carmen Jones: Film Spectacular in Color," *Commentary* 19/1 (January 1955): 74–77.

40. See also Susan McClary's penetrating discussion in *Georges Bizet: Carmen*, 130–35. Among the more interesting treatments of *Carmen Jones* are Garel and Salmon in "Cinéma et Opéra, III," *La Revue du Cinéma* No. 430 (1987): 78–79.

41. Technically speaking, a first version bowed at a theater at Columbia University; it was the revised version that ran on Broadway.

42. "Trente Classiques," 71. Siegfried Kracauer, who is generally negative toward cinematic opera, criticizes the film's combination of cinematic realism and operatic musical style, in *Theory of Film: The Redemption of Physical Reality* (London: Oxford University Press, 1960), 154–55.

43. As quoted in Bruce Archibald, "Menotti," *The New Grove Dictionary of Opera*, vol. 3: 332.

44. Her review appears in "Ivan the Terrible, Part 1" entry in *Cinemania 96* CD-ROM (Microsoft Corporation, c. 1992–1995).

45. Peter Symcox, "The Four Faces of Opera," *Opera Quarterly* 3 (1985), 2.

46. This is implied although not stated explicitly in Graf, *Opera for the People*, 217.

47. Useful sources are Graf, "Opera in Television," *Opera for the People*, 219–31; and Adler, "Opera on Television: The Beginning of an Era," *Musical America* 72 (February 1952): 29. For the following discussions I am indebted especially to Brian Rose's rich survey of the United States, "Opera on Television," *Television and the Performing Arts: A Handbook and Reference Guide to American Cultural Programming* (New York: Greenwood Press, 1986), 127–88. Lionel Salter's general historical survey is also excellent, "Television," *The New Grove Dictionary of Opera*, vol. 4: 680–82.

48. As conveyed in Rose, "Opera and Television," 129.

49. Salter, "Television," 680.

50. Adler, "Opera on Television: The Beginning of an Era," 29.

51. "Menotti Opera, the First for TV, Has Its Premiere," *The New York Times*, 25 December 1951, Section I, p. 1, as excerpted in Rose, "Opera on Television," 139. For an extended discussion of *Amahl* see Jennifer Barnes, "Television Opera: A Non History," *A Night in at the Opera*, 27–38.

52. Salter, "Television," 680. A thorough, international listing of opera on television through the 1960s is Helga Bertz-Dostal, *Oper im Fernsehen*, 2 vols. (Vienna: Gesellschaft für Musiktheater, 1970).

53. Adler, "Opera on Television," 29.

54. Rose, "Opera on Television," 142–43.

55. Philip Reed, "*Billy Budd* on Television," *Benjamin Britten: Billy Budd*, ed. Mervyn Cooke and Philip Reed (Cambridge: Cambridge University Press, 1993), 152.

56. Rose, "Opera on Television," 147.

57. Barnes, "Television Opera," 27.

58. Rose, "Opera on Television," 159. Jeremy Tambling discusses pacifism in

the work as well as its suitability for the medium of television, in *"Owen Wingrave* and Television Opera," *Opera, Ideology and Film* (New York: St. Martin's Press, 1987), 113-25. A more recent interpretation is Shannon McKellar, "Music, Image and Ideology in Benjamin Britten's *Owen Wingrave:* Conflict in a Fissured Text," paper presented at the Annual Meeting of the American Musicological Society, Phoenix, October 1997.

59. Arnold Whittall, "Owen Wingrave," *The New Grove Dictionary of Opera,* vol. 3: 803. The general decline in commissioned opera for television is discussed by Barnes, "Television Opera: A Non History," 25-51.

60. For a perceptive analysis of Browning's style, especially in comparison to that of Brian Large, see Brooks Riley, "Camera Angles," *Opera News* 54 (June 1990): 12-15.

61. Rolf Liebermann, "Mittelmäßige Massenmedien," *Erlebnisse und Erfahrungen vor, auf, und hinter die Bühne grosser Musiktheater* (Bern: Scherz, [1977]), 295.

62. Valuable sources on Liebermann are Joachim Hess, "Oper im Fernsehen," *Musica* 32/3 (1978): 237-40; Liebermann, "Mittelmäßige Massenmedien," 287-96; and "Liebermann et le film: Un nouveau monde pour l'opéra," *L'Avant-Scène Opéra* No. 36 (September-October 1981): 126-31.

63. Hess, "Oper im Fernsehen," 238.

64. Interview with Heinz Oepen, trans. Mary Whittall, in booklet in *Le Nozze di Figaro* video that was distributed in Britain (DGG 072 403-1); the interview originally appeared in the pamphlet *Musik im ZDF* 1976/77.

65. The best presentation of Ponnelle's views appears in *Imre Fabian im Gespräch mit Jean-Pierre Ponnelle* (Zurich: Orell Füssli, 1983), in the section "Film, Fernsehen, Videoplatte" (50-55); these pages were reprinted in *Opernwelt* 26 (1985): 81-83.

66. German critic Gerhard Persché, for example, who is generally negative toward films of operas, finds *Butterfly* one of the best examples of the genre, in "Lauter Mesalliancen?", *Opernwelt* 25/12 (1984): 64-65. Helen Greenwald discusses the film in her comparative paper, "Beyond Exoticism: Cio-Cio San's Screen and the 'Uses of Convention,'" presented at the International Musicological Society Convention, London, August 1997.

67. For a study of interior singing in Ponnelle's *Figaro,* see Marcia J. Citron, "The Elusive Voice: Absence and Presence in Jean-Pierre Ponnelle's film *Le Nozze di Figaro,*" *Between Opera and Cinema,* eds. Jeongwon Joe and Rose M. Theresa, Garland Press, forthcoming.

68. Critique appears in movie reviews, television reviews, opera reviews, and studies of Ingmar Bergman. Among the more interesting are Tambling,

"Opera as 'Culinary Art': Bergman's *Magic Flute*," *Opera, Ideology, and Film*, 126-39; Peter G. Davis, "Ingmar Bergman's Magic Fluke," *The New York Times*, 9 November 1975, Section 2, 1 and 17; Pauline Kael, "Walking Into Your Childhood," *The New Yorker* 51 (17 November 1975): 169-72; Rick Shale, "The Magic Flute," *Magill's Survey of Cinema: Foreign Language Films*, vol. 4, ed. Frank N. Magill (Englewood Cliffs: Salem Press, 1985), 1895-1900; Paisley Livingston, *Ingmar Bergman and the Rituals of Art* (Ithaca: Cornell University Press, 1982), especially 233-47; and "Bergman on Opera," *Opera News* 13 (5 May 1962): 12-14. Jeongwon Joe devotes a chapter to the film in her study, "Opera on Film, Film in Opera: Postmodern Implications of the Cinematic Influence on Opera" (Ph.D. diss., Northwestern University, 1998).

69. Especially by Tambling, "Opera as 'Culinary Art.'"

70. It is true that Schikaneder's libretto contains misogynist lines about how women talk too much and need a man's steadying hand. For stimulating studies on the maternal-paternal struggle in the opera see Catherine Clément, *Opera or the Undoing of Women*, trans. Betsy Wing (Minneapolis: University of Minnesota Press, 1988), 70-76; and from an anthropological perspective L. R. Hiatt, "Queen of Night, Mother-Right, and Secret Male Cults," *Musicology* (Journal of the Musicological Society of Australia) 5 (1979): 191-204. For these issues in the Bergman see Rose Laub Coser, "The Principle of Patriarchy: The Case of *The Magic Flute*," *Signs* 4/2 (Winter 1978): 337-48.

71. See Jeffrey Gantz, "Mozart, Hoffmann, and Ingmar Bergman's *Vargtimmen*," *Film/Literature Quarterly* 8/2 (1980): 104-15.

72. "Walking Into Your Childhood," 169.

73. See chapter 4 for a study of Syberberg's film *Parsifal*.

74. Earlier examples also exist, of course, such as the 1951 *Tales of Hoffmann* and *The Medium*, and the remarkable *Moses und Aron* of 1974, described in *L'Avant-Scène Opéra* as "the anti-Zeffirelli" in its dry style devoid of spectacle ("Trente Classiques," 75). But these were scattered chronologically and do not form a group. Joe notes the coincidence of the onset of postmodernism and the modern opera film, in "Opera on Film, Film in Opera," 7-8.

75. See, for example, a book devoted to the film that appeared when the film was released, Pierre-Jean Rémy's *Don Giovanni: Mozart-Losey* (Paris: A. Michel, 1979).

76. "Complete" is an ambiguous concept for this opera. The version we know today is actually a problematic merging of the original Prague version, of 1787, and the version for Vienna in May 1788. For details see the

Commentary in the *Neue Mozart Ausgabe;* for a summary Julian Rushton, "Don Giovanni," *The New Grove Dictionary of Opera* (London: Macmillan, 1992), vol. 1: 1206.

77. Alain Duault, "Le Film d'Opéra: Une Histoire, Des Questions," *L'Avant-Scène Opéra* No. 98 (1987): 5.

78. Considerations of space preclude a fuller exploration, but suffice it to say that the functions are probably not as clear-cut as they seem. For example, Ronnie's action recalls the opera visit the previous evening, and the background operatic music for Loretta could serve as a link to Ronnie as well as reflect her musing on the emotional experience at the Met the night before.

79. For *Malibran* see Ulrike Sieglohr, "Excess and Yearning: The Operatic in Werner Schroeter's Cinema," *A Night in at the Opera,* 195–215.

80. White, "Opera, Politics and Television: Bel Canto by Satellite," *A Night in at the Opera,* 267–94.

81. It is interesting to note that some stage productions of *Tosca* have attempted to reproduce the Roman interiors, as in Zeffirelli's lavish production at the Met, first staged in the mid 1980s and still in use in the 1990s.

82. For background see Boyd's interview with Lawrence Mass, "The Next Frontier for Opera," *Opera Monthly,* June 1988: 43–50; and for a review Richard Corliss, "Opera for the Inoperative," *Time,* 2 May 1988, 79.

83. For a postmodernist reading see the chapter on *Aria* in Joe's "Opera on Film, Film in Opera."

CHAPTER 3
A Matter of Belief: *Otello* on Film and Television

1. For example, Joseph Kerman, in his influential monograph *Opera as Drama* (New York: Vintage Books, 1956), 129–67.

2. Zeffirelli borrowed a few touches from this version. Two appear at the beginning: the stone "lions of Venice" as a visual motif over the credits, and the ship tossing on the waves in the storm.

3. Among the highlights are two productions of Puccini works: a *La Bohème* of 1982, from Covent Garden, directed for television by Brian Large; and a *Turandot* of 1987, from the Met, directed for television by Kirk Browning. Another production of *Bohème* that he designed, this one a 1965 studio-film version produced by Von Karajan, is also available on video. See chapter 2 for a discussion of the 1965 and 1987 productions and a still from *Turandot.*

4. For an exploration of the film see Roxanne Elizabeth Solomon, "A Critical Study of Franco Zeffirelli's 'La Traviata' " (D.Ed. diss., Columbia University Teachers College, 1987). This is a painstaking description of each camera shot rather than a critical interpretation. For a truly critical study, in both senses, see Jeremy Tambling, "Between the Spectacle and the Specular: *La Traviata*," *Opera, Ideology and Film* (New York: St. Martin's Press, 1987), 176–93.

5. Zeffirelli gives various reasons for making the film. See the chapter on *Otello* in *Zeffirelli: An Autobiography* (New York: Weidenfeld & Nicolson, 1986), 327–39; he sees the film on a scale equivalent to the great Hollywood epics (332). See also two interviews in *L'Avant-Scène Opéra* No. 90 (1986): 200–11, and No. 98 (1987): 99–101.

6. Interview in documentary, "Zeffirelli's *Otello*."

7. My points about television theory come largely from Ellis. See his excellent discussion, "Broadcast TV as Sound and Image," in *Film Theory and Criticism: Introductory Readings*, 4th ed., eds. Gerald Mast, Marshall Cohen, Leo Braudy (New York: Oxford University Press, 1992), 341–50; the essay comes from Ellis's *Visible Fictions* (1982).

8. Ellis, "Broadcast TV as Sound and Image," 342; Chion, *Audio-Vision: Sound on Screen,* trans. Claudia Gorbman (New York: Columbia University Press, 1994), 157. Rick Altman adds new perspectives to Ellis's theories, in Altman's "Television/Sound," *Studies in Entertainment: Critical Approaches to Mass Culture,* ed. Tania Modleski (Bloomington: Indiana University Press, 1986), 39–54.

9. Jean-Michel Brèque, "Le Film-Opéra: Vers Une Forme Cinématographique Autonome," *L'Avant-Scène Opéra* No. 98 (1987), 32.

10. Max Loppert, review of the film in *Opera* 37 (November 1986): 1318.

11. Leighton Kerner, "Messing with the Moor," *The Village Voice* 31 (30 September 1986), 70.

12. Maazel has considerable experience in film-opera, having also made the recording for Losey's *Don Giovanni* and Rosi's *Carmen* (for both see chapter 5).

13. Christopher Palmer, "Film Music," *The New Grove Dictionary of Music and Musicians,* 20 vols., ed. Stanley Sadie (London: Macmillan, 1980), vol. 6:550.

14. *Music for the Films: A Handbook for Composers and Conductors,* as discussed in Claudia Gorbman, *Unheard Melodies: Narrative Film Music* (Bloomington: Indiana University Press, 1987), 76–77. See also Hanns Eisler (and Theodor Adorno), *Composing for the Films* (New York: Oxford University Press, 1947), 92–93 and 109–11.

15. As stated in a BBC/Arts & Entertainment documentary on the making of the film, "Zeffirelli's *Otello:* From Stage to Screen" (1986).

16. Zeffirelli, *Autobiography,* 332. Maazel's willingness is curious in light of a published statement elsewhere, where he calls himself "the composer's *representative,* . . . a lawyer that defends the interests of the composer." See Maazel, "Je Suis L'Avocat Du Compositeur," *L'Avant-Scène Opéra* No. 98 (1987), 106.

17. Documentary "Zeffirelli's *Otello.*"

18. Interview in *L'Avant-Scène Opéra* No. 98 (1987), 100. For severe criticism of Iago's cuts, see the review by François Chevassu, *La Revue du Cinéma* No. 419 (1986), 25.

19. Brèque, "L'*Otello* de Zeffirelli," *L'Avant-Scène Opéra* No. 90 (1986), 215.

20. For an excellent critical treatment of the workings of film music, see the review essay by James Buhler and David Neumeyer in *Journal of the American Musicological Society* 47/2 (Summer 1994): 364–85.

21. For more on short forms, see Eisler/Adorno, *Composing for the Films,* 92–93.

22. Gorbman, *Unheard Melodies,* 5.

23. Philosopher Jerrold Levinson offers a stimulating theorization of the narrative sources of diegetic and non-diegetic music, in "Film Music and Narrative Agency," *Post-Theory: Reconstructing Film Studies,* eds. David Bordwell and Noël Carroll (Madison: University of Wisconsin Press, 1996), 248–82.

24. See perceptive discussions in Caryl Flinn, *Strains of Utopia: Gender, Nostalgia, and Hollywood* (Princeton: Princeton University Press, 1992); Gorbman, *Unheard Melodies;* and Kathryn Kalinak, *Settling the Score: Music and the Classic Hollywood Film* (Madison: University of Wisconsin Press, 1992), especially chapter 2. The Eisler/Adorno *Composing for the Films* is an important socialist analysis of the issue. See also chapter 2 of the present study.

25. Gorbman, *Unheard Melodies,* 55.

26. The documentary on the making of *Otello* shows some of the difficulties that occurred during shooting, particularly at Otello's first entrance on the magnificent "Esultate." Because of problems in lip-synchronization, Domingo's first few notes are filmed as a long-shot. Hardly visible, he scarcely seems like a victorious warrior. This is certainly a weak spot in the film. Moreover, the volume is inexplicably loud, even though he is far away, and it doesn't change when the camera shoots him (and his voice) in close-up.

27. Many reviewers criticize the volume level of the effects, which often com-

pete for attention or drown out the music. See, for example, Elizabeth Forbes, "Film," *Musical Times* 127 (December 1986), 704.

28. Tambling, *Opera, Ideology and Film*, 176. For other perspectives on the influence of the film musical see my discussion of Rosi's *Carmen* in chapter 5.

29. A preference for discrete moments in opera rather than a dramatic whole has been ascribed to "opera queens," in Mitchell Morris, "Reading as an Opera Queen," *Musicology and Difference: Gender and Sexuality in Music Scholarship*, ed. Ruth Solie (Berkeley: University of California Press, 1993), 197–98. This aspect of gay culture might have a connection with homoerotic features of Zeffirelli's film, a subject beyond the scope of the present study. See note 64 below.

30. For an overview of the workings of the relay telecast see Brooks Riley, "Camera Angles," *Opera News* 54 (June 1990): 12–15; Brian Large, "Filming, Videotaping," *The New Grove Dictionary of Opera*, ed. Stanley Sadie (London: Macmillan, 1992), vol. 2: 200–04; Lionel Salter, "Television," *The New Grove Dictionary of Opera*, vol. 4: 680–82; and Claude Brunel, "Opéra et Télévision," *L'Avant-Scène Opéra* No. 98 (1987): 90–93.

31. For a related point on the labor needed to produce opera, see the discussion of Syberberg's *Parsifal* in chapter 4.

32. The Royal Opera House itself is not exempt from domestic problems, as revealed in the documentary produced by the BBC, "The Royal Opera House," which aired on PBS in 1997. See also Rodney Milnes, "A Battle Royal, Smashingly Operatic," *The New York Times*, 5 April 1998, "Arts and Leisure" Section, 1 and 42.

33. Riley, "Camera Angles," 14.

34. James Jolly, "Video," *The New Grove Dictionary of Opera*, vol. 4: 988.

35. Max Loppert, contributor to the British magazine *Opera*, notes that Moshinsky's productions "are distinguished by their sharp intellectual focus"; see his entry on the director in *The New Grove Dictionary of Opera*, vol. 3: 483. For Large, see Riley, "Camera Angles," 15; Brunel, "Opéra et Télévision"; and Brian G. Rose, "Opera on Television," *Television and the Performing Arts: A Handbook and Reference Guide to American Cultural Programming* (New York: Greenwood Press, 1986), 164–70. In addition, the entry "Filming, Videotaping" in *The New Grove Dictionary of Opera*, which Large authored, illuminates his preferred techniques.

36. These observations are tempered by the use of "big-screen" television. This not only shows the influence of cinema in the home, but it has also affected the composition of shots for television. Some types of programs,

especially news and sports, now have simultaneous points of interest, for example, multiple images and boxes with information. This technique also derives from visual organization on the Internet and the general concepts of graphic-user-interface and pull-down menus.

37. Television relays require brighter lighting than a stage production, by as much as 25 percent (Riley, "Camera Angles," 14, and Large, "Filming, Videotaping," 203).

38. Large, "Filming, Videotaping," 201-02.

39. In the documentary on the making of the Zeffirelli film. Several reviewers of the Rosi criticize Domingo for his stiffness. See also chapter 5.

40. According to Riley, Large uses close-up much less often than Kirk Browning, the other major director of opera relays. Browning, whose experience dates from the 1950s (see chapter 2), was associated with truly live relays and still did them as of the date of Riley's article—a situation that John Goberman, his producer, calls "an aesthetic of risk" ("Camera Angles," 14-15).

41. For more on direct address with respect to televised opera, see chapter 6.

42. In the documentary on the making of the Zeffirelli film.

43. Eduard Hanslick, Review of *Otello*, originally in *Neue Freie Presse*, [April] 1887; quoted in Hans Busch, ed., *Verdi's Otello and Simon Boccanegra: In Letters and Documents*, (Oxford: Clarendon Press, 1988), 2:711-12.

44. Originally in *The Anglo-Saxon Review*, March 1901, reprinted in Busch, *Verdi's Otello*, 2:737.

45. Zeffirelli, *Autobiography*, 339.

46. Quoted in Robert Levine, "Zeffirelli's *Otello:* The Italian Director's Film of Verdi's Masterpiece is Certain to Create Controversy," *Ovation* 7 (October 1986), 32.

47. The mid-nineteenth-century Shakespearean tradition in Italy often presented Othello as a savage, especially when played by actor Ernesto Rossi. The portrayal was strongly influenced by A. W. Schlegel's earlier conception of the character, which brought matters of race to the fore. See the excellent discussion in James Hepokoski, "Shakespeare Reinterpreted," *Giuseppe Verdi: Otello* (Cambridge: Cambridge University Press, 1987), 164-72. My thanks to the members of the "Opera 1875-1925" seminar at Rice University in spring 1998, especially Rebecca Morris, for emphasizing the significance of this tradition.

48. As in the film *Brother Sun, Sister Moon* (1972); the television series *Jesus of Nazareth* (1976); and a televised production of *Otello* (1976) at La Scala, also with Domingo, apparently the basis of the Catholic interpretation

in the 1986 film. Peter Conrad offers perceptive comments on Catholic themes and gestures in Zeffirelli's *Traviata* film, in *A Song of Love and Death: The Meaning of Opera* (New York: Poseidon Press, 1988), 304.

49. Andrew Porter, "Verdi, Giuseppe," *The New Grove Dictionary of Musicians*, vol. 19: 642, 657.

50. See, for example, Katherine Bergeron's postmodernist reading, "How to Avoid Believing (While Reading Iago's Credo)," in *Reading Opera*, eds. Arthur Groos and Roger Parker (Princeton: Princeton University Press, 1988), 184–99. See also Julian Budden, *The Operas of Verdi*, 3 vols. (New York: Oxford University Press, 1981), vol. 3: 359; Peter Conrad, *Romantic Opera and Literary Form* (Berkeley: University of California Press, 1977), 66; William E. Grim, "Iago as Archetype: Radical Evil in Opera," paper presented at Annual Meeting of the Modern Language Association, New York, December 1992; Hepokoski, *Giuseppe Verdi: Otello*, 145–48, 181–83; his "Boito and F.-V Hugo's 'Magnificent Translation': A Study in the Genesis of the *Otello* Libretto," *Reading Opera*, 55–59; Kerman, *Opera as Drama*, 140; Frits Noske, "Otello: Drama Through Structure," *The Signifier and the Signified: Studies in the Operas of Mozart and Verdi* (The Hague: Nijhoff, 1977), 133–70; Benedict Sarnaker, "*Otello:* Drama and Music," *Otello, Giuseppe Verdi*, English National Opera Guide No. 7 (London: John Calder, 1981), 15–16; and Gary Schmidgall, "Incredible Credo?" *Shakespeare and Opera* (New York: Oxford University Press, 1990), 240–50.

51. Letter from Verdi to Boito, 3 May 1884, in which he praises the poet for his verses; in Busch, *Verdi's Otello*, 1:163.

52. From the Ricordi Production Book, as translated in Busch, *Verdi's Otello*, 2:485.

53. Quoted in Porter, "Verdi," 19:653.

54. Several reviewers criticize the Catholic theme; see especially Forbes, "Film," *Musical Times* 127 (December 1986), 704; and Thomas Voigt, "TV-Tagebuch: Zeffirellis 'Otello' Film," *Opernwelt* 29 (July 1988), 71. In contrast, Gerhard Persché finds it highly apt, in "Rumo(h)ren im Kastell: Franco Zeffirellis Film nach Verdi, 'Otello,'" *Opernwelt* 27/11 (1986), 57. For a musicological study that places metaphors of religion at the heart of the opera see James Parakilas, "Religion and Difference in Verdi's *Otello*," *The Musical Quarterly* 81/3 (Fall 1997): 371–92.

55. See, for example, William van Watson, "Shakespeare, Zeffirelli, and the Homosexual Gaze," *Literature/Film Quarterly* 20/4 (1992): 308–25; Tambling, "Between the Spectacle and the Specular: *La Traviata*," *Opera*,

Ideology and Film, 176–93; and various passages in Zeffirelli's *Autobiography.*

56. In general, Moshinsky opposes trendy postmodern productions and is committed to emphasizing the "human values" in Verdi; see his "Verdi: A Pox on Post-Modernism," *Opera* 43 (October 1992): 1164–68.

57. Ellis, "Broadcast TV as Sound and Image," 347.

58. Ellis, "Broadcast TV as Sound and Image," 344 and 347. Ellis uses the term "viewer" for television and "spectator" for television, believing that the former captures the casualness of television while the latter implies more intense looking (347).

59. Flinn, *Strains of Utopia,* 48.

60. Peter Conrad believes that Zeffirelli's opera productions in general sacralize the past, in *A Song of Love and Death,* 273–74 and 303–04. Adorno sees opera as a genre that glorifies the past and induces in the spectator a desire to belong to the past. See the chapter "Opera" in his *Introduction to the Sociology of Music,* trans. E. B. Ashton (New York: Seabury Press, 1976), 81–84.

61. See the documentary "Zeffirelli's *Otello.*"

62. For a contrasting view see Chevassu, *La Revue du Cinéma,* 25.

63. In linking regressive musical language with psychological regression, I am not suggesting an absolute or unitary coding between the two. In this instance, however, the obvious movement away from the direction of the tonic aptly expresses the textual and psychoanalytic processes of regression already implied by the libretto.

64. David Lawton, citing Alessandro Luzio's *Carteggi Verdiani,* vol. 2 (Rome: Reale Accademia d'Italia, 1935), 97, notes that the original draft of the libretto cast an ominous shadow over the Duet by having Iago mutter some lines in the background ("On the 'Bacio' Theme in *Otello,*" *19th-Century Music* 1 [1977–78], 217–18). For other discussions of the Duet see Conrad, "Operatic Shakespeare," especially 67–69, in *Romantic Opera and Literary Form* (Berkeley: University of California Press, 1977); Hepokoski, *Otello,* various pages; Roger Parker and Matthew Brown, "Ancora un bacio: Three Scenes from Verdi's *Otello,*" *19th-Century Music* 9 (1985–86): 50–62; Harold Powers, "*Otello* I.2, 3: A Case Study in Multivalent Analysis," paper presented at the Verdi-Wagner Conference, Cornell University, October 1984; and Sarnaker, *"Otello,"* 15. Another flashback occurs in the film, during Iago's recounting of Cassio's dream. Dubbed sensational by many reviewers, the scene implies homoerotic attractions among the leading male characters. For homoeroticism in Zeffirelli's work

in general see Van Watson, "Shakespeare, Zeffirelli, and the Homosexual Gaze." For a brief discussion of this flashback see my essay, "A Night at the Cinema," 723.

65. For a perceptive analysis of the theories of Kristeva and others, see especially chapters 3 and 4 of Kaja Silverman's *The Acoustic Mirror: The Female Voice in Psychoanalysis and Cinema* (Bloomington: Indiana University Press, 1988). See also Tambling, "Film Aspiring to the Condition of Opera," in *Opera, Ideology and Film*, 51–65; and Michel Poizat, *The Angel's Cry: Beyond the Pleasure Principle in Opera*, trans. Arthur Denner (Ithaca: Cornell University Press, 1992). Flinn's discussions in relation to film music are helpful, in *Strains of Utopia*, especially the chapter "The Man Behind the Muse: Music and the Lost Maternal Object," 51–69. For additional implications of the female operatic voice, see Carolyn Abbate, "Opera; or the Envoicing of Women," *Musicology and Difference*, 225–58.

66. Flinn, *Strains of Utopia*, 68.

67. Doane, "The Love Story," *The Desire to Desire*, 107.

68. This idea is based on Abbate's discussion of Elektra, in "Elektra's Voice: Music and Language in Strauss's Opera," *Richard Strauss Elektra*, ed. Derrick Puffett (Cambridge: Cambridge University Press, 1989), especially 125–27. See also my discussions in chapter 4 of voice-character relationships for Olympia and other figures in the film-opera *The Tales of Hoffmann*. For an excellent summary of the genesis of the "Willow Song," see Linda B. Fairtile, "Verdi's First 'Willow Song': New Sketches and Drafts for *Otello*," *Nineteenth Century Music* 19/3 (Spring 1996): 213–30.

69. Grover-Friedlander, "*Amor Mortis:* Death and Femininity in Verdi's Operas," paper presented at the second Feminist Theory and Music Conference, Eastman School of Music, June 1993. She also notes that Desdemona is turning to the world of women, not only in this number but in the "Ave Maria" as well.

70. Scheman, "Missing Mothers."

71. Of interest is a recent play in which Desdemona is everything Iago accuses her of being: Paula Vogel's "Desdemona: A Play About a Handkerchief." See Ben Brantley's review in *The New York Times*, 13 November 1993, 10.

72. For a feminist interpretation of woman's visuality in cinema that is pertinent to this situation see Laura Mulvey, *Visual and Other Pleasures* (Bloomington: Indiana University Press, 1989), x–xi.

73. As in the theories of Jean-Louis Comolli, as discussed in Silverman, *The Acoustic Mirror*, 1–2.

74. Silverman, *The Acoustic Mirror*, 2.

75. While it exceeds the bounds of the present study to explore related issues in the play, the following essays offer interesting analyses from a feminist perspective: Shirley Nelson Garner, "Male Bonding and the Myth of Women's Deception in Shakespeare's Plays," *Shakespeare's Personality,* eds. Norman N. Holland, Sidney Homan, and Bernard J. Paris (Berkeley: University of California Press, 1989), 135–50; Madelon Gohlke, " 'All that is spoke is marred': Language and Consciousness in *Othello,*" *Women's Studies* 9 (1982): 157–76; Kahn, *Man's Estate,* 140–46; and Scheman, "Othello's Doubt/Desdemona's Death: The Engendering of Scepticism," *Power/Gender/Values,* ed. Judith Genova (Edmonton: Academic Printing and Publishing, 1987), 113–42.

76. For an interesting assessment see Brèque, "L'*Otello* de Zeffirelli, ou Quand L'Opéra Devient un Véritable Film," *L'Avant-Scène Opéra* No. 90 (1986): 212–18.

77. My thanks to William Drabkin and Harold Powers for their respective expressions of this idea.

78. Documentary "Zeffirelli's *Otello.*" A probing yet sympathetic look at the genre appears in Brèque, "Le Film-Opéra," 27–35.

CHAPTER 4
Cinema and the Power of Fantasy: Powell and Pressburger's
Tales of Hoffmann and Syberberg's *Parsifal*

1. For an exploration of these issues see Jean-Louis Dutronc, "Les Contes d'Hoffmann: Une Genèse Contestée," *L'Avant-Scène Opéra* No. 25 (January–February 1980): 13–17. The entire issue is devoted to *Hoffmann.* Marvin Kaye has edited a new performing edition, issued by Schott, that draws together dispersed source material; see Anthony Tommasini, "A Tale of Two 'Tales of Hoffmann,' " *The New York Times,* 3 November 1996, H33.

2. Barry Millington, "Parsifal," *The New Grove Dictionary of Opera,* ed. Stanley Sadie (London: Macmillan, 1992), vol. 3: 895.

3. Roland Lacourbe, "Recouvrir Michael Powell," *Ecran* No. 76 (15 January 1979): 48. Rick Altman discusses the innovative features of *The Red Shoes* in *The American Film Musical* (Bloomington: Indiana University Press, 1987), 264–65. For a study of *Shoes* in connection with the film *Raging Bull,* see Lesley Stern, "Meditation on Violence," *The Scorsese Connection* (Bloomington: Indiana University Press, 1995), 11–31.

4. Many sources on Michael Powell mention this feature. Among them are Ian Christie, *Arrows of Desire* (London: Waterstone & Co., 1985), and

Powell, Pressburger and Others, ed. Ian Christie (London: British Film Institute, 1978); Nora Sayre, "Michael Powell—At 75, A British Director Receives a Tribute," *The New York Times*, 30 November 1980; Raymond Durgnat, *A Mirror for England: British Movies from Austerity to Affluence* (New York: Praeger, 1971), especially the chapter titled "Romantics and Moralists"; and Roy Armes, *A Critical History of British Cinema* (New York: Oxford University Press, 1978).

5. Volume 2 of Michael Powell's autobiography, *Million Dollar Movie*, provides most of the important details on the conception of the film, including Powell's views that are described here (New York: Random House, 1995), especially 84–120. See also Christopher Challis, " 'Hoffmann' Sets New Pattern in Film Making Technique," *American Cinematographer* 32/5 (May 1951): 194; Christie, *Arrows of Desire*, 86; and "Interview with Michael Powell," conducted by Kevin Gough-Yates, 22 September 1970 (unpaginated booklet in film library, Museum of Modern Art, New York).

6. Powell, *Million Dollar Movie*, 99.

7. For the last see Hans R. Vaget, "Syberberg's *Our Hitler:* Wagnerianism and Alienation," *The Massachusetts Review* 23 (Winter 1982): 593–612; my thanks to the author for bringing the essay to my attention. Thomas Elsaesser offers an extended critique of Syberberg in light of these films, in "Myth as the Phantasmagoria of History: H. J. Syberberg, Cinema and Representation," *New German Critique* No. 24–25 (1981–82): 108–55.

8. Barry Millington, *Wagner*, rev. ed. (Princeton: Princeton University Press, 1992), 258–59. The major violation of this prohibition was a performance at the Metropolitan Opera House in 1903.

9. *Parsifal: Ein Filmessay* (Munich: Wilhelm Heyne, 1983), 42–43.

10. In contrast, the *Ring* tetralogy bears the title "Bühnenfestspiel," thus without the sacralizing function.

11. For a study that links performance with larger concerns in cinema, see Lesley Stern, "The Tales of Hoffmann: An Instance of Histrionic Cinema," unpublished paper. My thanks to the author for sending a copy.

12. They were mainly worried about producers' costs and audience reactions rather than aesthetic matters. After the important premieres, the film went into distribution without the final episode, a decision apparently made by the producers. It is only in recent years, thanks to a restoration at the British Film Institute, that the film is available in its entirety and its original Technicolor glory; the video version is the restored film.

13. Many productions of the opera, however, have the Venetian sequence

third, after the Tale of Antonia. This illustrates the confusion over the structure of the original opera.

14. For example Bosley Crowther, "The Screen: 'Tales of Hoffmann' Arrives," *The New York Times*, 5 April 1951, p. 34; and G. L. [Glenn Loney?], in *Monthly Film Bulletin* 18 (June 1951): 278.

15. In the piano/vocal score published by G. Schirmer (edition no. 2639), for example, this occurs at the bottom of page 289.

16. See Nancy Newman, "The Maternal Superego and the Determination of Musical Culture in *The 5,000 Fingers of Dr. T*," paper delivered at Feminist Theory and Music Conference III, University of California, Riverside, June 1995.

17. This effect of fake running in front of a flat sylvan background is one that Bergman used later in his *The Magic Flute* film, when Papageno and Pamina escape from Monostatos.

18. This sequence is a variation on a similar one in the "Red Shoes" ballet, although in the earlier instance the conductor is the actual conductor of the ballet, who is the ballerina's demanding boyfriend instead of father.

19. Hadlock, "Return of the Repressed: The Prima Donna from Hoffmann's *Tales* to Offenbach's *Contes*," *Cambridge Opera Journal* 6/3 (November 1994): 221–43; Abbate, "Debussy's Phantom Sounds," *Cambridge Opera Journal* 10/1 (1998), especially 70–74; and Tambling, "Towards a Psychopathology of Opera," *Cambridge Opera Journal* 9/3 (1997), 270–72.

20. For a discussion of MTV in relation to screen opera see chapter 6.

21. See also Bruce Babbington and Peter Evans, "Matters of Life and Death in Powell and Pressburger's *The Tales of Hoffmann*," *A Night in at The Opera*, ed. Jeremy Tambling (London: John Libbey, 1994), 154–55. This essay, the first critique based on interdisciplinary film theory, explores a number of interesting aspects of the film. An earlier piece by Thomas Elsaesser, originally from 1968, is also informative, exploring its thematic position in cinema, its pessimism, and its Leftist implications ("The Tales of Hoffmann," in *Powell, Pressburger and Others*, ed. Christie, 62–65).

22. The Archers drew the ire of Churchill and other officials during World War II for their wry approaches to war; see volume 1 of Powell's autobiography, *A Life in Movies* (London: Heinemann, 1986). Powell was also aware of the growing power of Hollywood and he attempted to resist it; see both volumes of the autobiography.

23. Among the most useful sources for this section are Kaja Silverman, *The Acoustic Mirror: The Female Voice in Psychoanalysis and Cinema* (Bloomington: Indiana University Press, 1988); Mary Ann Doane, "The Voice in

the Cinema: The Articulation of Body and Space," *Film Sound: Theory and Practice,* eds. Elisabeth Weis and John Belton (New York: Columbia University Press, 1985): 162–76; Rick Altman, "Moving Lips: Cinema as Ventriloquism," *Yale French Studies* No. 60 (special issue, *Cinema/Sound*) (1980): 67–79; and John Belton, "Technology and Aesthetics of Film Sound," *Film Theory and Criticism: Introductory Readings,* 4th ed., eds. Gerald Mast, Marshall Cohen, and Leo Braudy (New York: Oxford University Press, 1992): 323–31.

24. Silverman, *Acoustic Mirror,* chaps. 1, 2, and 5; and Barbara Engh, "Adorno and the Sirens: Tele-Phono-Graphic Bodies," *Embodied Voices: Representing Female Vocality in Western Culture,* eds. Leslie C. Dunn and Nancy A. Jones (Cambridge: Cambridge University Press, 1994): 120–35.

25. Theodor Adorno, "The Curves of the Needle," trans. Tom Levin, *October* 55 (Winter 1990): 54. See Engh, "Adorno and the Sirens," for a contextual study.

26. For longstanding associations between female singers and the imagery of birds see Elizabeth Wood, "The Odyssey of Sirens and Songbirds: Opera and Its Prima Donnas," paper delivered at the Annual Meeting of the American Musicological Society, Austin, October 1989.

27. His observations on his role in the film appear in Monk Gibbon's flattering book, *The Tales of Hoffmann: A Study of the Film* (London: Saturn Press, 1951), 87.

28. The reason for Shearer not mouthing much of the time was apparently practical: it was physically impossible to do the demanding steps and lip-synching at the same time. See Powell, *Million Dollar Movie,* 105.

29. The idea has been suggested that the dancing foot also acts to destabilize her unified representation. My thanks to the unknown audience member who proposed this idea at a presentation I gave on the film entitled "Dance and Film-Opera: The Powell-Pressburger *Tales of Hoffmann,*" Society for Dance History Scholars Conference, Barnard College, New York, June 1997.

30. Historical anecdotes offered at the Barnard conference suggest that a doll listening to her own voice may have formed a trope in late nineteenth-century ballet. One scholar (of unknown identity) mentioned an Austrian ballet of 1888, *Die Puppenfee* by Joseph Bayer, as a famous example, in which a doll's variation has the dancer "listen" to her own voice, or rather instrumental representations of that voice, uttering "Mama" and "Papa."

31. Chion, *Audio-Vision: Sound on Screen,* trans. Claudia Gorbman (New York: Columbia University Press, 1994), 71–73, and also 126–31. See also Chion's *The Voice in Cinema,* ed. and trans. Claudia Gorbman (New York:

Columbia University Press, 1999), especially part 1, "Mabuse: Magic and Powers of the Acousmêtre," 15–58. Abbate elaborates masterfully on the concept in "Debussy's Phantom Sounds." Other essays that deal interpretively with the *acousmêtre* are Michal Grover-Friedlander, " 'The Phantom of the Opera': The Lost Voice of Opera in Silent Film," unpublished typescript; and Marcia J. Citron, "The Elusive Voice: Absence and Presence in Jean-Pierre Ponnelle's film *Le Nozze di Figaro*," *Between Opera and Cinema,* eds. Jeongwon Joe and Rose M. Theresa, Garland Press, forthcoming.

32. Chion, *Audio-Vision,* 129–30.

33. Chion, *Audio-Vision,* 72.

34. Bosley Crowther, "The Screen: 'Tales of Hoffmann' Arrives," *The New York Times,* 5 April 1951, p. 34; Virginia Graham, Review of *Tales of Hoffmann, The Spectator* 186 (27 April 1951): 553; Mary Ellis Peltz, Review of *Tales of Hoffmann, Films in Review* 2 (May 1951): 44–46; Catherine de la Roche, "Films of the Month: The Tales of Hoffmann," *Sight and Sound* 20 (May 1951): 17–18; Robert Sabin, Review in *Musical America* 71 (March 1951): 9; and Pauline Kael, "Tales of Hoffmann," in *Cinemania-96,* Microsoft Corp. CD-ROM, 1992–95. Siegfried Kracauer also criticizes its excess, in his discussion of opera films in *Theory of Film: The Redemption of Physical Reality* (New York: Oxford University Press, 1960), 155–56.

35. Durgnat, *A Mirror for England,* 210–11.

36. Lacourbe, "Recouvrir Michael Powell," 48.

37. A performance-art installation of major themes in *Parsifal,* which took place in Dresden in 1995, is treated in Norma M. Darr, "Reading the Body and Blood of *Parsifal:* Performance at Hellerau," *The Musical Quarterly* 80/4 (Winter 1996): 629–47. Like Syberberg's film, this performative re-creation dismantles and then reassembles layers of meanings in the work.

38. Syberberg, *Parsifal,* 251. The phrase also comes from Wagner himself.

39. As cited in Michael Tanner, "Transformation Music: Wagner *Parsifal*," *Times Literary Supplement,* 8 April 1983, p. 352.

40. See especially Jeremy Tambling, "The Fusion of Brecht and Wagner: Syberberg's *Parsifal,*" *Opera, Ideology and Film* (New York: St. Martin's Press, 1987), 194–212; and Tanner, "Transformation Music." An incisive essay on Syberberg's relationship with German culture, made prior to *Parsifal,* is Frederic Jameson, " 'In the Destructive Element Immerse': Hans-Jürgen Syberberg and Cultural Revolution," *October* No. 17 (Summer 1981): 99–118. For perceptive remarks on the significance of weighty

critique to the seductive appeal of Wagner's operas see Suzanne R. Stewart, "The Theft of the Operatic Voice: Masochistic Seduction in Wagner's *Parsifal*," *The Musical Quarterly* 80/4 (Winter 1996): 597–628.

41. Jeongwon Joe offers a postmodernist reading of the film in "Hans-Jürgen Syberberg's *Parsifal:* The Staging of Dissonance in the Fusion of Opera and Film," *The Music Research Forum* 13 (July 1998): 1–21.

42. Syberberg, *Parsifal*, 263.

43. Tambling, "Fusion of Brecht and Wagner," 196.

44. Jean-Jacques Nattiez, *Wagner Androgyne: A Study in Interpretation*, trans. Stewart Spencer (Princeton: Princeton University Press, 1993), 290–91.

45. See, for example, Theodor Adorno, *In Search of Wagner*, trans. Rodney Livingstone (London: Verso, 1981), 93–94; Friedrich Nietzsche, *The Case of Wagner* (Der Fall Wagner) and *Nietzsche Contra Wagner*, trans. J. M. Kennedy, vol. 8 of *The Complete Works of Friedrich Nietzsche*, ed. Oscar Levy (London: T. N. Foulis, 1911); Linda Hutcheon and Michael Hutcheon, "Syphilis, Sin, and the Social Order: Richard Wagner's *Parsifal*," *Cambridge Opera Journal* 7/3 (November 1995): 261–75; Robert Gutman, *Richard Wagner: The Man, His Mind and His Music* (New York: Harcourt Brace & World, 1968); Marc A. Weiner, *Richard Wagner and the Anti-Semitic Imagination* (Lincoln, Neb.: University of Nebraska Press, 1995); Alex Ross, "Grand Seductions," *The New Yorker*, 12 April 1993, especially 117–20; and Ross, "The Unforgiven: Why the Wagner Problem Won't Go Away," *The New Yorker*, 10 August 1998, 64–72.

46. Syberberg, *Parsifal*, 48.

47. The last is based on an engraving by André Gill, which appeared on the cover of *L'Eclipse* in April 1869. See the facsimile-photo section of Gutman, *Richard Wagner*, n. p.

48. See Gutman, *Richard Wagner*, 395–96; and Weiner, *Richard Wagner and the Anti-Semitic Imagination*, chapter 3: "Smells: The Teutonic *Duft* and the *Foetor Judäicus*," 195–259.

49. Syberberg, *Parsifal*, 266–67.

50. Bryan Magee found it quite disturbing, as mentioned in his review in *Opera* 34/6 (June 1983): 687.

51. Nattiez's study, *Wagner Androgyne*, is the focal point for androgyny in Wagner. See also Bryan Hyer's review in *Journal of the American Musicological Society* 47/3 (Fall 1994): 531–40; and Paul Robinson's review in *Cambridge Opera Journal* 7/1 (March 1995): 81–85. Both are critical of Nattiez's enterprise but for different reasons.

52. John Hoberman, "His Parsifal: Following the Syberbergenlied," *Village Voice*, 22 February 1983, 64.

53. For ambiguities surrounding the castrato see Joke Dame, "Unveiled Voices: Sexual Difference and the Castrato," *Queering the Pitch: The New Gay and Lesbian Musicology*, eds. Philip Brett, Elizabeth Wood, and Gary C. Thomas (New York: Routledge, 1994): 139–53; and in relation to the film *Farinelli*, Katherine Bergeron, "The Castrato as History," *Cambridge Opera Journal* 8/2 (1996): 167–84.

54. Debussy commented how Klingsor seems to be the only human character in the opera (Gutman, *Richard Wagner*, 429). For a related discussion see Adorno, *In Search of Wagner*, 93.

55. Richard Mohr, *Gay Ideas: Outing and Other Controversies* (Boston: Beacon Press, 1992), 214. Tambling discusses homosexuality in *Parsifal* in *Opera and the Culture of Fascism* (Oxford: Clarendon Press, 1996), 46–60. For homosexuality and Wagner see also Ross, "Grand Seductions"; and Mitchell Morris, "Tristan's Wounds: On Homosexual Wagnerians in the Fin-de-Siècle," paper presented at Gender and Opera Conference, State University of New York at Stony Brook, September 1995 (my thanks to Professor Morris for providing a copy).

56. Syberberg, *Parsifal,* 161.

57. For an exploration of the masculinist agenda of the opera, especially in relation to Kundry, see Barry Emslie, "Woman as Image and Narrative in Wagner's *Parsifal:* A Case Study," *Cambridge Opera Journal* 3 (1991): 109–24. Stewart offers a psychoanalytic analysis of the Kiss and its impact on Kundry and Parsifal, in "The Theft of the Operatic Voice," 615–22. For psychoanalytic implications in the film see Paul Coates, "Memory and Repression in Recent German Cinema," *The Gorgon's Gaze: German Cinema, Expressionism, and the Image of Horror* (Cambridge: Cambridge University Press, 1991), 127–29.

58. Hoberman, "Parsifal," 61.

59. For the wound and its reconciliation with the female chalice in the opera, see Hutcheon and Hutcheon, "Syphilis, Sin, and the Social Order." For other associations of blood see Gutman, *Richard Wagner,* 427. Slavoj Zizek explores psychoanalytic implications of the wound, the kiss, and the characters as archetypes in " 'The Wound Is Healed Only By the Spear that Smote You': The Operatic Subject and Its Vicissitudes," *Opera Through Other Eyes*, ed. David J. Levin (Stanford: Stanford University Press, 1994), 177–214.

60. As conveyed in Guy-Patrick Sainderichin, "Voyage à Munich: Hans-Jürgen Syberberg Tourne *Parsifal*," *Cahiers du Cinéma* No. 331 (January 1982): 29.

61. Elsaesser, Review of film in *Monthly Film Bulletin* (May 1983): 137.

62. Syberberg tells how Clever would arrive at the studio shaking like a leaf, and that even after the film was completed she had nightmares of Minton pursuing her (Hoberman, "His Parsifal," 64).

63. Poizat, *The Angel's Cry*, 194, 198–99.

64. This disjunction is also discussed in Tambling, "The Fusion of Brecht and Wagner," 199–200, who sees it as intentional.

65. Lucy Beckett, *Richard Wagner: Parsifal* (Cambridge: Cambridge University Press, 1981), 23; and also Gutman, *Richard Wagner*, 394–98.

66. The two main lines of interpretation of the film are Brechtian and Freudian, split about evenly (some treat both). For Brecht the main sources are Syberberg's *Parsifal;* Tambling, "The Fusion of Brecht and Wagner"; and Magee, *Opera.* It is also discussed, although peripherally, in Tanner, "Transformation Music"; Jameson, " 'The Destructive Element' "; and John Rockwell, "Film: Hans Syberberg's Adaptation of 'Parsifal,' " *The New York Times,* 23 January 1983, section 1, p. 46.

67. Syberberg has considerable experience with Brecht on the stage, and in 1952 he directed a film of Brecht's Berliner Ensemble in performance.

68. Syberberg, *Parsifal,* 244.

69. Syberberg, *Parsifal,* 249.

70. Poizat, *The Angel's Cry*, 195.

71. This has become evident from written sources, but a personal anecdote makes the point more vividly. After I presented a paper on *Tales* and *Parsifal* at the 1996 annual meeting of the American Musicological Society (Baltimore), an audience member related that she had seen the New York premiere in 1952. She recalls that *Tales* was advertised as a ballet film, featuring the dancing star of *Red Shoes,* Moira Shearer, and like its predecessor was geared to aspiring young ballerinas. *The Red Shoes,* incidentally, enjoyed its greatest success in the United States.

72. For a study of the opera that pivots around this idea see Michael P. Steinberg, "Music Drama and the End of History," *New German Critique* No. 69 (Fall 1996): 163–80.

CHAPTER 5

Opera *al fresco:* Rosi's *Bizet's Carmen* and Losey's *Don Giovanni*

1. For example, Jean-Michael Brèque, an editor of *L'Avant-Scène Opéra,* is a real fan; see his "Réaliste et Lyrique: Carmen Dans Sa Vérité," *Positif* No. 278 (April 1984): 13–18, and his précis of the film in the extremely valuable "Trente Classiques du Film-Opéra," *L'Avant-Scène Opéra*

No. 98 (1987): 84–85. Blake Lucas, reviewing the film in *Magills Cinema Annual 1985* (Englewood Cliffs, N.J.: Salem Press, 1985), considers it the best of the genre to date (104). Other voices of high praise are Stanley Kauffmann, "The Abduction from the Theater: Mozart Opera on Film," *The Yale Review* 81/1 (January 1993): 104; and Lawrence O'Toole, "A Temptress and a Toreador," review in *Macleans* 98 (4 March 1985), 54.

2. See the introduction to the discussion of the films of *Carmen*, in Susan McClary, *Georges Bizet: Carmen* (Cambridge: Cambridge University Press, 1992), 130–31.

3. As mentioned by Pauline Kael in her review in *The New Yorker*, 19 October 1984, 123–24.

4. As quoted in McClary, *Carmen*, 138.

5. This is the thesis of Leicester's "Discourse and the Film Text: Four Readings of *Carmen*," *Cambridge Opera Journal* 6/3 (November 1994): 245–82. Saura's *Carmen*, choreographed by Antonio Gades, dancer/choreographer of the flamenco in Rosi's *Carmen*, forms the second part of a Saura-Gades dance-film trilogy. The first, *Blood Wedding*, based on Lorca, has many similarities to the *Carmen* story; for more on the fascinating film see Michelle Hefner, "*Blood Wedding:* Tradition and Innovation in Contemporary Flamenco," paper presented at the Society for Dance History Scholars Conference, Barnard College, New York, June 1997. The third film is *El Amor Brujo* (1988). A prize-winning trilogy, the three were also wildly successful at the Spanish box office.

6. As expressed by opera producer Rolf Liebermann, the impetus behind the project; see Alain Duault, "Entretien avec Rolf Liebermann," *L'Avant-Scène Opéra* No. 24 (November–December 1979): 208.

7. For more on the relationship between fidelity and interpretation in Mozart opera see chapter 6.

8. Michel Ciment, "Rosi in a New Key," *American Film* 9/10 (September 1984), 41–42.

9. "Italy: Auteurs and After," *The Oxford History of World Cinema*, ed. Geoffrey Nowell-Smith (Oxford: Oxford University Press, 1996), 590.

10. Ciment, "Rosi in a New Key," 39.

11. Ciment, "Rosi in a New Key," 39.

12. For perceptive descriptions see Pauline Kael in *The New Yorker*, 29 October 1984, p. 124; and Vincent Canby in *The New York Times*, 20 September 1984, p. C21, and "Film View: Three New Movies Enrich Their Genres," *The New York Times*, 23 September 1984 section 2, p. 19.

13. Kael, Review in *The New Yorker*, 124.

14. For an extended discussion of the duet see Leicester, "Discourse and the Film Text," 270–73.
15. Several reviewers discuss the film's realism with respect to the genre of film-opera. See especially Gerhard Persché, "Auf bunten Flügeln ins Heimkino: Francesco Rosis 'Carmen'-Film als Video," *Opernwelt* 27/3 (1986): 27; Canby, "Film View"; and Alan Stanbrook, "The Sight of Music," *Sight and Sound* 56/2 (1987), 132.
16. The epigram forms an integral part of Jeremy Tambling's critique of the film, "Losey's 'fenomeni morbosi': *Don Giovanni*," in his *Opera, Ideology and Film* (New York: St. Martin's Press, 1987), 159–75. Gramsci published these lines in 1951.
17. As proposed in Kierkegaard's influential essay, "The Immediate Erotic Stages or The Musical-Erotic" in *Either/Or*, Part 1 (1843), eds. and trans. Howard V. Hong and Edna H. Hong (Princeton: Princeton University Press, 1987), 45–135.
18. Tambling might call these beneficial fissures, as they serve as important agents in the critique of totalizing theories that mask the presence of ideology. What I mean by seams here, however, is a problematic means for accomplishing this end, and not the goal itself. See his "Losey's 'fenomeni morbosi.'"
19. To be precise, Leporello has an aria of escape immediately after the Sextet. But because it occurs as a concluding piece to the action in the Sextet, at the same location, it effectively belongs with it. Thus my looseness in describing the sequence. For negative appraisals see Brèque, "Trente Classiques du Film-Opéra," 79; and Kauffmann, "The Abduction from the Theater: Mozart Opera on Film," 99. For a summary of the finale-like qualities of the Sextet see Julian Rushton, *W. A. Mozart: Don Giovanni* (Cambridge: Cambridge University Press, 1981), 48–49.
20. Brechtian distancing forms a major theme in Tambling, "Losey's 'fenomeni morbosi.'"
21. From an interview with Boulez, "Sprengt die Opernhäuser in die Luft!" *Der Spiegel* No. 40 (1967); English translation in *Opera* 19/5 (1968): 440–50.
22. Another layer of meanings may derive from the strained relations between Losey and Rolf Liebermann. Documents in the Losey Archive suggest that the two had a serious falling-out during the final phases of the film's production, over public remarks by Losey concerning the respective contributions of the two men to the film. While many differences were ultimately resolved, underlying tensions did not seem to disappear.

It is therefore possible that in the image of a burning Opéra, which Liebermann headed at the time, Losey may have also been criticizing Liebermann and his connection with institutional opera. Of further interest is the fact that Boulez's remarks were largely aimed at Liebermann and his (then) directorship of the Hamburg State Opera.

23. Foster Hirsch, *Joseph Losey* (Boston: Twayne Publishers, 1980), 250.

24. Kierkegaard, "The Immediate Erotic Stages or The Musical-Erotic," 92.

25. One reviewer, however, is very critical of the juxtaposition; see Stanbrook, "The Sight of Music," 134, who generally dislikes the film.

26. Alain Duault, "Entretien avec Rolf Liebermann," *L'Avant-Scène Opéra* No. 24 (November–December 1979): 209.

27. James Palmer and Michael Riley, *The Films of Joseph Losey* (Cambridge: Cambridge University Press, 1993), 12. In discussing general themes in his films, the authors list "the unresolved tension not just between social classes . . . but between places and the characters who live in them, between communities and those who intrude on them" (13).

28. Many if not most traditional stage productions, however, set the work at the time the opera was written, 1787, and thus this aspect of Losey's version is not startling.

29. Many stage productions emphasize the similarity between the two. Peter Sellars's production, for example, features identical twins (see chapter 6). The 1987 Salzburg production, broadcast on television, had Samuel Ramey and Ferruccio Furlanetto alternate in the two roles in successive performances.

30. Duault, "Entretien avec Raimondi," 213.

31. See chapter 4, especially the discussion of *Tales of Hoffmann,* for more on the relationship between silent film and dubbing.

32. For this issue in the opera see, for example, Bernard Williams, "Don Giovanni as an Idea," in Rushton, *W. A. Mozart: Don Giovanni,* 81, who rejects the notion of a homosexual Don; and Catherine Clément, *Opera, or the Undoing of Women,* trans. Betsy Wing, 36, who sees the Don as hiding his homosexuality (Minneapolis: University of Minnesota Press, 1988).

33. In the Losey Archive at the British Film Institute, Losey's description to Raimondi of his role says that the Don is not a homosexual, although he might well be bisexual. In published sources Losey writes, "His kind of sexuality can be seen as running away from facing homosexuality or using sex as a means to run away from social realities you can't do anything about. There is a guilt in him about enjoying things which he knows

he does not deserve" (in Ciment, *Conversations with Losey* [London: Methuen, 1985], 373).

34. Palmer and Riley, *Films of Joseph Losey*, 11.

35. Martyn Auty, Review in *Monthly Film Bulletin* 47 No. 560 (September 1980): 175.

36. Thomas Voigt, Review of the Video in *Opernwelt* 30/1 (January 1989): 60. Hirsch sees a parallel with Donald Sutherland's portrayal of Casanova in a Fellini Film, in *Joseph Losey*, 248.

37. I have in mind, for example, a production I saw at the old Metropolitan Opera House in the early 1960s, with Cesare Siepi as the Don.

38. Carcassonne, "Tombeaux de Mozart," *Cinématographe* No. 52 (November 1979), 12.

39. Archival materials of the director, at the British Film Institute, provide additional clues. Although Losey refuses to be precise about the identity of the valet, who apparently was added at the time of the second draft shooting script, he writes that the valet functions as an observer, but more than anyone else in the film represents the director's point-of-view. As guardian of Don Giovanni's doomed soul he watches over the destiny of an "homme exemplaire." Although the details of his birth are uncertain he may be an illegitimate son of Giovanni and a servant who died in childbirth. For critical commentary see especially Tambling, "Losey's 'fenomeni morbosi' "; Hirsch, *Joseph Losey*, 248; and Duault, "Entretien avec Ruggero Raimondi," *L'Avant-Scène Opéra* No. 24 (November-December 1979), 213.

40. Leicester, "Discourse and the Film Text," 275–76.

41. This is McClary's phrase for characterizing the action, and I find it apt (*Bizet's Carmen*, 145).

42. An earlier film of Rosi, the celebrated *Il Momento della verità* (1964), depicts bullfighting as a complex cultural symbol.

43. For general comments on Losey's treatment of women in the film see Hirsch, *Joseph Losey*, 249; and Ciment, *Conversations with Losey*, 369.

44. Ciment, *Conversations with Losey*, 370–71.

45. For a wonderful analysis of misogynist interpretation of the women in the opera see Clément, *Opera, or the Undoing of Women*, 33–36.

46. Composed after the death of Leopold Mozart, the opera is thought to play out the composer's troubled relationship with his father. See especially Brigid Brophy, *Mozart the Dramatist* (New York: Da Capo Press, 1988), 242–65; and Clément, *Opera, or the Undoing of Women*, 36. For extensive discussion of Leopold's psychological impact on his son see Maynard Solomon, *Mozart: A Life* (New York: HarperCollins, 1995).

47. The story appears in Rushton, *Don Giovanni*, 126–31. See also Williams, 83–84, in the same volume.
48. According to Rolf Liebermann, in his interview with Duault, 208.
49. It is used very successfully in one of his most respected films, *The Servant* (1963). A study of the nuances of the master-servant relationship, it has led one critic to see *Don Giovanni* as a "prequel" to the earlier film (Stanbrook, "The Sight of Music," 134).
50. Ciment, *Conversations with Losey*, 371. Tambling interprets Elvira's hysteria in the film as "the morbid symptom that has to do with the frustration of the female." Furthermore, "frustrated sexuality" is largely responsible for the three aristocrats' revenge on Don Giovanni ("Losey's 'fenomeni morbosi,'" 172).
51. See my discussion in *Gender and the Musical Canon* (Cambridge: Cambridge University Press, 1993), 73. For historical context see Wye Allanbrook, *Rhythmic Gesture in Mozart: Le Nozze di Figaro and Don Giovanni* (Chicago: University of Chicago Press, 1983), 238.
52. This may be an example of Losey's attempt to make the film cinematic as opposed to operatic, a problem mentioned by Kauffmann in his negative appraisal, "The Abduction from the Theater," 99. Harvey E. Phillips is also critical of the jumpy camera in his review of the video version, *Opera News* 53/5 (November 1988): 67. Regarding this instance of the Quartet, after my critique was written I found a similar objection in Andrew Porter's review, "Close and Effectual Don," *The New Yorker*, 21 January 1980, 121. The Losey Archive reveals that in an early shooting script the Recitative and Quartet were to occur in one location; by the second shooting script, however, the disposition is as in the final version.
53. Peter Sellars, however, assigns him greater weight; see the discussion in chapter 6.
54. Gerald Kaufman, *Opera* 31/12 (December 1980), 1260.
55. See McClary, *Bizet's Carmen*, especially 57–58, for Carmen's discursive mastery. One reviewer critical of the multiplicity is Persché, "Auf bunten Flügeln."
56. Chapter 3, a comparison of screen treatments of Verdi's *Otello*, discusses the connections between non-diegetic film music and a heavily rearranged opera score, especially in the context of Zeffirelli's *Otello*.
57. Among those who have mentioned the film's similarity with the film musical are Kauffmann, "The Abduction from the Theater," 104; and Kael, *The New Yorker*, 125, especially in the deployment of the choruses.
58. The extent of spoken dialogue in the opera is ambiguous because the very content of the opera, musical and otherwise, is open to question. For

the premiere in May 1875 Bizet had spoken dialogue, but for the Vienna performance after his death this was replaced by recitatives, written by his colleague Ernest Guiraud. These became standard in the performance tradition, at least until recently. Controversy surrounds other musical matters in the opera and many relate to the nature of the composer's intentions. The issues are brought to the fore by Oeser's revisionist score, published in 1964, which has sparked rebuttal from Bizet scholars Winton Dean and Lesley A. Wright, who defend the authenticity of the score published by Choudens. For a summary of the controversy see McClary, *Bizet's Carmen*, 25-26 and 152-53 (notes to chapter 5). For a conductor's reaction to the Oeser version, see Georg Solti's remarks on how he draws from both versions, in the liner notes to his 1976 recording of the opera (London 414 489-2).

59. See also McClary, *Bizet's Carmen*, 131-35. In addition to contemporary reviews in the usual outlets, see "Cinéma et Opéra III," *La Revue du Cinéma* No. 430 (1987): 78-81; "Trente Classiques du Film-Opéra," 73 (Claude Beylie); James Baldwin, "Life Straight in De Eye: Carmen Jones," *Commentary* 19/1 (January 1955): 74-77; and Otto Preminger's *Preminger: An Autobiography* (New York: Doubleday, 1977), 133-37.

60. The show musical is a sub-genre of the film musical, as designated in Rick Altman, *The American Film Musical* (Bloomington: Indiana University Press, 1987).

61. Of course, many film musicals depart from the archetype, such as *West Side Story,* which foregrounds cultural difference, and *Cabaret,* which amounts to a parody of American innocence and those very values listed. In general, the most useful interpretive surveys of the film musical are Altman's study, which pays a lot of attention to genre theory, and Jane Feuer, *The Hollywood Musical,* 2d ed. (Bloomington: Indiana University Press, 1993). A shorter study, Feuer's volume brings in critical theory and often reads against the grain.

62. For example, Lawrence O'Toole in *Macleans.*

63. Altman, *American Film Musical,* 286-87.

64. Altman, *American Film Musical,* 62-73.

65. Altman, *American Film Musical,* 65.

66. Leicester coins the phrase "musicalization of the noise track" to describe how noise is used in the film ("Discourse and the Film Text," 269).

67. Rushton, *Don Giovanni,* 80.

68. See note 39 above.

69. Some reviewers find this a problem in the Rosi. See Wulf Konold, "Ein

Opern-Mythos als Film? Viermal 'Carmen,'" in *Oper-Film-Rockmusik,* ed. H.-K. Jungenheinrich (Kassel: Bärenreiter, 1986), 42; Max Loppert, "On Film: Carmen," *Opera* 36/5 (May 1985): 582; and David Wills, "Carmen: Sound/Effect," *Cinema Journal* 25/4 (Summer 1986), 39.

70. As one of the few negative voices on the film, Carlo Piccardi offers an opposing view on realism. He believes that the Rosi is a failure because cinema can deal only in descriptive realism, while this opera is strong in literary realism. See his "Carmen tradito sullo schermo," *Dissonanz* No. 3 (February 1985): 15–17.

CHAPTER 6

A Matter of Time and Place: Peter Sellars and Media Culture

1. His main admirers are Andrew Porter, then opera critic for *The New Yorker;* Peter Davis of *New York* magazine; and Robert Marx of *Opera News.* The most negative voice is Donal Henahan of *The New York Times,* and another major detractor is essayist David Littlejohn. Among the many who are generally sympathetic but see a major problem in Sellars's conceptions are Andrew Clements (*Opera*), Edward Said (*Nation*), and John J. O'Connor (*The New York Times*). A few critics like the stage production but believe the video version ruined it, for example James Reel in *Fanfare.*

2. American by birth, Losey spent his mature career in England and Europe.

3. For an extended study of Sellars's stage productions in the context of European producers of opera see Tom Sutcliffe, "Peter Sellars: Americanizing Everything," *Believing in Opera* (Princeton: Princeton University Press, 1996), 195–226. For theatrical influences see Richard Trousdell, "Peter Sellars Rehearses *Figaro,*" *Drama Review* 35 (Spring 1991): 72; and Del Ray Cross, "Peter Sellars's Stagings of *Don Giovanni:* Directorial Intent and Critical Response," M.A. thesis, Bowling Green State University, 1992, 22.

4. See especially Robert Marx, "Grand Finale," *Opera News,* July 1989, 14–16, 33.

5. Quoted in Will Crutchfield, "Modern Twists Spice a Mozart Opera," *The New York Times,* 13 July 1986, section 2, p. 21.

6. For additional discussion in the context of traditional representations of women in Mozart opera, see my *Gender and the Musical Canon* (Cambridge: Cambridge University Press, 1993), 73–75.

7. Sellars's comments before Act II of the telecast version aired on PBS. Un-

fortunately, Sellars's "talking head" appearances in the three Mozart were removed from the video versions. Extravagant and fanciful, they provide a valuable clue to the mind behind the productions.

8. David Littlejohn, "What Peter Sellars Did to Mozart," *The Ultimate Art: Essays Around and About Opera* (Berkeley: University of California Press, 1992), 142.

9. Andrew Clements, "People 215: Peter Sellars," *Opera* 46/11 (November 1992): 1263.

10. Tom Mikotowicz, "Director Peter Sellars: Bridging the Modern and Postmodern," *Theatre Topics* 1/1 (1991): 94.

11. Cross, "Peter Sellars's Stagings of *Don Giovanni*," 38.

12. For Sellars on Brecht see Trousdell, "Peter Sellars Rehearses *Figaro*," 69–70.

13. "Shock value" is mentioned, for example, in his verbal introduction to the PBS broadcast of *Don Giovanni*, in January 1991.

14. Porter, for instance, cites himself as an example of someone who missed an important contemporary reference in *Così,* the popular sex therapist Dr. Ruth Westheimer ("Musical Events: And in My Lady's Chamber," *The New Yorker* [15 August 1988]: 63). Considered passé by the time the production was taped, Westheimer is replaced by Shirley MacLaine, whose book on spiritualism was then current.

15. In Will Crutchfield, "Modern Twists Spice a Mozart Opera," *The New York Times,* 13 July 1986, sect. II, 21.

16. Especially Donal Henahan, as in "When Auteur Meets Opera, Opera Loses," *The New York Times,* 9 December 1990, H23.

17. As quoted in Cross, "Peter Sellars's Stagings of *Don Giovanni*," 39.

18. Jeremy Tambling, "Revisions and Re-Vampings: Wagner, Marschner and Mozart on Television," *A Night in at the Opera: Media Representations of Opera,* ed. Tambling (London: John Libbey, 1994), 69–70. He suggests that "visual counterpoint" derives from film-music theorist Claudia Gorbman. But the concept is much older, having been theorized earlier in film-music composition, in which contrast and not necessarily opposition is stressed between music and image.

19. Andrew Clements, "Peter Sellars as Seen on TV," *Opera* 42/6 (June 1991): 642.

20. As proposed by Jane Feuer, whose ideas are presented in John Fiske, *Television Culture* (London: Routledge, 1987), 192.

21. Quoted in John Calhoun, "The 90s: Global Markets and Marketing— Peter Sellars, Creating a New Set of Classics," *Theatre Crafts* (January 1990): 67. For similar comments by the director see Brooks Riley, "Peter

Sellars Looks at Mozart Through a TV Lens," *The New York Times,* 10 December 1989, section 2, 39.

22. E. Ann Kaplan, *Rocking Around the Clock: Music Television, Postmodernism, and Consumer Culture* (New York: Routledge, 1987), especially 143–45.

23. Sandy Flitterman-Lewis, "Psychoanalysis, Film, and Television," *Channels of Discourse,* ed. Robert C. Allen (Chapel Hill: University of North Carolina Press, 1987), 195.

24. Fiske, *Television Culture* (New York: Routledge, 1987), 105. For an overview of flow see Richard Dienst, *Still Life in Real Time* (Durham: Duke University Press, 1994), 29–33. For another perspective on flow see Rick Altman, "Television/Sound," *Studies in Entertainment,* ed. Tania Modleski (Bloomington: Indiana University Press, 1986), 39-54.

25. Porter, for example, laments this feature, in "And in My Lady's Chamber." I also recall the reaction of a college-production director of *Figaro* at Rice University, whose greatest objection to Sellars was in his distortions in pacing.

26. For a good summary see Cross, "Peter Sellars's Stagings of *Don Giovanni,*" 33–34, 66–68.

27. Fiske, *Television Culture,* 103.

28. Flitterman-Lewis, "Psychoanalysis, Film, and Television," 197.

29. Fiske, *Television Culture,* 105.

30. Flitterman-Lewis, "Psychoanalysis, Film, and Television," 198 and 200.

31. One critic troubled by the device is Patrick J. Smith, in *Opera News* 57/11 (13 February 1993): 44.

32. This is not to say that the original operas, particularly the Mozart, are clear-cut in their endings. See, e.g., Bernard Williams, "Mozart's Comedies and the Sense of an Ending," *The Musical Times* 122 (July 1981): 451-54. My point is that Sellars overlays the operas with a much greater degree of uncertainty and thereby resists much more strongly any neat ending.

33. See chapter 2 for a discussion of this number in Ponnelle's *Figaro.*

34. For a discussion of this number in the Losey, see chapter 5.

35. For a discussion of the relay see chapter 3, which explores a video telecast of Verdi's *Otello.*

36. See Tambling's critique of the film in chapter 6 of his *Opera, Ideology and Film,* 126–39.

37. See Riley, "Peter Sellars Looks at Mozart Through a TV Lens," 39; and "Camera Angles," *Opera News* 54 (June 1990): 15.

38. Andrew Goodwin, *Dancing in the Distraction Factory: Music Television*

and Popular Culture (Minneapolis: University of Minnesota Press, 1992), 76–78.

39. Goodwin, *Dancing in the Distraction Factory*, 76.

40. For example, in Littlejohn, "What Peter Sellars Did to Mozart," 151.

41. The music of this Trio was used memorably in John Schlesinger's film *Sunday, Bloody Sunday* (1971), to capture the emotional pain of three individuals caught in a love triangle. For a perceptive discussion of nos. 9 and 10 in relation to larger themes of the opera see Scott Burnham, "Mozart's *felix culpa: Così fan tutte* and the Irony of Beauty," *The Musical Quarterly* 78/1 (Spring 1994), 79–84. Another sensitive visual rendition of the Trio occurs in Jean-Pierre Ponnelle's film for television (1988).

42. As in the title of Andrew Goodwin, *Dancing in the Distraction Factory: Music Television and Popular Culture;* Tambling's opening chapter, "Introduction: Opera in the Distraction Culture," in the edited volume *A Night in at the Opera: Media Representations of Opera;* and a likely source for the current usage, Walter Benjamin, "The Work of Art in the Age of Mechanical Reproduction," *Illuminations,* ed. Hannah Arendt, trans. Harry Zohn (New York: Schocken Books, 1969), especially 240–41.

43. Porter, "Musical Events: All-American Mozart," *The New Yorker,* 21 August 1989, 75.

44. For Tambling's assessment of the Sellars see his "Revisions and Re-Vampings: Wagner, Marschner and Mozart on Television," 63–74; and for *Parsifal* see "The Fusion of Brecht and Wagner: Syberberg's *Parsifal,*" *Opera, Ideology and Film,* 194–212. His general view of opera as a culturally regressive medium suffuses both volumes and becomes a major target of criticism in a lengthy review of a more recent book, *Opera and the Culture of Fascism* (Oxford: The Clarendon Press, 1996); see H. Marshall Leicester in *Cambridge Opera Journal* 10/1 (1998), especially 124.

45. For a fuller discussion of the values behind the Western canon see my *Gender and the Musical Canon,* especially chapters 1 and 6.

46. For example Littlejohn, "What Peter Sellars Did to Mozart"; MacDonald, "On Peter Sellars"; Albert Innaurato, "A Matter of Voice," *Opera News* 58 (September 1993): 16–18; and especially Donal Henahan, who calls Sellars "a blight of our time" ("When Auteur Meets Opera, Opera Loses," *The New York Times,* 9 December 1990, H23).

47. A fan of the stage productions, Patrick J. Smith finds the colloquial subtitles one of the drawbacks of the televised version ("Great Performances: Mozart-Da Ponte Operas," *Opera News* 56 [July 1991]: 42–43); Clements, "Peter Sellars as Seen on TV," *Opera* 42/6 (June 1991): 641–42; and John

O'Connor, "TV Weekend: Peter Sellars's 'Marriage of Figaro,'" *The New York Times*, 14 December 1990, C38.

48. As this chapter was drafted, I came across a notice that Austrian Airlines painted their aircraft with faces of famous Austrians. Composers and conductors make up the bulk of the group, and Mozart occupies the most prominent place, as the sole figure represented on the tail.

49. Sellars is aware of the dilemma. For his comments see the interview with Bruce Duffie, "Conversation Piece: Peter Sellars," *The Opera Journal* 25/2 (1992): 55.

Index

Page numbers in italics refer to illustrations.

Bierstadt, E. H., 25, 26–27
biopics, 32, 67
Bizet, Georges, score of *Carmen*, 194
Bizet's Carmen (Rosi), 4, 11, 61, 110, 161–204 passim; compared with film musical, 194–96; creation of distance in, 80; as "discourse-*Carmen*," 162; and outdoors, 4; spoken dialogue in, 277n58; use of noise in, 14
body as "discourse," 195
Bohème, La: filmed at La Scala, 50–51; on "Live from the Met," 48; in *Moonstruck*, 63
Bohème, La (Zeffirelli), 257n3
Boito, Arrigo, 93, 94
Bond, Dorothy, 116
Boris Godunov (Stroyeva), 39
Botstein, Leon, 28
Boulez, Pierre, 171
Brecht, Bertholt, 207; and epic theater, 32; and notion of distraction, 244
Brechtian alienation, 203; in *Don Giovanni* (Losey), 171, 188; in *Parsifal* (Syberberg), 155–56; in Sellars's works, 214
British Broadcasting Corporation, early opera telecasts on, 42–43, 47
Britten, Benjamin, 45, 47
Brown, Pamela, *122*
Browning, Kirk, 45, 47, 48–49, 257n3, 261n40

Cabaret, 194, 278n61
cable networks, 46; European opera on, 47
camera: cutting, 12, 142, 223–24,

228; in *Don Giovanni* (Losey), 170–71; as narrative force, 69; in *Parsifal* (Syberberg), 142; rhythm of, 12; and scale, 13; in Sellars's work, 219–37, 238; as tool, 12–13
camera and image, in *Otello* treatments, 82–96
Cannes Film Festival, 62
Carmen. See *Bizet's Carmen*
Carmen (Bizet), 36, 44, 45, 194
Carmen (DeMille), 26–27
Carmen (Mérimée), 27, 28
Carmen (Saura), 162, 181–82, 273n5
Carmen Jones (Preminger), 35–37, 194
castration anxiety: in *Parsifal* (Syberberg), 152; and sound-image separation, 130
Catholicism: Verdi's response to, 94; in Zeffirelli's *Otello*, 90–96, 261n48
Cavalieri, Lina, 27, 28
Cavalleria Rusticana (Zeffirelli), 71
CBS. *See* Columbia Broadcasting Company
CBS Opera Television Theater, 45
Chion, Michell, 73, 134–35
choreography, in Sellars's works, 237, 241–42
cinema: as medium, 8, 10–11; multiple perspectives of, 84; silent (*see* silent film); as successor to opera, 24; in U.S. vs. Europe, 21
class relations: in *Bizet's Carmen* (Rosi), 179–83; in *Don Giovanni* (Losey), 170, 173–79; scenery and, 174; in Sellars's works, 240–42
Clever, Edith, 149, 152–53, 272n62

lip-synching, 29, 259n26; in Fracassi's *Aida,* 34; in *Parsifal* (Syberberg), 13, 153–54; in *Salome* at NBC, 45; and sound-image relationship, 8, 13; in *Tales of Hoffmann* (P&P), 13, 117, 268n28; in televised opera, 43. *See also* sound-image relationship

"Live from Lincoln Center" series, 47–48

"Live from the Met," 48–49

liveness, 8, 24, 65–66, 86

Lloyd, Robert, 148

Losey, Joseph, 18; background of, 178; and cutting, 12; *Don Giovanni,* 1, 4, 11–12, 52, 110, 161–204 passim; on the Don's sexuality, 275n33; on function of valet, 276n39; and Liebermann, 274n22; social context and, 60

Louise (Gance), 33–34

Lumière Brothers, 24

Lyrica Society for Word-Music Relations, 2

Maazel, Lorin, 70, 74, 75, 259n16

Macbeth (D'Anna), 61

Macbeth (Verdi), Alden's production, 23

Madama Butterfly (Mitterand), 61

Madama Butterfly (Ponnelle), 53–55

Maddalena, James, 207, *235*

Magic Flute, The (Bergman), 1, 41, 56–59, *57;* audience and, 231; oedipal struggle in, 125

Massine, Léonide, 116, *122*

meaning, and use of nature, 164–73

media culture, 18, 206

Medium, The (Menotti), 35, 37–38, 45

Méliès, Georges, 26, *27*

Menotti, Gian-Carlo, 5, 37–38, 44, 45

Mérimée, Prosper, 27, 28

Metropolitan Opera, 30; telecasts from, 43, 45, 48–49

Meyerhold, Vsevolod, 207

Migenes-Johnson, Julia, 165, 195, *199*

mime, 39, 84; in *Tales of Hoffmann* (P&P), 128–29, 135, 160

mind-body split, in Sellars's works, 232

Minter, Drew, *232*

Minton, Yvonne, 152

mise en scène, 143, 161. *See also* setting

Mitterand, Frederic, 61

Mohr, Richard, 150

Moonstruck, 22, 63

moral tone, in *Parsifal* (Wagner), 114

Morandini, Morando, 165

Moshinsky, Elijah, *Otello* (with Large), 69–111 passim

movement: importance to Rosi's Carmen, 184; pacing of, 23; popular culture and, 242, 243; in Sellars's works, 237–43

Mozart, Wolfgang Amadeus, 246–47

Mozart-Da Ponte operas, Sellars's productions of, 205–48 passim

MTV, 66–67; Goodwin on, 236–37; influence on Sellars, 206, 219, 220, 221

music: in *Bizet's Carmen* (Rosi),

192–202; click track, 74–75; continuous, 6, 17; cutting, 32, 74, 75, 103; in *Don Giovanni* (Losey), 188–92; film-score model, 77–79; interiorized, 55–56; as major discourse, 17; rearrangement, 32, 74. *See also* continuous music

musical. *See* film musical

musical organization, in *Otello* treatments, 73–82

narrative: flashback, 84, 99–100; fragmentation, 18, 74, 78–79; memory, 156–58; rhythm, 188; in Sellars's works, 229–37

National Broadcasting Company, 42–45

Nattiez, Jean-Jacques, 143

naturalism, continuous music and, 6

nature: and interpretation, 11, 161–204 passim; used to shape meaning, 164–73

NBC. *See* National Broadcasting Company

NBC Opera Theatre, 43–45

NET Opera Company, 46–47

New York City Opera, 47

Night at the Opera, A (Marx Brothers), 22, *33;* and social role of opera, 32–33

noise: in *Bizet's Carmen* (Rosi), 179, 192, 197; sound-image relationship and, 14–15

non-diegetic music, 22, 63, 77–78, 79, 196; in *Carmen Jones,* 35; in *Tales of Hoffmann* (P&P), 123. *See also* diegetic music; music

Nozze di Figaro, Le (Ponnelle), 55–56

Nozze di Figaro, Le (Sellars), 205–48

objectification: in *Bizet's Carmen* (Rosi), 183–84; in *Don Giovanni* (Losey), 187–88

Offenbach, Jacques, 17, 112, 125, 126

opera: and England, 126–27; jazz as threat to, 30; live (*see* liveness); as model for sound movie, 31; as social critique, 20; social role of, 32–33; as star vehicle, 26; as target of satire, 139–40; on television, 40–59; useful to film industry, 32

opera buffa, 222

operetta, 32

Otello (Moshinsky-Large), 69–111 passim; Large's camerawork in, 87, 88–90; sound effects in, 81; on video, 106

Otello (Verdi), 10, 43; film and television treatments, 69–111 passim

Otello (Von Karajan), 51–52, 70, 109

Otello (Zeffirelli), 2, 6, 10, 12, 14, 16, 69–111 passim; Catholicism in, 90–96; diegetic sound effects in, 81; lost maternal object in, 101–2; producers of, 59; use of noise in, 14–15; on video, 106

Otherness, and Sellars's work, 215

outdoors. *See* nature

pacing: in Sellars's works, 221; in Zeffirelli's *Otello*, 74, 82

Pagliacci, I (Zeffirelli), 71

Paris Opera, 50, 171–72, 173, 192

parody: absent from *Parsifal* (Syberberg), 141; of relays, 170–71; in Sellars's works, 225–26, 239–40, 242–43; in *Tales of Hoffmann* (P&P), 115, 137–41, 159

Parsifal (Syberberg), 4, 60–61, 110, 112–60 passim, 141–58; absence of noise in, 14; gender in, 17

Parsifal (Wagner), 11, 13, 26, 112–13

pauses, insertion of, 74, 222–23, 227

PBS. *See* Public Broadcasting System

performance: ritualized, 167; in *Tales of Hoffmann* (P&P), 119–29

Perry, Eugene and Herbert, *209*

playback: Ponnelle and, 53; in screen opera, 18; and sound-image relationship, 13. *See also* lip-synching

Poizat, Michel, 153, 158

Ponnelle, Jean-Pierre, 12, 41, 52–56

popular culture: in opera, 66–68; and Sellars's video operas, 205–6, 219, 242, 243

Porter, Andrew, 244

Powell, Michael: *The Red Shoes*, 115–16; and silent film, 138; *Tales of Hoffmann*, 4, 38–39, 112–60 passim

Powers, Marie, 45

Preminger, Otto, 35–37

Prénom Carmen (Godard), 162

presence: television and, 73, 96; and use of videotape, 82–83

Pressburger, Emeric, 4, 38–39, 112–60 passim

Prey, Hermann, 55

Price, Leontyne, 45, 67

props, as symbols in *Parsifal* (Syberberg), 145–47

Public Broadcasting System, 47–49, 210

puppets: in *Parsifal* (Syberberg), 117, 145–46, 157; in *Tales of Hoffmann* (P&P), 128–29, 139–40

Raimondi, Ruggero, 176, *177*

RCA, 66, 67

realism, 161–204 passim; in cinema, 8; use of noise, 14–15

Red Shoes, The (P&P), 39, 115, 115–16, 272n71

regression: and lost maternal object, 101; in treatments of *Otello*, 96–106, 263n63

relay telecast, 5, 13, 15, 41, 230; camera techniques in, 84–86; curtain calls in, 97–98; favored in Europe, 49–50; as main format for televised opera, 46, 62; rootedness of, 83–84; sophistication of, 48–49; technical requirements for, 40; technological advances and, 47; use by Great Performances, 47–49; and use of videotape, 82–83

Rent, 67–68

reproduced art, screen opera as, 7–8

Revue du Cinéma, 61–62

Ricciarelli, Katia, 69, *78*

Riegel, Kenneth, 191

Riley, Brooks, 218

Robber Symphony, The (Feher), 22, 31

rock-opera, 67–68

Rosenkavalier, Der (Czinner), 39–40

Rosenkavalier, Der (Strauss), 28

Rosi, Francesco: background of, 164; *Bizet's Carmen*, 4, 11, 14, 61, 80, 110, 161–204 passim, 277n58; and cutting, 12; social context and, 60

Rounseville, Robert, *122*

Rushton, Julian, 203

Russell, Ken, 67

Sabaneev, Leonid, 75, 110

Salome, NBC Opera Theatre production of, 45

Sarnoff, David and Robert, 43–44

Saura, Carlos, 162, 181–82, 273n5

Scheman, Naomi, 104

Schoenberg, Arnold, 25, 31

Schwarzkopf, Elisabeth, 39, 40

screen opera: effect on distance, 7; in Europe vs. U.S., 20–22; as form of *Gesamtkunstwerk,* 19; genre defined, 9; influence on stage opera, 22–23; in Italy, 34–35; as product of media culture, 18; setting in, 11; and spectator-ship, 7; and technology, 6

Sellars, Peter, 4, 10, 18; background of, 206–12; cultural resonance in, 243–48; and cutting, 12; and direct address, 234–37; *Don Giovanni,* 109, 187; dualities in, 213–19; and media culture, 205–48 passim; movement and gesture in, 237–43; and notion of distraction, 243–45; and popular culture, 66; and space, 229–37; and television as medium, 10; on updating, 213; use of close-ups, 12, 15–16; and video camera, 219–37

Senso (Visconti), 34–35

separation: and image, 115; of sound and image, 129–37, 154; as theme in *Parsifal* (Syberberg), 148–56

setting: authenticity and, 165–66, 202; for *Bizet's Carmen* (Rosi), 166–67; for Moshinsky-Large *Otello,* 86, 98; in screen opera, 11; as symbolic in *Parsifal* (Syberberg), 143–45

Shearer, Moira, 116, *122,* 127, 132, 268n28, 272n71

show musical, 194

silent film, 24–30, 117; literary source and, 28; overview, 24–30; similarities with opera, 24; sound-image relationship in, 29; "soundless opera" in, 25; as vehicle for actors, 27

Silverman, Kaja, 104–5, 130

Smith, Craig, 207

soap opera, influence on Sellars, 206, 219, 220, 221, 222–29

Solti, Georg, 70, 74

Sontag, Susan, 142

sound: advent of, in film, 30; effect on realism-artifice relationship, 8; as first human perception, 101; vs. image in television, 73

sound effects, in Moshinsky-Large *Otello,* 81

sound era film, overview, 30–40

sound-image relationship, 8; and disembodied voice, 14; disjunction, 148, 149, 190; embodied sound in, 8; and lip-synching, 8, 13; in Moshinsky-Large *Otello,* 82; in *Parsifal* (Syberberg), 148; and playback, 13; in relay, 84;